Free Your Child's True Potential

Free Your Child's
True Potential

Martyn Rawson

Hodder & Stoughton
LONDON SYDNEY AUCKLAND

British Library Cataloguing in Publication Data
A record for this book is available from the British Library

ISBN 0 340 75643 8

Typeset by Avon Dataset Ltd, Bidford-on-Avon, Warks

Printed and bound in Great Britain by
The Guernsey Press Co. Ltd, Channel Isles

Hodder & Stoughton
A Division of Hodder Headline Ltd
338 Euston Road
London NW1 3BH

To my wife and family from whom I learn so much

Contents

Acknowledgments

I would like to express deep gratitude and respect for Judith Longman of Hodder & Stoughton for having had faith in the project and for the remarkably supportive yet professional attitude she has shown me. I would also like to thank Carrie Walker who did such an excellent editorial job in helping to shape this book.

Introduction

This book aims to help parents to understand and support their children in both their general development and their education. It shows that there is much that parents can do to nurture, stimulate and sometimes challenge their children in helpful ways. I'm going to describe some of the pitfalls that exist, but I also aim to give parents hope, courage and inspiration to find real joy in bringing up children. We can also learn about ourselves and develop with and through our children: as the great researcher into child development, Jean Piaget, said, *'The child explains the adult more than the reverse.'*

Love is all they need

The educator and philosopher Rudolf Steiner once remarked that there are three effective ways of educating children – fear, ambition and love – and we can do without the first two.

What does love mean? Surely all parents love their children? And don't children need other things as well? Of course they do, but all

1

the other things need to be accompanied by an inner attitude of love. Love is a way of relating to others that fully respects them as individuals and puts their needs first without any expectations of a pay-back. Love is the welcoming space we create for our children to become what lies within their potential.

Love is also understanding with feeling and the ability to feel with understanding. It is neither pure emotion, unguided by insight, nor cold, intellectual logic. As Leonardo da Vinci put it, '*Great love is the daughter of great understanding*'. All true love is altruistic and never egotistical.

But love of and for children is even more than this. It is not theoretical; it is essentially practical. It is not about merely thinking or feeling but about actually *doing*. That means translating whatever good thoughts and feelings we have about our children into concrete actions that will benefit them. It is about what underlies our relationship with them, about who we are and what we do. Universal love is the highest state we can hope to achieve, but that shouldn't daunt us. Love is not a goal but a path, one that starts today, one that starts with the next step.

What does love mean in terms of raising children? In my view of 'love', this can mean, for example:

- recognising your children's individuality and supporting their development
- having a vision yet letting them become what they *can* become
- recognising our own strengths and weaknesses and working on being a better person for our children's sake
- creating an environment from which children can draw meaning and values
- having courage for the truth and not selling children short
- doing whatever we can to provide children with what they need and protecting them from what they don't need
- stressing the positive yet not running away from the negative
- facing the negative with courage and hope
- expecting the miraculous but accepting the humble.

A new image of childhood

> The history of childhood is as long as the history of humankind. The fact that we have such a long childhood is one of the central factors in what makes us human, fundamentally different from even the most intelligent animals.

Attitudes towards childhood and children vary between cultures and evolve over time, even from generation to generation, along with other aspects of culture. The era of flower power in the late 1960s, as well as protesting against war, nuclear weapons and environmental destruction, ushered in a period, at least in Western countries, of anti-authoritarian education. Its proponents advocated moving away from the view that children should do what they are told and be drilled into good citizens. But this led to a generation of children who were often left precariously to their own devices.

Like most extremes, both the authoritarian and the anti-authoritarian approaches were mostly wrong, neither understanding what children *actually* need. Both had more to do with egotistical adult needs. In reality, children need role models rather than rigid authority, guidance rather than commands, participation rather than determination. Above all they need to be recognised for who and what they are and not bent by 'society's pliers' (as the singer Bob Dylan memorably put it at the time) into somebody else's predetermined shape.

However, although I would never advocate the traditional authoritarian approach to bringing up children, which personal experience has shown can leave you with too much repressed emotional baggage, freedom from authority can, on the other hand, mean a complete absence of authority, and children can't cope with that either. Such freedom tends to mean freedom for parents to get on with their own lives, and the children will, so the theory goes, more or less grow up on their own. But most don't.

Nevertheless, like most revolutionary groups, the hippies of the 1960s, themselves the product of a parental generation who prized cleanliness, obedience and order, did bring about some important changes, the most important for our purpose being a greater level of independence for children.

Children are resilient, capable and active

In many other respects, our understanding of childhood has changed too. Modern research has provided many remarkable insights into how children develop – how active a part they play in their own development, how adaptable they are to changing circumstances, how they can, in certain situations, cope with major burdens with great resilience. Contrary to the view held almost universally by educationalists and childcare experts, children *can* cope with high-risk situations and do more than simply survive.

Let me elaborate. Two long-term studies have shown that up to 30 per cent of children identified as living in very high-risk situations – exposed to poverty, conflict, family separation and medical problems – managed to become well-adjusted, confident, capable, individuals able to sustain stable relationships and cope well with the demands of work and leisure. Seventy per cent of the children, however, showed a range of symptoms that indicated an inability to cope with their lives.

So what characterised the 30 per cent who did well? First, they seemed to be possessed of certain personality traits such as flexibility and adaptability, self-esteem and a positive self-image, confidence, an ability to find ways of coping with stress, an ability to take responsibility and good communication skills.

Second, there appeared to be factors in their social environment that had helped, such as an intense bond to at least one adult – a parent, grandparent, neighbour or friend. When such individuals were a little older, they were adept at finding substitute parent role models within their social context. They were popular at school and had a wide circle of friends and associates, and they were able to accept and use offers of help in a constructive way.

If we analyse these findings, we can arrive at a core of ideals for all parents and educators to work towards in order to provide the right kind of support. The successful children in this study may have possessed something intrinsic in their personality but they needed the opportunity and support to develop it. Merely telling children how to 'be' is hardly effective: they must witness how it works. Children need role models who will nurture their self-esteem and who are socially competent, ready and able to help others and who can carry responsiblility.

But how happy? Fulfilled by what?

The title of this book promises happy and fulfilled children. Before you reach for the Trade Descriptions Act, let me briefly qualify that claim. Obviously no book can guarantee anything as all-embracing as happiness and fulfilment, not least because these terms are highly relative and individual. Really the title should be something like: 'Teach yourself to develop the inner qualities and insight necessary to strive towards creating the best possible conditions within which the potential of each individual child can unfold and develop'. But that really is a bit of a mouthful!

Children and adolescents are happy when they can be themselves, when they sense that their lives have meaning and context, and when they feel that they have the abilities they need. This is not just a momentary happiness or good humour but a long-term underlying mood of being able to get on with the business of life, unburdened by worry, tension, anxiety or fear.

> Being happy means having a positive outlook, being able to cope with the demands of life, being interested in life, facing challenges and knowing you have the ability to tackle them.

Being happy is being positive

Being a happy person also makes you a generous person, in terms of giving not just things, but also time, attention and space, of being able to let go – in short being able to love. An unhappy or anxious person is inhibited and cannot give as freely. Being able to stand back yet continue to have interest brings happiness and radiates positive energy into the world. It is also good for you: scientific research has confirmed that happiness, especially laughter, is good for your heart and your general well-being.

Happiness is, however, not truly possible without its sister emotion of sadness. A healthy soul can encompass the full spectrum of human feeling from greatest happiness to deepest sadness, the art of life being to balance both extremes and to feel them as circumstances demand. Above all, a healthy, well-balanced individual can return healed from the depths of sadness and come down calm and composed from heights of joy. That is what is meant by emotional competence.

The path of fulfilment

Fulfilment is harder to define because it appears so final, as if it were the balance we draw up at the end – *'Yes, she led a very fulfilled life and died having achieved all she wanted to.'* Or it can be too relative, like a young footballer looking back over a successful career – *'Yes, I won all the medals I wanted to.'* But what is this young man going to do with the remaining 40 years of his life?

The trouble with the idea of fulfilment is that it gets confused with success. It is, however, possible to find failure a very fulfilling experience. I like to think of fulfilment as an ongoing attitude, one suggesting that we are at one with what has happened to us and what we have become. It is the sense of satisfaction we have when we have given our best and can accept the outcome, whatever that is.

Fulfilment is also an expression of love. It is an interest in and an acceptance of 'what is'. This means appreciating our own and others' successes as well as coming to terms with our failures, and, because things are rarely straightforward in love, understanding the balance of gains and losses. So if you can contribute to your children being basically happy, creative, generous and interested people, you will derive much happiness for yourself too. And if they are able to find ongoing fulfilment in their lives and go on growing inwardly you may, as parents, find fulfilment too.

What do people need today?

Although exam results will continue to be the gold standard of academic achievement for some time to come, the leading shapers of tomorrow's world have long since recognised that much more is needed. The business, commercial and industrial world is clear what the future needs in terms of real qualifications. Assuming that people have basic literacy, numeracy and information and communications technology skills, what they really need is:

- practical morality
- social competence
- team skills
- creativity
- initiative
- problem-solving skills
- judgement
- interest and enthusiasm
- communication skills
- flexibility

By practical morality, I mean the ability to act in a moral and ethical way out of personal insight rather than because someone tells you what to think.

Few of these skills play a prominent role in conventional educational approaches: they may be considered instead to be a lesson from the School of Life. Although they are central to the Steiner educational approach, other schools will also need to pay far greater attention to them. Parents too can do much to cultivate them, primarily by valuing them as qualities, but also in practical terms, which will be addressed throughout the book.

Parenting today

Parenting has never been easy. It has long been one of the most crucial yet underrated tasks in society. But anyone who has ever reflected on the role of parenting will realise that it makes a vital contribution not only to individual lives, but also to the health, and probably wealth, of the nation. What is more, although parenting has traditionally been women's work, it is task in which male and female roles are equally important.

Times have changed radically and the challenges of parenting have not become any easier. The entire cultural landscape – work, sense of community, the nature of human relationships themselves – is different and will continue to change. We are concerned here not with the reasons underlying this change, but with its net result. Even if we cannot explain all the factors that make up this tangled web, it is worth listing a few – some good, some bad – that have a direct bearing on parenting.

The (mostly) good news

- Women are no longer tied to the kitchen sink and nursery. There are in fact more (paid) working mothers than ever before, and in some communities, more women than men are at work.
- More men actually want to have an active role in parenting, even of very young children.
- Both fathers and mothers feel a greater need to be with their children more often.
- Many family traditions and cultural structures that have helped to bond communities have largely disappeared. For some people, this has been a liberating experience, offering greater freedom from class restrictions, greater social mobility and more scope for individual expression.
- Domestic life has been made incomparably easier through affordable technology and labour-saving devices such as washing machines and central heating. Thus, family life has gained time.
- Most of us have access to a wealth of leisure activities and travel opportunities unimaginable to earlier generations.
- Society is now much more liberal, which makes diversity of lifestyle much more acceptable. We have far more choice in areas such as clothing, literature, health care and gender orientation.

The not-quite-so-good news

- One in five children suffers from nervous stress and psychological problems requiring treatment.
- About a third of children are born outside marriage, about a third are raised in single-parent families, and up to half of all marriages end in divorce. Behind these facts lie hugely complex situations, and despite what some politicians think, no simplistic conclusions can be drawn nor solutions proposed.
- In spite of the liberation from some inhibiting traditional values, many people yearn for some kind of community and the support it gives. The loss of community has tended to emphasise the nuclear family of mum, dad and a couple of kids. This can make the family isolated and if there is no wider network of relatives, long-standing friends and neighbours, many parents who are separated or divorced are on their own without meaningful support.
- With men and women (more) equally able to pursue a career there are new tensions between husband and wife over whose role it is to be there for the children. Many parents become absent parents through the pressures of work.
- Our lives are filled with time-saving devices at home and at work, yet who does not feel under time pressure? We can barely imagine what life must have been like when the family washing had to be done by hand, when we had to go down to the corner phone box to make a call, when coal fires had to be lit and kept in all night. But what do we do with our time? The most common experience shared by parents is the urgent need to carve out quality time because we seem to have so little of it: men spend on average 8 minutes a day with their children. Children on the other hand have a lot of free time, so parents are under pressure to help them fill that time in a constructive way.
- There have been major demographic changes, with a large number of people living in totally new surroundings. From the 1970s onwards, millions moved out of the towns in pursuit of what they imagined to be a village ideal in the country or suburbs. At the same time, increasing dependence on the car killed off village life as a result of traffic, large supermarkets and the sprawl of housing estates. Such new estates are often devoid of what

makes for community life, while the old inner city communities have largely disappeared, their substandard but friendly housing replaced by shopping malls and car parks. Most living spaces, in town and country, are unsuitable for children. Those of us who remember playing in the streets until bed-time experienced something that very few children today have: even parks and playgrounds have to be supervised.

- Leisure activities and consumption go hand in hand, and quite apart from the expense of meeting their children's strong demands for both, many people question whether too much of either is good for them anyway.

- Childhood is increasingly under pressure from the loss of awareness of children's need for play, the aggressive marketing of consumer products, the pressure to achieve at school, the lack of secure role models, the drug culture, the uncertainties of future employment and much more besides. The most worrying aspect is, however, a lack of understanding of children's real needs within our society.

- What one might euphemistically call 'traditional' pressures such as poverty, social exclusion, deprivation and violence have sadly not disappeared from our welfare state, instead developing new faces and new causes. Their effect of stunting children's development remains as real as ever.

- We wish to be free of all predetermining factors such as race, social status or gender and yearn to be able to define our own identities, yet so many people struggle with identity crises of one kind or another.

- In an age of pluralism, we have wide choice in most things *except* education. Those who have no choice or wish to choose state education have the National Curriculum, probably the most prescriptive curriculum in Europe, if not the world. Real choice is limited because the schools at the top of the league tables obviously cannot take all those who apply, and not everyone can afford to transport their children to preferred schools elsewhere. Private education with very few exceptions, offers essentially the same education but in a different packaging.

It may seem from all this an impossible task to *raise our children sensibly in these conditions*. Little from our own past can help us because so much has changed. But this challenge also carries with it many opportunities for bringing new meaning into our family life.

Why this book?

In preparing this book, I asked myself first and foremost, '*Is this book really needed?*' There are already many good books on the subject, some of which I too have found helpful in my own search to understand the task of parenting. My research helped to crystallise the next question: '*What can I add that has not already been said?*' I came to the conclusion that, as a result of my work over the past 20 or more years as a teacher and educator in Steiner Waldorf schools, I could offer a less well-known but, I believe, valuable new perspective.

The Steiner approach

There are around 860 Steiner Waldorf[1] schools in around 50 countries, as well as nearly 2000 early years and childcare settings, about 50 adult education centres, hundreds of schools, homes and communities working with children and adults in need of special care and many social projects such as family centres. Related to this educational work are other diverse projects, including bio-dynamic farms and agricultural produce businesses, hospitals, an international network of companies producing complementary medicines, hygiene and cosmetic products, publishers, producers of children's goods and even management consultancies.

What all of these share is a philosophy based on the work of the Austrian educator and philosopher Dr Rudolf Steiner (1861–1925). There is extensive literature available on the many aspects of this approach, a few key texts being referenced in the bibliography.

Underlying the many applications of this philosophy to real-life

[1] Some of these schools call themselves Rudolf Steiner schools after the founder; others use the name Waldorf because Steiner was asked to establish the original school for the children of the factory workers at the Waldorf Astoria cigarette factory in Stuttgart. The original school was therefore known as *die Freie Waldorfschule*, the Independent Waldorf School.

situations is an understanding of the nature of the human being that not only recognises biological explanations for human nature, but also takes spiritual factors into account in a practical way. Furthermore, Steiner's approach, which he himself named *'anthro-posophy'* – a term based on the Greek for *'knowledge of'* and *'through the human being'* – offers various paths of moral and spiritual development that can enhance our awareness and help to focus our endeavours to become more effective, that is selfless and socially competent, individuals. In short, anthroposophy as a path of know-ledge can help people from all cultures to become more complete as human beings, to address what is universally human in each of us.

What is more, anthroposophy differs from religious philosophies in many ways, most importantly because it allows – in fact actually *requires* – individuals to think for themselves. It is a modern path of self-knowledge and social renewal that can work hand in hand with or even within different confessions. Thus, there are Steiner Waldorf initiatives in Islamic Egypt and Hebrew Israel (both with state recognition and support), in Buddhist Thailand, in black townships in South Africa, in schools for the children of MIT professors in Boston and in D.H. Lawrence country in the UK's East Midlands. UNESCO and the European Union recognises the Steiner Waldorf movement as a non-governmental organisation, and recent public recognition by the Secretary of State for Education in the UK has been most welcome.

With this in mind, I feel that I can offer new perspectives on the nature of child development, education and upbringing. As well as focusing on the child, I will also address issues that concern us as adults and how we can prepare ourselves to meet the needs of our children in such a way that we too can grow in the process.

> The more we know who we are, and the more able we become, the easier it is for our children to grow into happy and fulfilled adults and parents themselves.

How this book is organised

Some of the issues in this book touch on some of the deepest aspects of what it is to be a human being, including questions of morality, ethics and personal development. These can be challenging to address, but to ignore such aspects for parenting and child development would be like taking a cookery course that simply taught you how to heat up precooked meals.

My experience is that parents do not wish to be offered simplistic recipes describing how to bring up their children. They want to know not only *how* but also *why*, for the obvious reason that real life presents us with situations for which no recipe of options can prepare us. What we need are new abilities based on insight. Having said that, I realise that readers have probably not bought this book because they are interested in philosophy or educational theory. Nevertheless, I believe that they want to understand *enough* to know what to do.

Therefore I have tried to find a balance. There will be sections that you may want to think about. You may even want to pursue the subject further, so I will give a few references to other literature. Other sections will be easier to read, although perhaps not necessarily easier to put into practice!

The main point to remember is that you are the one who has to find a way, you are the one who has to get up in the night, you are the one who has to make the difficult decisions. All a book of this nature can hope to do is help you to look at your own attitudes and values anew and perhaps show you aspects of childhood of which you were less aware. What I hope to do is to stimulate, perhaps occasionally initiate something in you that you then take on and own, but the days of prescriptive teaching manuals are over.

> The only real way to work is on yourself, and my aim is to offer you help towards that self-help.

1

Attitudes

Children learn how to be by observing us. Who we are helps (and may hinder) them become who they are.

Rudolf Steiner

Before we start exploring the tasks of parenting in more detail, I would like to address a range of issues relating to attitudes. If you recognise any of these in yourself, don't worry, we all do to some extent. But we need to recognise the emotional and habitual tendencies we have and reflect on their influence over how we are with other people, especially our children. This is the first step towards the self-knowledge we need.

Let us start with the thoughtful words of the Lebanese poet Kahlil Gibran, spoken by his famous creation the Prophet. These thoughts express the inner attitude we have to cultivate as parents. They are in some ways challenging and unattainable, but so are all ideals. Their purpose, however, is to give us something to aim for and an inexhaustible source of strength.

Your children are not your children.
They are the sons and daughters of Life's longing for itself.
They come through you but not from you,
And though they are with you, yet they belong not to you.
You may give them your love but not your thoughts,

For they have their own thoughts.
You may house their bodies but not their souls,
For their souls dwell in the house of tomorrow,
Which you cannot visit, not even in your dreams.
You may strive to be like them, but seek not to make them like you.
For life goes not backward nor tarries with yesterday.
You are the bows from which your children as living arrows are sent
*   forth.*

The Archer sees the mark upon the path of the
Infinite, and He bends you with His might that His arrows may go
*   swift and far.*
Let your bending in the Archer's hand be for gladness;
For even as He loves the arrow that flies, so He loves also the bow that
*   is stable.*

Kahlil Gibran, The Prophet

Self-esteem

Parenting is in many ways about self-esteem, ours and our children's, and self-esteem is about being realistic and honest. Most of the time, we are good, well-balanced people. Some of the time, however, each one of us is self-preoccupied, egotistical or anxious. Individually, it is a matter of degree. Children need us to come to terms with these negative qualities so that they themselves can gain in self-esteem.

Children (and adults) with self-esteem are:

- more able to develop their potential
- more confident and willing to learn
- more able to show interest in the world around them
- more able to deal with problems and cope with adversity
- more able to overcome difficulties or live with permanent limitations
- more generous and caring towards others
- more socially competent
- more likely to find satisfaction and happiness.

Expectations

> In parenting, much depends on our expectations: too many and the child is inhibited; too few and the child becomes insecure through knowing no boundaries.

Our expectations must not crush the emerging individuality of the child, force her[2] into a mould that we have designed but into which she doesn't fit. If she doesn't live up to our expectations, it can be a tremendous burden for her and a source of misery for her parents. On the other hand, if we don't live up to *her* expectations, this can also be painful. And if our children sense that we really have no idea what we want, either because we *do have no idea* or because we are afraid of imposing something inappropriate onto them, they may feel uncertain.

Making comparisons

Comparing children with others, such as a successful older brother or other children in their class, can also undermine their self-esteem. When we ask rhetorical questions of our children such as *'Why can't you sleep all night like your brother or play quietly like Susan?'*, we only put them under pressure. If they were able, they would answer, *'Because I am not my brother or Susan, I'm me!'* Even worse is to accuse a child of being, *'as bad as your mother'*, *'as stupid as your uncle Ted'*. Such comments are unhelpful and confusing for the child and demeaning for all concerned.

Doing your best is best

> The best standard we can set ourselves is to do better than we have so far managed.

---

[2] For simplicity, I will refer to the child as 'she', although of course both girls and boys are meant.

Learners are their own best standard. Learning is all about growth and development, not winning races or competitions. A big step for me might be a small step for you. Some of us can put in huge effort and, relative to someone else, achieve little. Another person may achieve a great deal through little effort. Which is more valuable?

Generally speaking, things worth achieving require greater effort and what demands greater effort means more for the development and self-esteem of the individual. Someone with a natural capacity for mathematics may be incredibly shy and their efforts and achievements in the social realm will be of far greater significance for their development than will the effortless solving of equations. Put another way, the things that come easily to us are in some way or other the fruits of our previous endeavours. What we have to overcome *now* helps shape our future. The future is where our potential lies.

If we set standards for our children, we have to make them relevant and attainable. A child can be motivated to go beyond her own previous limits, but it can be demoralising always to fall short of someone else's standards.

> You are never a failure as a whole person if you have done your best.

Expectations that become burdens

Although this is now probably less common, many parents want their children to follow in their footsteps and go into the family profession or the family business. Three generations of doctors, lawyers or farmers is a hard act for offspring *not* to follow, but many increasingly manage to go their own way. It is rare these days that dress-makers' daughters become dress-makers, and almost unknown for the children of systems analysts, accountants or supermarket shelf-stackers to follow in their parents' footsteps, except by pure chance. This is as it should be. We want our children to have their own careers, make their own choices.

Yet wanting the best for our children can become a very limiting burden. If we want too much, they may rebel and turn their backs on us, or they may feel crushed into submission, resentful and insecure.

> We have to learn to respect who our children are and celebrate their abilities and personalities, whatever these are.

The only legitimate disappointment we may have is that *we have failed them*. The professor who can fully accept that her son has chosen to work in a market garden rather than pursue the hoped-for academic career will be a happier parent and probably have a better relationship with her son. The land-owning farmer who can welcome his son's choice to become a musician will perhaps also find greater fulfilment in the long run.

Men probably suffer more than women from failing to meet their parents' expectations, if only because parents once used to expect less from their daughters. Giving advice is not the same as wanting your child to become what you want her to be. Like love and trust, both of which can only be given freely and never demanded, the expectations we have for our children must help them to find their way rather than forcing them to become what we want. They, like us, have their own destiny to fulfil. I all too often encounter parents worried about their children's progress, the underlying thought being '*I'm so intelligent/successful/motivated, how could my child fail to be the same? It must be (anybody's) fault (but mine).*'

The right kind of expectations

It is quite appropriate to say to a child, '*I expect you to put all your toys away*', reminding her that we put our own things away in their proper places and that it is accepted to do so. Or if I say, '*You can do better than that*', the child is stimulated to say, '*Well, yes I can*' and mean it. If she couldn't have done better, I should have known and not demanded it of her. The right kinds of expectation involve the recognition of a child's abilities, setting reachable and meaningful goals. These can sometimes be hard for the child to understand at the time, but in the long run they will reap recognition and thanks.

So, in summary:

- try to be clear what you expect from your children
- make your expectations clear by explaining them
- try to give guidance that helps but leaves children free to be themselves
- our highest expectation should be for the child to develop to her full potential.

Trust and boundaries

> One of the incredible things about children is that they trust us, even though they hardly know us, at least in terms of our adult personalities.

Young children are simply too young to understand what we think, yet they trust us in ways that we can barely fathom. The basis of this lies in the fact that they come to the world with an instinctive thirst to learn how we do things, how we communicate and behave. They desire to learn how 'to be'. They imitate our language, our gestures, our habits (good and bad), our attitudes. In short, they assume that we know how to be people so they copy us. This imitation is an elementary expression of trust since they do not select who or what to copy. This trust often expresses itself in the form of expectations. They instinctively expect us to know what *we* are doing and, above all, to know what *they* should be doing. They also expect us to provide for all their needs. Not least, they expect us to have all the answers.

Although I am talking primarily about young children, teenagers also expect this. They expect to disagree, but that's another story. They would rather disagree with somebody who knows what he or she stands for because this at least provides them with the kind of resistance they need to develop their own power of judgement. Teenagers lose their respect if we give in too easily and let them have what they want because they have high ideals, not least with regard to *our* wisdom and integrity. Confronted with our accommodation or, worse, abdication of responsibility, they lose not only their belief in us, but far more seriously, their faith in themselves, becoming cynical and losing the motivation to try to live towards their own ideals.

Children and teenagers expect us to determine the boundaries. They do so not out of insight or superior knowledge but almost instinctively because it is existentially vital to them. The boundaries we impose should not, however, be arbitrary or unrealistic, or we will undermine our own authority. Limits must make sense for essentially practical, objective reasons – although we obviously can't expect either children or teenagers to agree with us on their usefulness!

No one has difficulty saying, *'Don't touch the cooker, you'll get a nasty burn.'* But saying, *'No, you can't have another chocolate'*, let alone *'I think you are too young to sleep with David'*, is much harder. You don't have to persuade your child of the reasoning, but you have to *persuade yourself* that there are good reasons for the boundaries you set. This usually means having an established code of practice of a more general kind, such as:

- we don't eat between meals
- it is nutritionally sensible to limit the amount of chocolate children eat
- or even (albeit less convincing in the long run) because I expect you to do what I say.

Having thought the matter through and arrived at some kind of judgement, perhaps in consensus with your partner and family, it will be much easier to reinforce, and if necessary *enforce*, the boundaries. As a rule, children look back on their childhood and appreciate the implementation of rules even if, from their adult perspective, they think the rule itself crazy (we say grace before meals, we go to church on Sunday, etc.). And the same goes for moral values.

> If children grow up in an environment in which we offer hospitality and help to the needy, respect to all regardless of colour, caste or creed, they are far more likely to behave in this way as adults.

Being kind, loving, generous and honest is a deep-seated form of behaviour. At its best it is unreflected behaviour rather than the response to an externally imposed code. The more un-self-consciously we act in these ways, the more impact it will have on our children's behaviour patterns. This is what is known as schooling the will. Gestures here speak louder than words and are far more effective than schooling the intellect. It is one thing to think what is right. It is another thing to simply *do* the right thing. If such experiences are also associated with good feelings, they will be even more effective in helping the child to develop the basis of a truly moral attitude. Many of the practical examples I talk about later have this basic concept at heart.

Mapping out life's journeys

Children's sense of orientation in the world has essentially two co-ordinates: them and us. We are the harbour from which they set sail and to which they return. The length of their voyages of discovery progressively increases, until the child, at a certain age, disappears over the horizon and loses not only sight, but also consciousness, of home. This can be a worrying time for the parents waiting at the quayside. If, however, the invisible band of trust has been woven and tested throughout childhood, they will come back when they are ready. Their joy at returning will be no less than ours – only they tend not to show it as much! These are highly significant moments in a child's biography.

This unquestioning expectation that we provide them with a point of safety is, if they but knew it, a massive act of trust. How do they know we are able to provide this? It is like their expectation that we will feed and clothe them, even though their expectations are often unreasonable: '*If I can't have those jeans*' – naturally the most expensive designer brand – '*I will be a social leper. I will never be able to leave the house and might as well die!*' Children can and do survive without designer jeans but *not* without orientation. Without boundaries, children lose their orientation, lack certainty and can become anxious.

So then:

- children need clearly demarcated boundaries
- these boundaries have to be realistic

- parents must know why they insist on such behaviour
- limits must be enforced with kindly but firm persuasion
- we must expect children to want to go beyond the boundaries we set for them, and welcome them home when they return.

Be positive, keep talking

> Being positive does not mean mindless optimism in the face of evidence that life can be a difficult thing. Being positive means acknowledging the pain, the loss, the failings and the uncertainties while addressing the things that can be dealt with.

I once asked a friend from Bosnia, who had lived through the siege of Sarajevo with a group of children, how they managed to keep the children's spirits up. She replied that once they had realised that it was impossible to hide the terrible realities from them, they kept the children informed in a matter of fact way while constantly reaffirming their commitment to the children. They found that this approach was much better, at least at the time, although who can tell what the long-term effects will be? Yet all the evidence suggests that children are incredibly resilient as long as they know what is happening. What concerns them most is where *they* stand, what will happen to *them*.

What my friend did not realise was that those children were incredibly fortunate to have someone like her, a tower of calm strength, practical wisdom and good humour. She also knew that the children needed the opportunity to talk about their experiences, best achieved through the medium of story. They needed to see how everything related, especially what their part in the story had been. For children who were too traumatised to talk, playing with dolls often provided the same experience. When asked by a TV journalist what the Sarajevo children needed, my friend replied, '*Time to play.*' Play is the other healing side of talk and stories. We will consider play and stories quite a lot in following chapters because this is central to being human, and children can rarely get enough of it.

Fortunately, most of us do not have to go through such traumatic life experiences, but our children frequently face disturbing challenges such as accidents, illness, bereavement, separations and bullying. We will tackle some of these issues later, but for now it is worth bearing in mind the fact that children need to know what is going on:

- children should not be kept in the dark about what is happening: find a way of telling them that they can understand
- children need the opportunity to talk about what is happening to them
- above all, children need to be reassured that they will be looked after.

Don't say don't

> If we can possibly avoid using negative commands, we should. It is always better to stress the positive.

Say what a child can or should do rather than what she can't or shouldn't. This is sometimes very hard, and in emergencies we do have to resort to 'Don't'. Nevertheless, positive reinforcement works best in the long term to strengthen a child's self-esteem.

Children have powerful imaginations. When we say something, they instinctively form a strong mental image of this, so abstractions are of little use – what kind of image can you form from a phrase like, '*Be good*!' Conversely, if we suggest the worst, it is more likely to occur! If we imagine the sensible, safe thing to do, they are more likely to do it. In addition, if we give children clear pictures of what we want them to do, it is much easier for them to understand.

So saying '*Don't run out into the road because you might get run over*' leaves a fairly fearful image, the alternative being to say something like, '*Now remember, when we go down the road, people walk on the pavement because the road is for cars.*' Or try to stress the better form of behaviour: instead of '*Don't fight with Jacob over the bicycle!*' say '*Why don't you two boys have fun sharing the bike?*' (Now this is a '*don't*' you can use!)

Changing the subject is a simple and often effective way of diverting a child from rude, unpleasant or destructive behaviour. Children (and adults) often get stuck in a rut and need to be guided into something else. As in much of parenting, timing is crucial, a skill best learned in the practice of music, drama or sport.

Another aspect of positive reinforcement is to be hopeful, to show children that we can hope things will work out, that it will stop raining on camp, that exams can be survived. Again, this not a matter of being unrealistic. It is no good promising in November that the weather will soon get warmer: it is better to look at the enjoyable aspects of winter weather. If we do this out of a genuine enthusiasm for life children will be greatly helped in developing a positive attitude. Even if older children see through our efforts at positivity, they will appreciate that we at least tried.

To sum up:

- avoid saying don't as a command
- stress the positive rather than the negative
- be hopeful, finding something good about a situation.

Making mistakes

We should at all costs avoid making mistakes while also facing the fact that we will fail in this. We *will* make mistakes, many small ones and a few really big ones. Yet life says '*Go on!*' We can't give up just because we've messed up! We have to pick up the pieces, swallow our pride, apologise, whatever, but in the end we have to carry on.

However, for those listening carefully, the voice of life also adds, '*But learn to learn from your mistakes.*' This is crucial. Our children too suffer from the mistakes we make, yet they grow in the certainty that we will not just give up and walk away. Learning from one's own mistakes is probably one of the greatest lessons we can teach our children. Mistakes are bad, but not making things better is worse.

Children are immensely forgiving, and I've often wondered why. While recently reading the childhood recollections of the musician Binjamin Wilkomirski, an answer began to dawn on me. Wilkomirski's moving book *Fragments* describes childhood experiences in the Warsaw ghetto and a series of death camps. Even by the standards of Holocaust literature, this book is especially poignant because it reconstructs, through fragments of memory, a child's experience with utter objective authenticity. What is so astonishing is the child's will to survive. His is a will that trusts that all will be well and meaningful despite the most appalling evidence to the contrary, even though that trust was gradually eroded to the extent that he had difficulty believing the sincere efforts of those trying to rehabilitate him on his escape from the death camp.

Such is a child's will to grow and develop, to become what she is not yet, that she will be drawn to any opportunity that presents itself. Of course, her will may, at some point be driven out into apathy or turned inwards towards self-destruction, but this usually occurs when the child no longer feels that what is happening to her has any meaning.

Any effort on our part to put things right releases a flood of renewed vitality, energy to grow and develop, but the effort to do better on our part must also be sincere. We must face up to our mistakes, trying as best we can to understand them, accepting rather than denying their consequences. This does not mean becoming morbid or obsessed with our failings, becoming wracked with guilt; it means looking our mistakes in the eye, and saying 'Sorry, I will learn from this and do better', and then really doing it.

We need to realise that:

- learning from our mistakes in a positive way has a strengthening effect on our children
- children can be forgiving if they sense that we are learning. This gives them a sense of meaning in life
- real forgiveness doesn't mean just forgetting: it means owning the mistake
- feeling guilty puts an extra burden on the child.

Being sentimental doesn't help

Most of us have a tendency to be sentimental about children, especially when we are apart from them. By 'sentimental', I don't refer to those powerful feelings of blatant, honest love, the kind we feel when we tiptoe in to tuck them in at night once they are fast asleep and the battle of bedtime is over. Nor is sentimentality what we feel when they have touched us to the quick with some genial comment. Being sentimental means projecting an image, often stereotyped, onto children that does not reflect who they actually are. Fathers tend to be more sentimental than mothers because they generally have less contact. Sentimentality, by its very nature thrives on distance from reality. People without children are often the most sentimental of all.

Sentimentality is usually harmless, but it can place burdens of expectations on children that they cannot live up to, and this leads to disappointment all round. Sentimentality comes in a variety of flavours: seeing children as delightful, innocent creatures dressed in frilly (often Edwardian) clothes; a fondness for large stuffed furry comfort creatures, the larger the better, presented to children (and to girlfriends they call 'Baby') usually after an absence; a tendency to use baby talk, avoid real-life issues and make promises that cannot be fulfilled. If this behaviour occurs *between adults*, the adults can at least usually distance themselves if they wish, but children can't do this because they trust that everything is as it seems.

Unfortunately, sentimentality can be easily marketed, and we are surrounded by temptations that suggest it to be a norm – slushy birthday cards, and dolls stacked seductively at the cash desk in airport shops blinking their eye-lashes at guilty fathers on their way home. But does a father really need to bring anything other than himself? Isn't there a danger of gift inflation? Or wouldn't something simple and interesting from that country do? A colleague of mine always brings fresh bread from wherever he goes. Such a simple gesture can provide a far more interesting conversation around the breakfast table on his return.

The trouble with sentimentality is that it doesn't respect the real nature of childhood or the particular child, leaving too little room for the child's own personality. In extreme cases, the child becomes a figment of the adult's fantasy. Child-centred parenting means understanding childhood, respecting it and taking it seriously. Thus:

- being sentimental may mean imposing an image on the child that is not true to her nature
- sentimentality can be a burden for children if they fail to remain true to the stereotype projected onto them.

Being tough is just as bad

Another attitude to which we are all prone is assuming that children *can* and *should* be able to cope. This is in some ways the opposite of sentimentality, although it equally disregards the true nature of childhood and the child in question. This view expects too much of children, especially emotional competence and the ability to make decisions. It is essentially an adult-centred perspective.

We all know how it feels to be told *'Pull yourself together!'* But there is nothing more demoralising in a difficult situation than to hear this, especially if the speaker is not aware of the complexity of the circumstances. Children are even more prone to the sense of inadequacy that accompanies such comments, either because they really don't understand what is expected of them or because they are incapable of being what is demanded of them.

Criticism, if it has to come, should be helpful, comprehensible, constructive and never angry. This doesn't mean being 'nice' all the time. It means addressing the matter in a concrete and friendly way. Children can't understand abstractions and often don't know what the matter is when adults are upset with them. Even words such as 'silly' or 'stupid' assume that the child understands what is expected and what is not. Perhaps the most meaningless phrase used on children is *'Behave yourself!'* If only they knew how! If there is a problem, it needs to be described in words that children can understand.

> Children's self-esteem is greatly supported by understanding, positive reinforcement, praise and clarity.

Above all, whatever we say has to be sincere and a genuine reflection of what we really think, and it has to address children in terms they can understand. Take the following, for example:

- 'Aren't they beautiful to look at! They're very delicate. That's why Mummy leaves them on that shelf,' *rather than* 'For goodness sake, don't touch those!'
- 'I can't seem to find any of those toys, let's sort them all out and put them back where they belong so we can find them tomorrow,' *instead of* 'Clear up that mess!'
- 'You know, when I get tired, I like to lie down and have a rest for a few minutes, why don't you take five?', *rather than* 'Sit down and shut up!'

Looking back over situations once the heat of the situation has dissipated is much more effective than trying to sort things out in the middle of an argument or tantrum.

- 'You know, when Daddy says, no you can't have another ice lolly, that's because he knows that you won't have any room for that delicious supper he's made you.'
- 'Now that I'm out at work and have lots to do, it would be a great help if you picked up all your own clothes from the bathroom floor. In fact, I could show you how to use the washing machine by yourself. It would be a great help if you could learn to do that.'

Dealing with naughtiness after the event in a calm, objective way is also important. Children should have the opportunity to see their behaviour in a way they can identify with, while avoiding unresolved guilt. Being genuinely contrite is far more likely if a child actually understands the intended or unintended consequences of her actions. The following steps can serve as an example:

1. Try getting her to tell you exactly what she did.
2. Then describe to her in a matter of fact way what effect it had. In some situations, you can get the 'victim' to say how it felt being pushed over or teased. You can tell the child that everyone was really worried when she didn't come back until very late, how their plans were spoiled and so on.

3. The child can then be encouraged to identify with what happened and feel what it might have been like for the others involved.
4. Finally and most importantly, the child should be asked if she can think of a way of making amends and avoiding this problem in future.
5. If a punishment is to be given, the child should have it explained to her in advance and be told what it is for.

Expecting self-control of children can be reasonable if it is done in a way that strengthens the child's resolve. If it is done in a way that weakens that resolve, it is totally counterproductive. As a child I remember vividly once being told to pull myself together and failing disastrously: I wanted to go to the toilet when it was not convenient. I was so shocked by the shame of being ridiculed that I promptly wet my pants. Looking back, I'm sure I could probably have hung on, but the way I was spoken to made me lose the very self-control that was being demanded of me. And it was probably almost as embarrassing for the teacher as it was for me.

So:

- don't expect children to cope with too much before they are ready, especially emotionally
- don't use abstractions: explain to children how you expect them to behave or not behave
- don't blame children for things over which they have no control (such as their clumsiness)
- respect them through positive communication.

It's who you are and what you do that counts

Children are particularly sensitive to body language, facial expression and tone of voice, in short all the non-verbal aspects of language and communication.

Children, especially young children, are highly observant and responsive to all modes of communication, many of which we are largely unaware. This can sometimes lead to embarrassing moments – '*Daddy, why does that man smell?*'

Because they are young and so open, they are also unreflective. This means they cannot to any degree consciously overlook some odd behaviour or undertone in another person. They cannot make allowances for someone's mood or circumstances (such as being tired following a hard day at the office). They take everything at face value.

The way we stand when talking to children is very important. We can be quite intimidating simply because we are so big. It is much easier to listen to a child, to make her feel that we are attending to her, if we come down to her physical level or lift her up to ours. Making sure our words and gestures communicate the same meaning is important too. Once children have noticed the discrepancy between words and actions, they will exploit it mercilessly. Parents would do well to try observing body language.

Perhaps the most important gesture we can show children is our ability to listen and empathise. Children who feel listened to will feel more confident, secure, valued – in short, loved. They will also find these feelings much easier to develop if they have observed the adults around them doing this. Being able to participate, especially in conversations, is another aspect (I will return to this in Chapter 10). Touch is also very important.

The key thing here is that what we *do* makes a far greater impact on children than what we *say*. If we are kind in our actions towards others, if we are observant of nature, if we are respectful of other people's space, our children will learn from this. The negative side of this hardly needs stressing: anger breeds anger and fear (most violent adults were treated violently as children; most child-abusers were themselves abused).

In summary:

- body language is as important, if not more so, to children than words
- non-verbal communication must not contradict the words we say
- show children how 'to be' by being attentive, calm, brave, cheerful and honest yourself.

Don't imagine that they don't understand

Let us also not forget that children listen to everything we say, even when they don't appear to be listening. In fact they take all kinds of linguistic signals to heart long before we think they can understand or even talk! Most of us have observed that children can mind-read and even spell at a very early age: Mum says to Dad, '*Shall we let him have some I-C-E-C-R-E-A-M?*', and junior says, bold as can be, '*I want an ice cream.*'

This apparent capacity to read our thoughts is very interesting. I doubt that children are really telepathic; they are simply so good at reading all our verbal and non-verbal signals that they can instinctively make the jump from hearing and seeing to grasping the thought being communicated. This faculty is most pronounced when the subject matter directly involves them.

This is a relatively harmless aspect of what is a very serious business indeed. This capacity means that children can read the signals when something is wrong but is not being directly discussed. They can hear the strained undertones between two parents who are trying to cover up the fact that they are not getting on. Children can read the underlying mood far better than adults because they are unable to filter it out.

The long-term effect of such situations is to make children feel insecure, as they always do when they feel that something is going on that may concern their security but from which they are being excluded. If adults have to disagree in front of the children (because there is no other way of dealing with it), it is probably better to be direct and say, '*You know, Mum and Dad don't agree on this one, but we're going to try and sort it out.*' The key coded message that the children have to receive is that although there *is* a problem here, whatever happens they will be all right, everyone still loves them and all are trying to sort the problem out as quickly and as well as possible. It is of course better not to let things get that far, but, being realistic, this will happen to the best of us at some time or other. But although our children are highly receptive, they do not necessarily understand. They can be deeply influenced by what they see and hear yet are often unable to digest it. If we speak about our children as if they were not present, especially if what we say is critical or disparaging, they will carry that with them for a long time. Think what children may make of the following comments regularly used by their parents:

- *'He just isn't coping at school'* ('I *can't* cope at school.')
- *'Her ears stick out; goodness knows what she'll look like.'* ('My ears stick out; I'm ugly.')
- *'Having another child was the worst thing I could have done.'* ('She never wanted me.')

We must therefore remember that:

- we can't (and perhaps shouldn't) hide our moods and feelings from children
- if we can't control our feelings, we should attempt to address this for the sake of our children (and ourselves)
- children's self-esteem can be seriously affected by how we speak to them or even about them.

Offering choices that children can't make

Young children actually don't have much choice except to try to do what we expect of them or show them. Left to themselves, they will not always choose what is good for them. Nor of course do adults, but there is a significant difference. Adults are in a far better position to evaluate the consequences of their actions, even though they may decide to go ahead and take a risk. It is, however, unreasonable to expect a young child to deduce the medium- or long-term consequences of her actions from experience. Short-term consequences are far easier to understand: the radiator is hot, the cat scratches, eggs break.

> If adults are incapable of behaving reasonably or in a healthy way, it may well be because in childhood they were given too many choices that they were unable to make.

Until children are surprisingly old, they do not have any real basis for making sensible decisions or judgements of the kind we expect ourselves as adults to make. They also have little sense of time, do not know what is harmful and cannot sort out rational priorities (wanting to play *just one more* game at 10.30 in the evening).

Knowing what *is* reasonable to expect of children is very individual, but there are general guidelines based on an understanding of child development which I summarise in Chapter 5. Learning to observe your children's reactions can help to ensure that they are not being asked too much of, both in terms of emotional choices and at the mundane level of knowing what's good for them:

- we must not expect children to make judgements if they are too young
- remember that children live mostly in the present.

Treating children as adults

As parents, we have every right to pursue our careers, our hobbies, our lifestyles, but this doesn't work if we treat our children as if they were consenting adults who had the option of saying, no thanks. To treat them as if they ought to be able to understand our needs and priorities places a huge burden on them and can make them very insecure, not to mention downright unmanageable. When we expect too much too soon, too soon we get too little. I once actually heard a distraught parent say to a 6-year-old, '*Do you want to live with Mummy or Daddy?*' (But the child in question astonished us by replying matter of factly along the lines of '*If I live sometimes with Daddy and sometimes with you, Mummy, then you won't have to argue.*') So:

- don't ask children to make choices when they have little or no experience on which to base a judgement
- don't be surprised if they are remarkably matter of fact about things we find embarrassing or shocking.

But they are wonderful!

I confess that whenever I see children being special – a group of 5-year-olds listening intently to a story or a spotty teenager playing her heart out in a role too big for her in a school drama production – tears come to my eyes. This is of course a kind of sentimentality against which I somewhat haughtily warned about, but I can't help being touched by the magic of childhood. I console myself with the thought that it is not *my* fantasy they are playing out. They are simply being a special version of themselves, and it is this that is so very moving.

2

Introduction to the exercises

What can I do to help my children?

There are many practical things you can do to help, which are listed in the various chapters. You also learn about children as understanding who they are and how they develop is of enormous importance. The more you can intuit why your children are as they are, the more *they feel* understood, and that gives them a valuable sense of security. The information I have given on child development can lead to insight if it is supported by an observation of children. But what helps link the practical with the theoretical is how we digest this and how we prepare ourselves inwardly. That is what the exercises are all about. They involve quietly sitting down and thinking, but this is unfortunately not as easy as it sounds!

The exercises are designed to help you establish an inner and outer quiet in order that you can reflect on some important aspects of parenting. Many people find it helpful to write their thoughts down – although others find this such a stressful challenge that they will avoid it at all costs. The writing is only a support if you want it but it can help to clarify what you think. It may also be of interest in looking back on your initial experiences and seeing how they develop.

There are basically two kinds of exercise:

- questions to think about, then writing down your thoughts
- regular meditation exercises.

Meditation

Please forgive any not-very-subtle teacher-like tones that you may detect in these instructions: as a teacher, I spend a lot of time suggesting sensible things to adolescents in such a way that *they* are supposed to realise that the advice is the most obvious in the world and that *they* knew it all along, and this tends to stick. The important thing is that you choose to do these meditation exercises – Exercises 1–3 – freely out of your own interest, and you can vary or adapt them to suit your needs.

It is also important to know that you can't do anything wrong. You might not do an exercise for very long, you may feel like not bothering, you may spend 10 minutes simply trying to get comfortable, but *you can't actually fail*. In the 24 hours of busy living (sleep being a busy time too, at least for the mind), 5 or 10 minutes spent on yourself will certainly do no harm and can only do some good. This can create an active still point in a whirl of activity.

So make yourself comfortable, but not *too* comfortable or you'll fall asleep. Choose a comfy chair, somewhere where the phone won't ring and people won't talk to you. Tell the family you are going to reflect on the day for 10 minutes and that they can have their turn afterwards.

How to do it

Take 5 or so minutes to compose yourself, catch your breath and get comfortable. Don't worry if you're not in the mood. Just *do it*. You can watch the time, but don't clock watch! Then do the meditation exercise. Afterwards, as soon as it is time to go and you are more or less ready, carry on with what you have to do.

Exercises 1–3 are daily exercises and benefit from being undertaken as a regular and more peaceful moment in the day. Do not do this while driving or being otherwise responsible for others. If your only space is on the bus or tube, that will have to do. A good time is just after the children have gone to bed or are out.

While doing the exercise, I can guarantee that your mind will wander. As soon as you notice this happening, gently come back to the matter in hand. Don't get annoyed with yourself; be tolerant. Treat yourself with the same friendly compassion you would use towards a child who is upset or a friend who needs your support. *You* are someone who needs your support here! It may be that you spend the entire 10 minutes exercising this tolerance, but don't worry. That is just as important as the exercise itself. In fact, you can consider this effort of tolerance *the* most important part of the exercise.

It will be a great help though if you do a meditation exercise before you tackle the exercises at the end of each chapter as it will help to relax you and focus your mind.

Exercise 1

Choose a time and place where you can regularly do this exercise. Have a clock or watch in front of you (preferably not one with an annoying tick). Sit quietly, close your eyes and gradually allow a feeling like a warm glow inside you to spread from your middle outwards and upwards into your head. Feel yourself slowly filled with warmth. While this is happening, watch yourself with friendly compassion, as you might watch a sleeping child. Do this initially for 5 minutes, then open your eyes and, when you are ready, get up and carry on with your life. When you feel comfortable with this exercise, extend it to 10 and ultimately 15 minutes. That's it. If you are not comfortable with your eyes closed, keep your eyes open but dim the light.

This is the primary exercise designed to create a peaceful space in which you can focus on yourself. It is the starting point for all the subsequent exercises and you can do it any time you feel the need to calm down – such as at the dentist's! Some people find it helps to light a candle to create a mood of concentration. They can then 'transfer' the light and warmth of the candle flame to their own body.

Exercise 2

After practising Exercise 1 for a few weeks, extend it as follows. Sit quietly and gradually allow the warm glow to spread from your middle outwards and up into your head, as in Exercise 1. Once you have got used to letting this warmth fill you, imagine it to be accompanied by golden light, warm Mediterranean sunshine for example, not a dazzling light but more like a radiant sunset. Try to feel yourself physically uplifted by this, as if you were actually lighter in weight.

After a week or so of trying this, move on to the final and complete stage of the exercise.

Exercise 3

Start as described in Exercises 1 and 2. Having established the feeling of being filled with warm light, focus on the breath at your nostrils when you breathe in. The air we breathe in is usually slightly cooler, and you can feel this at the edge of the nostrils. Don't change your breathing in any way, just observe the feeling of the in-breath in a composed and detached way. This acts to focus your attention.

When your mind drifts away, as it frequently will, don't worry. As soon as you notice you have stopped feeling the breath, just simply go back to watching it. After 5 or 10 minutes, calmly open your eyes and, when you are ready, rejoin life. After a while, you will find that you can judge the right length of time without having to look at the clock. When you feel comfortable with up to 10 minutes, extend it to 15. It is unnecessary to sit for more than 20 minutes, but if you can manage it, try doing the exercise twice a day.

Homework

Now we come to the first 'homework assignment'. Some of the questions may take quite a while to work through. Think of them somewhat like doing a correspondence course with the Open University. The exercises that need repeating can be done on a daily basis and should not take more than a few minutes.

You will need a notebook (or a PC), one big and sturdy enough to last for some time. You may wish to decorate the cover to remind you of the book's importance.

A wide margin down one side of each page can contain the date of each entry. Note the question and write your thoughts on the rest of the page. When you return to each entry, you can add new thoughts, explanations, comments or further notes and references in the margin. Separate each entry by a space (so you can add things later), and don't worry about writing in full sentences or spelling correctly. This book is just for you.

Read your last entry each time you start again. Periodically, when you have time, go over the entries again, noting further thoughts in the margin. This makes your notebook into a kind of research journal.

Outer preparation

It is worth choosing a regular time to do these exercises, if only because once it becomes a habit, it is easier to find the right time and space. When and where this will be is very individual, but too early or too late in the day, is not always suitable. The important thing is regularity. The questions are best answered once a week like doing a homework assignment.

The following tasks can be done independently of the meditation exercises, although meditating first may help.

Exercise 4

Think back to the happiest moments of your childhood. Choose one and describe as much as you can remember. Try to recall how old you were at the time. Once a fragment of memory crops up, watch it for a while. Then begin to build up the detail with questions such as, 'Where was this?', 'What kind of place was it?', 'Was it warm?', 'Who else was there?' If you feel like it, write down your thoughts.

Through this, you can start to gain some insight into how your own children feel.

Two kinds of memory

There are basically two different kinds of memory perspective when recalling scenes from long ago. The *observer* perspective is from the outside, like looking at a photograph. In this, one can build up more external details such as who was there or where the scene took place. The other view is that of the *participant*: you experience the scene as if you were inside it. This is much harder to describe because it tends to blur external details and concentrates on feelings, which are harder to put into words. Some people find the observer perspective much easier, others go straight for the participant view, but try to add something of both to your description.

Exercise 4 can be repeated, choosing a different memory each time, so you can begin to build up empathy for what it is to feel like a child. To bring some objectivity to the question, try to identify what age you were at the time. Notice too, if you can, how much of this memory is original and how much arises from the situation having been discussed in the family: '*Do you remember when . . . ?*' Or is it based on family photographs or videos? It is interesting to note what makes a group family memory and what is, as it were, individual and private.

If you want to know more about memory, read Daniel L.

Schacter's *The Seven Sins of Memory: How the Mind Forgets and Remembers*.

A word of warning

Let me add something here. If, when you try to recall memories of childhood, things arise which are painful, try to ask yourself, *Do I want to go into this?'* In a way, there is not much that one can do: a memory is a memory and one can hardly forcibly suppress it. Nevertheless, it is not necessary to dwell on it. It may be that it is helpful to look at the situation from the perspective of the present, but I would first consider the situation and come back to it if necessary.

Also, try to balance such bad experiences by recalling a genuinely happy moment. There is much to be gained by reflecting on what makes for painful memories, but please be compassionate with yourself, and share the experience with a trusted friend.

3

Why do we have children?

Every child proves God's renewed faith in humankind.
                                    Rabindath Tagore

'Why do we have children?' may seem an odd question in a book about raising children. If you already have them, isn't it a bit late to be considering this? Yet the answers we find may help us to understand our role as parents.

The reasons for having children have obviously changed over the years. If we go far enough back in time, people had children for the same reasons that birds build wonderfully woven nests and salmon travel thousands of miles to lay their eggs in the mountain stream of their own birth, a journey that in effect kills them. Humans originally had children because of the instinct to breed. Later, as humankind developed societies, this instinct was complemented by cultural and economic needs. Today, however, people actually have the choice of whether or not to have children. This choice is part of human freedom, something that marks us as unique in nature, that raises us above the animal kingdom. Having said this, the means of preventing children being conceived or born are widely but not *universally* available or even used when available. For all kinds of reasons, millions of children are born unwanted, despite contraception.

> Like most freedoms, the freedom to have children requires
> a high degree of conscious choice to be exercised.

Conscious choice is one thing, but even when every precaution in the book is *consciously* used, children still arrive! Most of us know families who have 'slipped up' and are (when they get used to the idea) usually pleasantly surprised. It seems that some individuals go to incredible lengths to get themselves conceived and born, whether or not they are wanted.

The traditional reasons for having children

As I said above, having children was once an economic necessity. Someone had to look after us in our old age. Furthermore, the means for doing this had to show continuity, whether through hunting and gathering or through farming. The skills required had to be learned and practised for a long time. The most effective transmission of such skills was from parent to child or, as was often the case, from close relative to children. Once humankind largely became settled and worked (if not actually owned) the land, continuing the economic process that sustained the family became even more necessary. Useful skills, possessions and property had to be retained within the family for this continuity to be maintained.

A sense of identity through family

The psychological necessity of maintaining the family traditions and the family line was probably once as significant as material needs. The topic of family traditions, especially issues of inheritance, is fascinating and hugely complex. Sometimes it is tragic too, especially when one considers how some societies have denigrated girls to the advantage of boys, as is apparent in some parts of the world even today. On the one hand, there was the need for the father to hand the family economic concern – land, trade or profession – on to a son or sons; on the other, there was the need to secure the family's social ties to the rest of the community by intermarriage. Both aspects were economic as well as psychological.

The need for continuity of identity plays an important role in both processes. The complex web of family relationships and the economic basis of subsistence are usually bedded into a wider cultural setting by a common language and traditions. The individual within this complex of relationships secures her identity through the recognition of her place within the whole. 'I am my father's second daughter, my uncle's niece, my grandmother's fifth grandchild' etc.

Family identity and place

For much of human history, the connection between family identity and place has been a strong one. The aristocracy has retained this aspect the longest, the family seat going back centuries symbolically representing this unity. But the poor too often identified themselves strongly with their village or region, especially if they were forced through poverty or conflict to leave it. To a large extent we are losing this family connection to place.

Family problems

So having children was essential not only to provide for one's old age, but also to perpetuate the social and psychological structures from which people derived their security and identity. This factor of social relationships was so compelling that it may have led to economic disadvantage and even long-term social instability. It has not only been royal dynasties who have experienced constant conflict because of the quandry of inheritance: this happens at all levels of society, especially in societies in which land and economic resources are not in common ownership. The question of which of the children should inherit the estate and what happens to the others has been the cause of social strife and civil conflict down through the centuries.

So matters of inheritance tended in historical times to respond more to cultural factors, including religion, than strictly speaking to what made economic sense. With industrialisation and the break up of traditional farming communities, the problem of inheritance must have become less significant for a large number of people: for the poor industrial working class, there was little to inherit anyway. Uprooted from their homes, people also had little sense of coherent community in the vast sprawling industrial slums, similar conditions still existing around the world where vast shanty towns full of dispossessed people gather around the cities of the developing world.

Why then do such people continue to have children when it simply means more mouths to feed and little bodies to shelter? I have yet to come across any research that really helps to explain this. On the one hand, we have to say that many children arrive in such situations unwanted, unplanned, the result of brief passions. In such social contexts, where most people have lost touch with their roots and traditional values and have little education or guidance, it is not hard to see how living for the moment can explain this. But it is also true that many of these children are abandoned to their own devices at a frighteningly early age, becoming the street children who inhabit the underworld of big cities such as Bogota, Delhi and Bangkok. Even the cities of wealthy Europe have many such children too, albeit of a slightly older age. There are simply millions of homeless children throughout the world. It is not only a tragedy but also a riddle.

Children bring hope

It is, however, unfair to assume that this is the norm even in conditions of social deprivation. Most people lovingly do their best for their children, are happy when they arrive and derive joy from their presence. Those children may represent a form of hope for a better future. They have an innocence that reminds us that life has its pure and noble side. Having children actually provides a focus for such families, providing them with the motivation to try against all the odds to make something of life. Children make family life out of chaos; family life means community. And in spite of everything, these children appear to *want* to be here too.

Too many?

UNESCO recently symbolically celebrated the birth of the 6 billionth citizen of this planet. The baby in question was born in a Kosovan refugee camp, chosen no doubt because of the poignancy of the situation, yet somehow the issue of global overpopulation is difficult for us to take on board. Are we really expected to feel guilty that we have children? Are we expected to act like responsible world citizens and stop having children, or limit ourselves to just one?

Let us just consider for a moment some of the arguments against overpopulation. The overcrowding, starvation, pressure on diminishing resources and conflict that are the consequences of these conditions are powerful arguments for *other* people not to have children. We probably imagine these '*other*' people to be living in the developing world, where most of the problems seem to be. It makes sense, we may be tempted to think, for *them* to have fewer children.

Baby boom or bust

In fact, the complication for us as Westerners is that our own populations are in decline. In many European countries, the birth rate is now so low that there will not be enough young people to do all the work and, more importantly, to pay the taxes needed to support an ageing population. In the former Western Germany, for example, the current birth rate is less than one child per woman, but it needs to be 2.2 to maintain the current population level. Birth rates are even falling in Catholic countries, where contraception and abortion are officially restricted if not actually illegal: Italy has the lowest overall birth rate in Europe, with a figure of 1.3 children per woman. Christopher Wills' book, *Children of Prometheus*, provides us with a fascinating discussion of such issues.

An ageing population

Some European countries have been actively encouraging their citizens to have more children by offering tax breaks and guaranteed nursery provision. Their main motives, however, have nothing to do with a love of children but reflect socio-economic realities, some pragmatic and sensible, others more morally dubious. Along with a falling birth rate, we have increased longevity, living on average twice as long as our great grandparents. With an increasing percentage of the population over retirement age and more in need of expensive medical and social care, governments are staring at a looming budgetary nightmare. If the tax-paying section of the population is declining, who is going to pay for all this? One of the answers is immigration. This can unfortunately bring as many social problems as it solves since there appears to be a deep-seated and sometimes violent distrust of foreigners.

Having children responsibly

But do population issues actually influence people in their decision to have children? I think it is rare that people let global concerns influence such intimate matters, but whether this is right is hard to judge. My feeling is that the problems of overpopulation have to be addressed in other ways, in terms of distribution of wealth, renewable energy resources, ecological industrial practices and sustainable food production methods.

In exercising our freedom to have as many children as we want, it is reasonable for society to expect that with freedom comes the responsibility to ensure that the children we have get the best we can offer in terms of our love. They will then be more likely to make a contribution to society rather being a burden through their social incompetence. And, as I have already stressed, this is not necessarily related to issues of wealth or poverty. Although social exclusion and a lack of personal competence are more likely in a context of poverty and deprivation, this is sadly not always prevented by access to wealth and opportunity: wealth can be a serious handicap for some children.

We also have a moral responsibility to make our children aware of their social responsibilities. They need to learn:

- that every person on earth is an individual with rights and a destiny just as complex as everyone else's
- that the world's resources are not unlimited and that, in small

domestic ways, we can avoid waste as a matter of habit
- that sharing is (along with listening and observing) a primary social skill
- that there are challenges in the world – environmental protection, peace – that need capable young people to address them with their skills, creativity, energy and will – a version of US President John F. Kennedy's famous appeal to young people, 'Don't ask what your country can do for you, ask what you can do for your country.'

Do they choose us?

Now here is a radical thought for the modern mind. Just imagine that children, in some deeply unconscious way, choose to be born to us, here, now. This would mean that they somehow pre-existed before their conception, that they were somehow around before the embryo began to be an individual. This would mean that a child exists in some form that is not constricted by our bodies.

I am suggesting here that individual uniqueness and destiny cannot be explained simply by assuming that it arises solely out of the biochemistry of our growing bodies or that it is somehow induced in us only by our parents or our upbringing, however much they do have an effect. But if we are not the sum of nature and nurture, we must exist as something beyond that, something that I will call the human spirit.

The human spirit is the core of individuality, and it wants to become, to develop. It can, however, realise its potential only if it grows within a body through which it can experience the world and act out its intentions. It needs to become someone who can feel, think and, above all, act. To do that it needs to be here, in this world, in a unity of body and spirit.

And that is where parents come in. First, we provide the genetic material, the energy and resources to build a body. Then we provide the nurture and nutrition that any living being needs to get started. Furthermore, we provide a social and cultural context because humans are social beings. And since we are such incomplete beings, we need to learn – from family, friends, school and social contact.

But human individuality contains far more within it that also needs to develop. It needs challenges, tasks and choices, both practical and moral. It needs resistance to push against with its own strength. It needs something to cut its teeth on. Something to compare itself against. The opportunity to expand inherited faculties as well as developing new ones.

Development has to involve transformation and the progression from one stage of life to another. As we shall see in our exploration of child development, abilities developed at one level transform into abilities at new, higher levels. Individuality comes to expression in the way in which this transformation occurs, whether at the physical or the psychological level.

Another mystery of human development is that we do not exist in a vacuum. What and who we are is inextricably related to other people.

The extended family provides the first community a child inherits. Who we are as parents matters to how the child develops her individuality. Where we live, the language we speak, the historical context into which we are born matter too. Individuality is all about how we relate to all these.

The bias of the unborn

Unborn children need people like us if they are to come here, have their own experiences and live out their own destinies. In the end, who knows who they are and what they bring to humankind? Maybe they make subconscious connections to us long before the moment of conception. Those with spiritual leanings may propose that this connection to an unborn human spirit may lead us to other relationships and decisions. If the spirit of the unborn child is calling us, perhaps it prompted us (mother and father) to get together in the first place. Mind boggling, isn't it?

Women, who are the far more intuitive members of the species, often have a strong premonition that they will get pregnant in certain circumstances. This may even influence their choice of man, in spite of all rational evidence to suggest that he is *not* Mr Right. Do the unborn exercise far more pull than we realise with our modern scientific brains?

Some people see a kind of inevitability in such relationships – she *had* to be born to us because of what we have to do with each other. We have things to work out with each other, issues necessary for all our development. Later relationships, often imbued with great meaning, with friends, teachers, strangers and partners will help the individual to develop her individuality.

These relationships will vary in intensity and duration but each plays its part in the drama that is a life. The woman I met for a day and a night on a beach in Crete may have given me something that only she could. The colleague whom I continually annoy by my very presence has something to do with me that clearly neither of us understands – but would no doubt benefit from if we could somehow work it out. Viewed in this way, human individuality becomes a quality to be respected and nurtured, giving us a special responsibility related to the care of our children.

Life tasks

One of the central tasks in life is to understand who we are, which we do through learning about those we encounter. As parents, we have a very special task to provide one or more individuals with everything they need to be independent beings. The relationships involved clearly have great, albeit variable, significance.

It is by no means ordained that the genetic inheritance is the most important one: it is perfectly possible for me to provide an individual with my genes but for someone else to provide her with the nurture she needs, as is the case with adopted children. Life events also play a part. Today, the needs of individuals will clearly be met in multiple ways as families become more and more flexible in their arrangements. The blood ties that once were socially so important are not necessarily the ones that matter.

What is crucial is that the adults who are and feel themselves to be responsible for the upbringing of a child respect the inner connections that underlie their relationships even if they do not understand them with their conscious minds. I believe that our subconscious understands far more than we are aware of, this showing itself in our actions and attitudes. We need to respect a child's higher or unknown being.

The best parents are those who can love a child in the full sense of the word. These may be step-parents, foster parents, a gay couple, a grandmother or a carer in an orphanage. The child may be an abandoned orphan, a niece or a child from someone else's sperm. What matters is that the child finds adults with whom she can develop, maybe even different people at different times.

So why do we have children?

We don't really *need* to have children, especially if we are certain that we will earn enough money to ensure that we are cared for in our old age. So here are a few ideas why we *should* have them:

- the joy that children bring is, in spite of all the hard work and the problems, immense: experiencing them grow and develop has to be just about the most amazing phenomenon on earth
- having children around us brings a vitality into our lives because they bring so much energy with them
- having children means creating a family, and family gives us a real focus for structuring our lives
- having children helps us to step outside our adult preoccupations, gives us another focus and draws on all our best qualities
- assuming that children want to be born, we can provide them with the opportunity and support needed to help them to develop and experience all there is in this wonderful (and sometimes terrible) world.

A few questions before you start . . .

In case you do not yet have children and are considering it, you might like to think about the following, perhaps surprisingly direct and challenging, questions. The '*you*' in the questions is addressed to both the individual and the prospective parent pair.

- Are you willing to give up a large amount of your time, energy and resources to someone else who may or may not grow up to be grateful? Children have to come first, at least in the first 7–10 years. If you want to give your children the best start, this can mean sacrificing or at least deferring your lifestyle and career for them to be the most important people in your life. Once you have your own children, for example, you may finally have to stop being someone else's child.
- Are you prepared to welcome an individual into your life who may not be your first choice of person, who may have totally different needs and gifts from the ones you hoped for? Can you let your child become something different from what you want?
- Are you prepared to offer everything with no expectation of reward or at least with rewards that are much harder to gain than we would normally expect? This may seem a little drastic, but the parents of autistic, physically or mentally handicapped children will be faced with massive challenges in deriving the deepest happiness from their children.
- Are you prepared to work on yourself to make family and parenting work? Few people have a natural talent for this most challenging skill; most manage but could do a lot better. If you really want to optimise your child's chances of growing up happy and fulfilled, you will have to work on yourself.
- Can you take on the long-term responsibilities that come with parenting? Of course, no one can really answer this question. The best we can do is be prepared to continue asking, 'What is required of me, however much relationships and outer circumstances change?'

Having answered all these questions in the affirmative, let us proceed. Even if you do not have your own children, you may come into contact with other people's children. These are even more difficult to deal with, so this book may still be of use to you. If you are planning to have children, try drawing up a list of practicalities to focus your mind:

- Decide whether your home is big enough to have children. This goes for the car too.
- Plan which room would be for the children and decorate it in

suitable colours, preferably with non-toxic paint.

- Take time to visit friends who have young children to begin to get used to how life is.
- Discuss how you want to plan your lives once the children are there: how long the mother will take off work, whether the father can make changes in his career to be more available to give help. It may not be possible to control these factors, but it is worth exploring all the options with your employers beforehand.
- Start collecting useful equipment (a pram, a cot, a baby bath, baby clothes). If you are well off, there is plenty to choose from in the baby market. If you have less money or are into recycling, start collecting good-quality used items from friends or charity shops. As much of this equipment will be used for only a relatively short period, it can often be used again and again.
- Start reading good literature on pregnancy, birthing and early childhood so you can deal better with difficult choices (see the Bibliography).

Exercise 5

If you *don't have children*:

- Write down a list of all the positive things you can think of to do with having children, how it would change your life in good ways, what it might mean for you and your partner, for your work, lifestyle and so on. You don't need to go into detail.
- Then write down a parallel list of all the reasons for not having children, all the possible unwanted changes this might bring.

When you have done this, repeat the exercise a week later, compare the results and discuss them with your partner. Explore the reasons you have noted and above all the uncertainties, the things you can't decide on. Please don't use this exercise to make a decision about whether or not to start a family: just use it to clarify your present thoughts.

As a third step, write down all the conditions you would expect to fulfil if you were to start a family at some point in the future. Consider all the outer circumstances – housing, work, timing – and then consider what conditions you would set yourself in terms of relationships, attitudes, feelings and so on. What you would like family life to be like? What dreams do you have? – I'd like to have five children and live in a farmhouse with horses and a Land Rover. My partner would devote him/herself to home, family and farm, and I would spend each weekend riding over the heath and sitting by the fire. You might then like to take a critical view of this dream and see what weaknesses and practical limitations might there be: schools, lack of willing partner, isolation, cost of idyllic farmhouse, etc. The difference between fantasy and reality can be somewhat sobering.

For people reading this who already *have children*, try this variation of the above:

- Write down all the positive changes that having children has made in your life.
- Write down all the aspects of having children that you feel you could do without.

Repeat this exercise a week later and (if you are brave enough) discuss it with your partner.

As a third step, sit down (preferably with your partner) and reflect on what might help to change the negative aspects you have identified. And while you are at it, enjoy once more reflecting on all the joy your children have brought into your lives.

4

The early years

The most important years of our lives

Yes, I'm afraid it is true. The early years of childhood are by far the most important in terms of subsequent development. More significant things happen developmentally to human beings in those 3 years than in the whole of the rest of their lives. Just think about it. We get born, we start to breathe, we grow more than at any other time, we develop the most important structures of our brains, we learn to balance in an upright position and walk, and, perhaps the crowning glory, we master some of the most complex phenomena known: speaking and thinking. If we get the first 3 years right, we will have set our child well on the way to happiness and fulfilment.

But if we get things wrong, there may be lasting effects. It is of course possible to put things right later on, but it will be much harder. The good news, however, is that most of the healthy development happens with relatively little input from us. The best we can do, and this will prove to be challenging enough, is to enable all this self-activity on the part of the child to occur without undue hindrance.

> ## The golden rules are
>
> * let the child be
> * don't force things
> * provide only what the child can deal with and needs.

These are actually quite big demands as it is harder to do less than more. We may also be tempted to do the wrong things for the right reasons.

Learn from your mistakes

I do not mean here the kind of daily mistakes we make out of inexperience, such as not knowing how to hold a child properly, or getting the bath water too hot or too cold, or mistaking teething problems for meningitis, or letting the cat sit on the baby. Children survive all this. They are in fact as important as learning experiences for the children as they are for us because *they learn how we learn!* As long as we are observant enough to find the cause of their discomfort and learn to avoid it, they are happy – or at least not permanently unhappy. But if we keep on getting it wrong, or if we get angry because *we* have got it wrong and *they* have cried, we may hinder their healthy development. As the child psychologist Hellgard Rauh put it:

healthy children give their parents about two years to learn their difficult craft. For this length of time they will forgive small everyday mistakes, as long as they don't get regularly repeated or become habitual. Parents should orientate themselves by following the rule that whatever is enjoyable for both partners, child and parent, is usually OK.

(Quoted in *You Are Your Child's First Teacher* by Rahima Baldwin Dancy)

Who knows best?

It is getting harder to know what is the best way to act. Parents are more inexperienced than ever before because *their* parents were inexperienced. Those who were poorly parented tend to make poor parents, but everyone can learn how to be a good parent if the will is there. Traditional wisdom about how to bring children up has disappeared, and people generally do not know what is right, although if they followed their intuition rather than their intellect, they would probably fare better. The sad paradox is that more information about children is available today than ever before.

As we know, however, information does not always translate into wisdom. Certainly the commercial, and to some extent the scientific and medical, world has got it wrong. There is a massive industry trying to sell us things we don't really need or are totally inappropriate for young children.

Furthermore, we live in a world whose commercial media are concerned to wire people up, connecting children to their electronic umbilical cords as early as possible, telling us that it is good for them. But in reality it damages their development and gets them hooked for life. At the risk of sounding unreasonable, I would like to suggest that, when it comes to young children and their development, there is overwhelming evidence that much that is offered to children in terms of nutrition, lifestyle and sensory stimulation is positively bad for them.

But don't they have to grow up in an electronic world? Don't they have to cope with a modern environment? Isn't it natural for infants to go everywhere with their parents? Shouldn't they get used to the real world as early as possible? Parents have many similar and related questions.

Basic principles of early development

Before going into more detail about what is good and bad, let me first say what, for me, the basic principles of early development are:

To start with, human beings have evolved to what they now are over several million years. All the most precious faculties we have, our brains, our senses, our wonderfully gifted hands, our unique upright posture, have evolved under conditions that were until very recently very different. Humans have grown up in modern, electronic environments for only a tiny fraction of time. For example, we evolved our remarkable colour sight and visual system to distinguish features in a non-urban setting rather than to hurtle along in vehicles or coping with rapidly appearing pixels on a TV screen!

Second, these wonderful sensory organs and our ability to direct them to give us an accurate picture of the real world are not fully functional at birth. They first have to be fine-tuned, mastered and developed. If we overload them before they are fully functional, we limit their potential enormously, with the consequence that we impoverish the picture of the world that we are able to construct in our minds as well as our understanding of it.

Thus, the development of our brain and senses, as well as the mastery of our motor co-ordination, is an essential prerequisite for healthy psychological and cognitive development. Modern research fully bears out the old adages that you can't run before you can walk, and that nimble fingers make nimble minds.

Fourth, all human beings have to make themselves at home in their own body. This does not happen instantly but takes many years.

Next, it has been shown that the basis for all fine judgement is real experience. Thus, the greater the primary experience of natural qualities that children can have, the sounder their basis for making judgements in life. As complex judgements are based on simple ones, so each individual needs a rich spectrum of primary experiences.

Sixth, understanding the world is based on recognising processes in context, context being what gives the real world its meaning, its sense. Random, rapidly appearing and disappearing sensory impressions that have no context provide no meaning, leading to alienation, fear and anxiety. Meaning instead arises for the child when she can see that the impression has several dimensions and relates to other things that can be experienced. Experiences have to be sorted out into categories of meaningful connections before abstract concepts can be grasped.

Children thus first need to experience the world in concrete, tangible terms. If we flood them with essentially artificial images, they will find it so much harder to make sense of it all. We are first and foremost natural creatures, still relating to the natural forms that are true to our senses, even if our intellect tells us that there are other explanations. We *see* rainbows. We *see* the horizon as a straight line. Our minds need a literal explanation first before taking theoretical (albeit true) theories on board.

Finally, the most crucial aspect of early childhood development for me is that children learn direct communication with and through living people. The many techniques involved in communicating, including spoken language, body language, tone of voice, gesture, eye contact and the rhythms of human dialogue, have to be learned at source. Not to have acquired an intuitive sense of give and take, of the alternating rhythms of speaking and listening, of the structure and stages of narrative, is to be severely limited in life. Listening and hearing are also the basis for hearing what is not said, for intuiting what a person really means. The world is unfortunately full of people who can't listen, can't hear or understand what is really being said and can't say what they really mean.

But this most subtle and vital of human skills does not come ready made. There is no gene for being able to listen and communicate: it has to be learned. This has optimal conditions, which we should strive to attain, conditions that require a child to be able to hear and distinguish sounds and their meanings, that require periods of peace and quiet if reflection is to occur. If children always have to compete with other sounds, they just get louder and hear less.

In summary then, these principles require:

- time for the child to develop
- an environment that encourages, engages and supports the child but does not force her to take steps she is not ready for
- sensory impressions that she can digest and process
- the child to feel safe

- the creation of a listening, responsive, communicating and, above all, human environment.

Now that we have some basic guidelines, let us explore some of the key areas of development encountered during the child's first 3 years.

Pregnancy and birth

This book is not big enough to go into great detail about the specialist areas of pregnancy and birth. There is a wealth of good literature on the subject and wise advice to be had, not least from your National Health Service midwife and from the National Childbirth Trust (see the section on Other organisations).

From the wealth of available literature, I would recommend to any parent-to-be two authors in particular. First is Sheila Kitzinger, whose books *The Experience of Childbirth* and *Freedom and Choice in Childbirth* changed the way in which many people thought about birth, providing information and offering an inspiring and common sense approach, especially to the psychological challenges of pregnancy and childbirth. The other author is the American midwife and parenting counsellor, Rahima Baldwin Dancy, whose book *Special Delivery* offers not only practical advice and information, but a recognition of the spiritual issues of childbirth too.

The home birth movement reflects more than just a reaction against the impersonal environment of large hospitals, representing instead a sea change in attitudes. Birth has become an act to celebrate in a meaningful way. Rather than being a nightmare suffered passively by women while the men waited outside and prayed (or drank) for a successful outcome, it has become a process that actively involves both partners. Whether at home or in hospital, birth has become something in which we can participate.

> The *way* in which a child is born has become as important as the technical things that are done to manage the process. The *how* has become as, if not more important than the *what*.

Women have claimed responsibility for their bodies and won some measure of self-determination for what happens to them rather than being in the hands of professionals, however efficient and authoritative. This is especially important in giving a woman self-esteem and is crucial to what the mother can give the child, especially in those early months. But perhaps most importantly, the home-birthing movement has led to a new awareness of the child as a sensitive being for whom the act of giving birth has profound meaning.

Not-so-natural birth

Like many other things in life, birth has become a 'natural' issue, but the concept of 'natural birth' is something of a misnomer. It is evident that human birth has for a very long time, perhaps the past million years, been a highly risky process requiring help from an experienced midwife. This results from our upright stance and large brain, both uniquely human traits.

Being upright places constraints on how wide the female pelvis can be: too wide and we would be unable to walk or run efficiently. Even then, our thigh bones slope inwards to the knees, placing great stress on our hip joints, which wear away, leaving many elderly people in need of a hip replacement. However, the *narrowness* of our pelvis, an advantage for running, is a big disadvantage for giving birth, especially since humans have by far the largest heads for their body size of any mammals.

Nature has come up with an extraordinary set of solutions to this biomechanical problem. First, the baby's head bones are not fused together but overlap in the birth canal to make the head smaller. Second, the baby's brain is delayed in its development and therefore size until after the birth. Third, the frontal part of the mother's pelvis can soften up and stretch slightly during the birth. Fourth, the baby turns its head sideways half way down the birth canal to get round the narrowest part. But it is still a very tight squeeze, requiring massive muscular contractions, a lengthy labour and often support to turn the baby's head.

Birth in human beings is only really possible (with any degree of safety) with experienced support and a knowledge of how to manage the contractions. This knowledge has to be passed on from generation to generation, and specific techniques have to be learned. No animals known to us have any regular difficulties with birth, or need to be trained in it. In other words, birth has long been a cultural activity.

A new consciousness for birth

It is wholly appropriate in our times that birth should be a cultural act. Since the traditional cultural rituals surrounding birth have (in most cases thankfully) been forgotten, we have the freedom to create our own. Those people who have done their own birth thing (either at home or in sympathetic hospitals) will testify what a meaningful time this was. Such experiences not only support the mother and reduce the likelihood of post natal depression, but also create the most welcoming environment for the child. The important point here is not to turn our backs on modern medicine but to make birth a sacred moment in the lives of those directly involved by placing the mother, child and family at the heart of the process.

Creating the right environment will be a highly individualised task. It is also about allowing the normal process to unfold in its own time. Experienced midwives will know how to support the process in the best possible way, using technology and medicine as needed. As long as health is not at risk, birth should be a celebration of life rather than a medical operation, the mother a celebrant rather than a patient, the midwives the servers at the ceremony, and the father on hand to help or disappear as necessary.

Preparing for a child

Before a child arrives, there are many things parents can do to prepare themselves. As well as attending antenatal classes and informing yourself about pregnancy and birth, for example reading the books I recommended earlier, there are some practical steps you can take to create a welcoming space for the newcomer. If this is your first child, such activities can help you to adjust to a totally different lifestyle, becoming more accustomed to the slower pace of family life and the need to invest in a new kind of quality time.

Outer preparation helps you to find solutions to life's little problems, an inner ability much needed by parents. The thoughts and feelings that accompany our preparations also create an environment for the child, who inhabits an unconscious world that we already share with her. You will need to think about the following:

- The child will need a bed of her own. If this is your first child, you will be faced with many alternatives. You could, for example, ask your friends, family and neighbours whether anyone could lend you a crib or Moses basket. While this may seem odd, things with a lived-in feeling are much more welcoming than something that still smells of newness. Our daughter Ruby had a crib, hand-made by its original owner that had the names of 18 previous occupiers written on its base over a 20 year period. It had practically never got cold!

- If you are at all handy, try making a crib yourself. This can be very simple as the newborn child does not need anything elaborate or fashionable. Just simple and friendly. Your love and care will imbue it with a special quality. Try using wood that has been waxed or oiled rather than painted or varnished since the smell of fresh paint lingers for a long time. Lavender oil is a lovely choice.

- The same principle applies to preparing a room for the baby. Keep it natural and as free as possible of chemical smells, make it an environment that is warm, enclosing and quiet, not only in terms of noise, but also in terms of colour, shape and brightness as the human infant is still in a kind of embryonic phase. If you have to paint the room and furniture, spend a bit more and buy non-toxic paints, and see if you can arrange for subdued, natural lighting.

The care and attention you put into such preparation help you as parents to think about the child and inwardly prepare for receiving her. If we think of every child as a special guest come to stay with us, they will, unconsciously but nevertheless effectively, feel our welcome.

The magic world inside the womb

Another tip I would offer expectant parents is to get hold of a book of photographs, taken non-invasively, of the developing embryo.

The classic example is the magnificent book *Being Born* by Sheila Kitzinger and Lennart Nilsson, but less expensive versions include Geraldine Flanagan's *Beginning Life*. Such images help us to imagine something of the world that the child comes from, a world not of conscious experience but of sensitivity and timelessness. This may be of special benefit to the father in trying to understand the world of the foetus about to be born.

Recording the birth

The birth of a child is one of the most magical moments in anyone's life. Once the child has arrived safely, and mother and baby are seen to be well, it often feels as if time has stopped, and for many people the aura of love and heightened sensibilities borders on the religious.

This is a moment to treasure forever, so does making a video of the event seem a good idea or taking a few photographs perhaps? The look on a newborn baby's face is unique. In those first few hours, babies show something of their innermost being that is soon hidden again. Yet even the best photographs often fail to record these visions. My own feeling is the moment is too special to miss by being behind the viewer of a camcorder. The images always look so different from the actual experience that they can at best serve only to jolt our memories. Certainly, there are few women who really want to be reminded of what it all looked like!

What does help, though, is to take the first opportunity that comfortably suggests itself to talk about the experience and go over it in detail. As long as this is agreed by the mother, it can bind together those who shared the experience and possibly deter postnatal depression. The baby too will be able to hear and recognise her parents' voices and emotions.

After the birth

Having a baby is a shock. Rahima Baldwin Dancy describes her own experience in her book *You Are Your Child's First Teacher*:

Like most people, I had grand ideas about being a parent before I had children . . . but when Seth and Faith actually came into my life, the reality of the situation came as an abrupt shock. All of my idealism had in no way prepared me for the minute-by-minute, day-after-day encounter of living with a child.

One of Rahima's pieces of advice is to maintain contact with those mothers you got to know during the antenatal classes:

as you become friends share your thoughts and feelings about being pregnant, giving birth, being a parent. You can help these friends by doing things for them in the weeks after their baby is born. And you can help a new mother, as well as learning more about being with young babies, by making yourself available for your friend to leave her baby for an hour or two while she goes shopping or does something by herself.

This strikes me as very good advice. Not all women have (or want to have) the benefit of their own mother's advice, and the self-help that new mothers can give each other is probably equally, if not more, valuable.

The development of the child over the first 3 years

The following sections give an overview of the key stages in child development. I have separated this into:

- biological development
- language development
- social and behavioural development.

These different strands obviously interrelate but have been teased apart for simplicity. My overview is intended to provide only an *outline*, more detailed information and descriptions being found in the recommended literature. *Please remember there is huge variation between children: some start late, others early.* If you are at all worried, please contact a health professional. Above all use your common sense, following your innermost feelings after quiet reflection.

Biological development

At birth

At birth, the baby's *head* is about 35 cm in circumference, her average length about 52 cm and her weight about 3.5 kg. Her brain weighs 350–400 g, about 30 per cent the weight of an adult's. The brain is about one-ninth of the weight of the whole body but over the first year consumes between a fifth and a quarter of all the body's energy. The brain will grow to about 1000 g, more than half its final adult weight, within the first year. The bones of the head are soft and not yet fused, the fontanelle at the front often remaining open.

The *heart* too is proportionately much larger, and at birth the pulse is fast and unstable (around 180 compared with an adult's 72 beats per minute), settling down to a resting rate of between 120–140. The frequency of breathing is between 38 and 42 breaths a minute. At birth, the baby's temperature is slightly higher than the mother's, at 98.8°F, but it drops by 5°F within 2 hours, which means babies need to be kept warm. For the first 2 weeks, they cannot shiver to generate heat and need to be wrapped up quickly.

The legs are short, with the knees turned outwards and the soles of the feet facing each other.

At birth, babies have several strong *reflexes*. These include the obvious ones such as breathing, sucking and swallowing and also the *rooting* instinct; this causes the baby to open her mouth, screw up one eye and turn her head towards the nipple, and can be caused by touching the baby's cheek. The *Moro or startle reflex* causes the child when startled or roughly handled, to throw up her arms, tremble and then pull her hands back as if grasping something. The *grasping reflex* makes the child grasp things that touch her palm, and the *walking reflex* causes her to make walking movements if held upright with her feet touching the ground (but do not try to make a newborn stand!). Related to the latter is the *stepping reflex*. These so-called primitive reflexes are usually replaced by learned responses and behaviour after about 3 months, but their presence at birth indicates a healthy nervous system.

At birth, babies can *digest* colostrum, a thick liquid released by the mother's breast that is rich in proteins and helps to establish the child's immune system by lining the stomach walls with a protective layer against invasive bacteria. Babies can digest true milk at about 2–3 days, but cows milk can generate allergies at this early age.

Newborn babies *sleep* most of the time.

1 month to 1 year

After a *few weeks*, the baby can lift her chin up when lying on her front. She sleeps for 16–18 hours a day.

At *2 months*, the baby can lift up her head and can raise her chest when lying on her front.

At *3 months*, she can reach for but usually misses objects in front of her, can play with her own fingers and can prop herself up on her arms.

At *4 months*, the baby can sit up with support.

At *5 months*, she begins to grasp objects. Breast-feeding gives way to 'solid' food such as purées and mashed bananas.

At *6 months*, the child can sit on a chair and reach for and catch objects dropped into her hand. She can grasp objects and pass them from one hand to the other, as well as turn over. The brain has reached about 50–60 per cent of its adult weight, indicating a rapid growth of nerves and their connections within the brain, and the formation of neural networks. The first teeth begin to come through.

By *7 months* of age, babies can usually sit unsupported for at least a minute and can grasp their own toes.

At *8 months*, the baby can stand with some support. Objects can be held using opposition of the thumb and fingers (the pincer grip).

At *9 months*, she can hold on to the furniture and can stand alone while holding on.

10 months of age sees babies crawling rapidly and with co-ordinated movements, thus travelling remarkably far in a short time. They can sit down by themselves without falling over and some can already walk holding an adult's hand. They can pick up balls and bricks using their index finger and thumb like tweezers.

At *11 months*, most babies can walk holding onto a hand. They possess the ability to point to things they want (and to throw tantrums if they can't have them).

At *12 months*, the child uses furniture to rise to standing position and can pick up smaller objects with some precision.

1–3 years

By *13 months* of age, babies can crawl upstairs.

At *14 months*, they stand alone and unsupported.

At *15–16 months*, the baby walks alone with some certainty. Manual skills involve being able to drop things from her hand at will (often from her high chair onto the floor to see your reaction). The breathing frequency is now 23–24 breaths a minute and the pulse 120 beats per minute. The child's immune system has been strengthened by many minor infections.

By *2 years*, the child can run, pick things up from a standing position without overbalancing, climb steps alone and jump with two feet. The brain has now reached 80 per cent of its adult weight. She can also unscrew bottles and hold a pencil like an adult.

At *2½ years*, she can stand on tiptoe.

At *3 years*, the child can balance on one foot and ride a bicycle. The (20) milk teeth are usually complete. She can begin to get herself dressed and undressed. The child has on average grown to 88 cm and 12 kg.

Language development

Here, I will present a summary of the general stages, going into more detail in Chapter 10.

First year

During the first *1–2 months*, not much happens that could really be described as language, but the child is developing her speech organs, both those for speaking and those for speech perception. Babies react to noises around them and soon learn to tell neutral sounds and human speech apart.

They soon develop a repertoire of cries, grunts, gurgles and clicks that relate closely to the experiences of breathing, feeding and digestion. The sounds babies produce are closely linked to their breathing rhythm. The range of sounds include '*eh*', '*ah*', '*hah*', and '*eh-eh*' (*eh* being pronounced as in '*air*'), all of which are variants of breathing out without articulation, that is, sounds produced at the back of the throat.

By *3 months*, the tongue has moved forward into the mouth, making it possible to shape the vowel sounds more effectively. In response to being spoken to, babies will form sounds such as '*goo*', '*coo*', '*la*' and '*aah*'. Smiles and laughs enter their vocabulary, to the delight of all concerned.

By *4 months*, the melody of their cries begins to vary and is no longer so obviously linked to breathing out. Individual sounds can now be articulated, new sounds including '*rrr*'.

By *5 months*, the child begins to articulate the sounds characteristic of her mother tongue instead of a more universal range of sounds. She begins to play with sounds to express her feelings, new sounds include lip-sounds such as '*m*', '*b*' and '*v*'.

By *6 months*, children begin to understand and respond to the emotional meaning of words and phrases. Their own sounds begin to be more rhythmical, and they play with sequences of sounds.

Between *7 and 8 months*, children begin to 'chatter', using long sequences of sounds, often double syllables such as '*da-da*', '*ba-ba*' and '*dee-dee*' (at which stage parents believe that they have been named!). Babies imitate spoken speech melody and play with variations of volume and pitch, especially when lying on their own in a relatively quiet environment in which they can clearly hear their own voice. At this age they begin to respond when called. This is known as the *babbling* phase and is common even to children who are deaf and dumb. It is a crucial period of exploratory play and learning.

By *9 months*, children usually understand (even if not accept) 'No'.

By *10 months*, they usually delight their parents by saying '*Ma-Ma*' or '*Da-Da*' and meaning it. They also clearly recognise the meaning of familiar words and names, such as 'Nana' 'supper' and 'beddy-byes'.

By *11 months*, children lose certain consonants that are not distinguished in their mother tongue, such as 'l' and 'r' for Japanese children.

By *12 months*, they can vary combinations of syllables, such as '*neh-nee*' and '*da-dee*'. They can babble whole sentences of gibberish with great conviction in the melody of their mother tongue and can also speak three or four clear words that apply to a wide range of situations. This forms what is known as the 'one-word sentence' phase, which lasts between 2 months and 1 year. From this stage onwards, language development becomes highly individual. Some parents are lucky enough to recall their children's first words. Most of these one-word one-liners – cow, teddy – refer to familiar objects, although some refer to actions; '*eat*', '*open*'. Children sometimes say whole phrases as one-word sentences, for example 'all-gone-now' or 'see-you-soon'.

1–3 years

At about *18 months* of age, language usually takes off. Statistically, children will eventually reach the rate of learning a new word every 2 waking hours, starting from a vocabulary of about 20 words. They progress from one-word to two-word sentences, and with these syntax begins. Their inner grasp of the relationships that syntax expresses (who did what to whom, when and how, for example) precedes the construction of their sentences. Two-word micro-sentences contain far more implicit sense than appears when we see them printed on the page.

Children acquire recognisable regional accents at this age and enjoy little rhymes and songs. They begin to try to tell us about their experiences, which can be quite a frustrating business and requires great listening skills on the part of adults.

Between *2 and 3 years*, three- and four-word sentences that have a subject ('Daddy'), a verb ('gave') an indirect object ('Susan') and an object ('a biscuit') begin to appear. Vocabulary increases, now demonstrating plural forms. Counting begins, and children start clearly to describe events in their lives.

Social and behavioural development

At birth

The baby can recognise her mother's voice within 12 hours of birth and can also recognise her mother's smell and taste via her milk. Within 6 days, the baby can imitate facial expressions made by the mother or another familiar person.

Babies, as we well know, cry when they are uncomfortable, frightened, hungry or in pain and are usually comforted by being cradled in the arms, spoken to gently and rocked. They enjoy company but also like being left alone in their bed. They usually enjoy being bathed too, and they make eye contact.

2 months to 1 year

By *2 months*, babies react to and follow objects moving near them, initially from side to side.

By *3 months*, babies can follow objects that go up and down. They listen to singing and music, follow sounds in their environment with their eyes and smile when encouraged by close-range attention.

By *4 months*, the child can follow a moving face, often imitating facial expressions and even lip movements. She can respond to friendly attention with what is known as 'social smiles'. Babies at this age can explore a new environment with their eyes.

By *5 months*, babies respond with vocal expression and show excitement and anticipation at being picked up or played with. Their expressions of joy at being tickled, for example, become more elaborate, but so to do their reactions of displeasure and protest. They respond with alert attention to music, especially live singing. They will turn and respond to a specific sound coming from a definite direction, such as a telephone ringing.

By *6 months*, babies 'speak' using their range of sounds with friendly people. They will respond to specific sounds, which indicates that they can focus their hearing.

By *7 months*, babies react in definite ways to different people they know and don't know. There is often an initial reticence with strangers, people who look in some way significantly different from those they are used to (e.g. men with beards or people with unusual spectacles, although they appear not to notice different racial characteristics). They reach out to familiar people in the expectation of being picked up. They also look down at objects that have fallen from their grasp, usually from their high chair.

By *8 months*, those around them are observed with great interest. Babies may react to their own reflection in the mirror, although not necessarily with self-recognition.

9–10 months is the age at which babies begin to discover the joys of peek-a-boo and hide and seek games. Peeping from behind a chair, or even their own fingers produces profound enjoyment. Toys will be hidden and found again. They begin to react to the mood of their parents and familiar people, imitating anxiety or cheerfulness. They can sit for longer periods on the floor and play. They also begin to imitate simple actions such as hand-washing or hammering.

Very significantly, at between *10 and 12 months*, although some-times later in boys, pointing starts, often in connection with wanting to have something. They will point to some desired object out of reach and then look from mother to object and back, followed by hefty screaming. This wonderful behaviour indicates a first ability to use symbols, since the gesture is meant to mean something: '*See that, I want it.*' This is a prerequisite for language and conceptual thought and is associated with children showing an interest in pictures and their ability to identify what is portrayed. They can then point to named objects.

At this age, they also begin to refuse to do things by wriggling or crying. They can resist having things such as scissors or toys taken away from them. In little games of exchange, they can begin to take the initiative. They enjoy waving, clapping and playing simple pat-a-cat games. Their motor co-ordination enables them to hold small objects and begin to use spoons.

1–3 years

From *12 to 18 months*, young children begin to be able to play with other children, although this is only at a very simple level of showing, giving (and mostly) taking. However, they take account of the other baby's presence in a new way. They begin to respond to simple requests such as '*Give me the cup please*', but they can also begin to be deliberately awkward. In play, children can push toy cars or trains around making 'brmm' sounds. They also begin to build towers with blocks, starting by simply putting one on top of the other.

At *18 months to 2 years* of age, toddlers begin to be able to choose what they like and dislike; they can in fact, if allowed to, become quite fussy. They love to listen to simple stories and follow picture book stories. They can point to named parts of the body and familiar objects.

From *2–3 years* – the 'terrible twos' – is strongly a 'me too' age. Children want to join in all kinds of suitable and unsuitable activities but have no real sense of the purpose or use of household appliances, and therefore no sense of danger. They open and shut drawers and doors noisily. They 'sweep' the floor, thus distributing the dirt very effectively everywhere. They will stand for hours turning taps on and off until their little hands are blue with cold.

They can increasingly play with similarly-aged children. They can also cope, with their own agreement, with being separated for short periods from their mother as long as they are in a safe and familiar situation. Play becomes more complex and elaborate. Towers can be built and joyfully knocked down again. Shops can be set up and played with, dolls dressed and put to bed, bottles unscrewed.

Between the ages of 2 and 3, most children go through their first real psychological crisis as their sense of self develops. They can express this most obviously by saying 'No!' The mood of 'me too' gives way to 'I don't want to.' But they also insist on attempting all kinds of technically impossible tasks such as tying their shoelaces, fastening their car seat belt and plugging in the hair drier on their own.

Children can, however, also become fearful of being alone. They suddenly need to have the light on at night or, worse still, come into Mummy and Daddy's bed. There isn't a moment's peace!

Exercise 6

This is a hard one and will require several attempts. Sitting quietly, look back and try to recall your earliest childhood memories. You may require some help here. If your parents are around, ask where you lived when you were a young child and see if you can remember anything about the house. Look at relatives' old photographs and see if you can make a connection. Try to stick to objective facts rather than being influenced by others' opinions of what you were like.

Once you have located early memories, recall them two or three times, each time looking for more detail. When you have any coherent images, try writing them down. Describe the place, other people, any situations you can recall and what you felt. Finally, write down what you feel you want to.

The actual task begins once there are a few early memories and you feel comfortable with them. It really doesn't matter how accurate they are, just try to be honest

---

with yourself. The exercise itself is to try to feel what it is like to be very young, to put yourself into the place of a very young child.

To complement your own experience, you can try to observe young children as and when the opportunity presents itself. Just watch them with a warm, friendly empathy and try to imagine what they are seeing, thinking and feeling. But don't ask them anything, and if you sense that they feel watched, stop as this exercise should be totally unobtrusive.

You don't need to write a Booker Prize-winning recollection of your childhood in Tipperary. Just jot down whatever comes to mind in the way of detail. Once you have some images of things, people or places, try to recall what it felt like – put yourself back in your old shoes, slip into your favourite jumper.

If you find you have mixed memories from various indistinct ages, this doesn't matter too much at present. Grouping them in association with places will help to sort them out later. We are going to try to compare different phases in the next exercise.

5

The nature of development

Let them develop

Children were traditionally thought of simply as being less competent, more dependent people. They were given as much care as they needed until they could be effectively trained for their role in life. From an early age, they were expected to be as useful as possible and, if not actually required to help, then expected not to hinder the important business of life. This seems harsh to us today: our instincts tell us that if we want children to grow up as free individuals, they need to be nurtured as children.

> Childhood consists of a series of developmental stages usually marked by significant changes such as losing our milk teeth or becoming sexually mature. No other creature on earth has such a long period of childhood with as many complex phases and transitions.

Understanding our children and offering them the best support we can means learning the nature of each phase of childhood and recognising the ways in which children differ in each of the main phases (see Chapter 3).

The ordinary miracles of growing up

I think everybody intuitively knows how important childhood is, but precisely because it is so important, we sometimes expect and demand too much. Sometimes what we demand is inappropriate and may in fact limit our children's development. To quote my colleague and friend Michael Rose in *Ready to Learn*:

> *Childhood is a time of miracles and the whole of the rest of life is its outcome. However, as a culture we have become impatient with ordinary miracles. We have been drawn to perform miracles of our own.*

There are two dangers here. One is standing back and leaving children to their own devices; the other is trying to engineer the outcome through too much intervention. That's what Michael is referring to. This approach includes everything from using genetic engineering, to choose traits for our children, to forcing children to do things before they are really ready.

Hurry up and grow up!

It's often very tempting to hope that children will move on from the phase they are currently stuck in.

> If we don't really understand that childhood is a valid time in its own right, we may be tempted to assume an attitude that urges the child to hurry up and make progress.

Our attitude need not even be spoken out loud. As we have seen, children are masters at reading our body language, our suppressed impatience, even before they can understand the words we use. The attitudes we have, even barely conscious ones, can be very influential. Attitudes can in effect say, *'For goodness sake, use the toilet'*, *'Why can't you put your own clothes on?'* *'Can't you see that I'm not in the mood?'* And so the child comes under pressure to be something she is not.

Less haste, more speed

The price of hurrying childhood is the potential loss of qualities we urgently need as adults: openness, enthusiasm, flexibility, imagination and creativity, boundless energy, an instinctive sense of wonder. As adults, we may have to work very hard to regain these and even harder to develop them from scratch, so such qualities should be allowed to develop and flourish in children. And if we, as parents and educators, can participate in the process of child development, we may once more catch at least some of their sparkle.

Lost youth

It is not only the magical qualities of early childhood that I am referring to. Who would not wish to have again the qualities of a youngster between the age of say 15 and 21? Who would not want to have the body and energy of a 17-year-old, albeit with the mind of worldly-wise thirty-something? Think of how we as adults consciously and unconsciously strive to retain or regain the quintessential qualities of youth – beauty, energy, freedom, sexual allure, adventurousness. How much of our culture is devoted to perpetuating this state; how much money is spent trying to achieve it?

Sex, violence, power-trips and insecurity

But just imagine what it would be like if we never really grew out of our youth. Let us for a disturbing moment think of the two aspects of youth that become the most problematical: burgeoning sexuality and a newly awakened awareness of physical strength without the experience, maturity or common sense to handle them. All forms of sexual deviancy and violence are exaggerated forms of the forces of sexuality and power that develop in adolescence. You could say that they are unredeemed by conscience. Let us be honest too and admit how we have never quite outgrown the more problematical areas of youth, such as self-consciousness and concern about our appearance.

Sadly, many of the people who never fully grow out of their adolescence cause us all problems. We can see this in the disturbing evidence that football hooligans and holiday yobs often turn out to have respectable jobs, families and mortgages, yet have a need to get drunk or behave in a violent or sexually abusive way. It is as if they are stuck in early adolescence but with an adult income to satisfy their desires.

Interestingly, this is the thing adolescents are least tolerant of in adults. Adolescents expect more of us. They expect maturity, they even expect us to be wise, and in my view, they have every right to do so. They expect us to have broken out of the vicious cycle of parents projecting their unfulfilled wishes and dreams onto the next generation.

It is often those people who have least advanced who like to lecture young people. It is bad enough when parents do this, but when politicians and tabloid journalists start telling youngsters what they should be, and how to think and behave, we begin to find the roots of social problems and alienation. In my experience adolescents have a fine sense for hypocrisy.

> If we want young people to outgrow their adolescence and become mature adults, we have to help them and, above all, set a good example. This means that we have to understand something of the developmental process itself.

What is development?

Childhood and adolescence are all about development, and the art of living is to be able to go on developing throughout our lives. As the singer Bob Dylan memorably put it back in the 1960s, '*He not busy being born is busy dying.*' So what is development? Let me put it as simply as I can.

Development is more than mere *change* because it implies not merely a modification, but a transformation of what is there. Nor is it the mere addition of new parts, like adding new software to your PC. Development always involves two aspects:

- who I already am: the stage of development I have already attained

- who I will become: the potential in me that wants to be realised.

Each individual has something inside herself that wants to become more. This something is an inner self that other people cannot necessarily see and of which the individual is usually only dimly aware. It is a kind of energy source from which we derive our motivation to try new things, take new risks and open ourselves up to others. Much of our everyday behaviour is habit, conditioned by our upbringing and by the way in which other people relate to us, but when we act out our inner self, it often leads us to break the mould. It can be the source of new ideas, showing us life and others through 'new eyes'.

The lower and higher selves

But this inner self also has a lower and a higher mode of being. The lower part leads us to behave egotistically, to gratify our desires and to lessen our pain, be it emotional or physical. Our lower inner self leads us above all to respond to our bodily drives. It is the source of our will to survive and breed. Its effectiveness can be traced back to what is referred to in biology as our *selfish genes*, which for many biologists is all we have. This basic drive is thought by some to explain *all* human behaviour, whether it is the work of an artist or just being a good mother.

The better person within us operates without our knowing, leading us towards what we need to experience. It is far wiser than we are, for it contains the unrealised future. People once spoke of having a guardian angel who watched over them and guided them, which can be thought of, depending on one's philosophical or religious views, as a spirit guide, or the god in whom we believe. I simply call this being my higher self, the spiritual part of me that is linked to the spiritual worlds. Knowing that it is there helps me to know that I can become a more complete, a more conscious and a more capable person. In times of great need, it can be a comforter.

It seems to me that human behaviour is far better understood and explained by recognising that we possess this higher inner self, which carries with it the potential for me to become wiser, more integrated as a whole person, more aware of the world and others and therefore more able. This inner self strives to make me a more complete and therefore a better person, real growth implying moral as well as physical development.

I am an 'I'

When we refer to ourselves, we say 'I', this 'I' being the inner principle that drives our development. The best way of describing it is perhaps to call it our 'self-activity', the motor of development, continuously striving to bring our true self ever more completely to expression through what it already possesses, namely a body and a bundle of abilities. Our development through our lower self is limited. It is only when our higher self penetrates and transforms the lower self that we really become better people. Thus, our task as human beings is to transform the natural processes of our lower self into higher cultural attributes. But what does it mean in practice?

> Out of the child's curiosity has to grow a genuine, open-minded interest in the world. Out of bodily hunger must grow a need to 'take in' what we can of the world. Out of the desire to have sex and reproduce must grow the capacity to love and be creative. Out of the energy we use to assert ourselves in the world comes the ability to be active in the pursuit of higher goals. Out of aggression and self-protection can grow qualities of leadership, endurance and self-sacrifice in the service of others.

Where is our 'I'?

When all the cells in our body have been worn out and replaced by new ones, a continuous process, what is left of us? What perpetuates my identity and keeps this vast array of cells *me*? That invisible quality is our 'I', our inner self, our self-activity, but where is it located? It cannot be located in our body, not in our brain, nor in any other single part as our cells are constantly being exchanged. In fact, science does its best to avoid answering this question altogether. Yet we are somebody. When we wake up in the morning, we know who we are. There is continuity in our lives. So because this 'I' has no physical location, it cannot be material: it must be spiritual. All living beings have a core of existence that is not limited to their physical bodies, but what differentiates human beings is our personality, our individual identity and our self-consciousness.

The individual spirit

> At the core of each one of us is something unique, an *individual spirit*. Growing up is the process of the individual spirit striving to realise its potential, working to master what it has inherited, seeking to find its own voice and direct its own development.

It is important to distinguish between this individual spirit and any form of self-centred egotism. We all put our own needs first, sometimes extending this to what we consider to belong to us – our children, spouse and so on. But what is the difference between egotism and a healthy care for ourselves and those close to us? With other people, it is easier to say: it is healthy when we respect another person's right to be who she is. Projecting our wishes onto her is not. With regard to ourselves, egotism is simply selfishness, putting our wishes before those of others.

Who is the moral voice within?

Our lower self, our everyday personality, is mostly selfish, self-centred and loud. Our higher self, our 'I', is also our inner voice of conscience, so when it comes to hard moral choices, it is easy to distinguish the lower from the higher self. The lower self wants satisfaction *now* and will take the easy way out; the higher 'I' will know what is good for us and those around us in the *long run* but its voice is quieter. Because children's own 'I' is often not yet fully conscious and accessible to them, they need an 'I' in the form of a parent, friend or teacher to guide them.

Religious and community values can help guide us to such a

recognition, but in the end only we as individuals can determine what is really egotistical and what is morally right. And experience shows how much this depends on circumstances. There are very few absolutes: in some situations, our 'I' knows that it is necessary and morally right to put ourselves first.

The greatest challenge is to be able to free ourselves enough from the clutter of feelings and moods that we can hear our own true inner voice. This is essential in order to know what to do as a parent, to nurture the emergent 'I' in our children. After all, we want our children to be their best selves *our* selves. The world is clearly in need of young people capable of taking the initiative, but they can only really do this from within themselves.

What else is an individual?

In a previous chapter, we talked about how an individual is more than the sum of inherited characteristics and the influence of culture and upbringing, although many may disagree with this view. (Those interested in taking this further can refer to the Further reading section at the back of the book.) I suggested that something else is also at work, an 'I' or human spirit, which governs how we make use of the genetic and environmental gifts we have been given. It is the 'I' factor that determines why brothers and sisters, even twins, can be such different people despite having pretty much the same bunch of genes, having eaten the same food, put up with the same parents and grown up in the same socio-economic milieu.

Of course, no two people, even identical twins, ever have quite the same experiences. Parents treat the first born significantly differently from the fourth of their offspring. Some children favour fruit and vegetables, others meat, regardless of what is served up at the domestic table. Different teachers can make a huge difference even within the same school.

What is individual destiny?

These arguments for difference in spite of growing up together beg a further question about individuality. What determines whether you are born first or fourth in a family? What determines whether you sleep well or have nightmares as a child? What determines why, having been given all the musical gifts anyone could wish for, all the opportunities for genius to develop, a supremely talented individual such as the pianist Glen Gould comes to hate performing? What determines an individual's destiny?

The conventional scientific answer is that this is merely the product of chance and circumstance acting on what is laid down within our genetic code. But we know from experience that it is not just a matter of having certain genes or of being in the right place at the right time (or the wrong place at the wrong time). Having particular genes does not absolutely predetermine you to be a certain person, nor do environmental influences entirely shape who you become. Why do some people survive deprivation and social disadvantages to become happy and successful while others who apparently have every advantage going fail to cope? It is helpful to consider here the determining role of our individuality, our 'I', as chance cannot explain all that happens.

Destiny is the freedom to get a life

Of course we can also be terribly fatalistic about destiny, assuming that what will be will be, that everything is 'written in the stars'. However, even astrologers see the influence of the stars not as binding, but as reflecting a certain starting position that still leaves room for individual choices (and mistakes). I do, however, believe that we do have a destiny, the nature of which is to present us with opportunities for development. We then end up with the opportunities, limitations and obstacles that we have created for ourselves through our freedom of choice.

> We have free will to the extent that we can recognise our destiny and do something about it, or do nothing and suffer the consequences. That's what makes us in the end – despite all the factors that make us what we are, including our genetic and cultural inheritance – individual.

What does it mean to be an individual?

Being an individual means that we are a riddle to ourselves and to others, and it is this riddle that we spend our lives trying to understand. It is also ultimately what gives our lives meaning. We pose the question '*Who am I?*' in countless different ways at each stage from our birth onwards. As infants and children we are not even conscious of the question, but our behaviour and even our bodies continuously put the question. We only begin to ask consciously in adolescence.

The core of the individual, the 'I', develops in ways other than merely physical increase or the addition of knowledge. It develops by taking hold of and transforming the body it has inherited, establishing an orientation in what it experiences of the world and the people around it through its sensory experiences. Once this orientation has been basically established, the 'I' has to order and master the experiences it discovers within itself.

But development is not only about taking in and processing what has been taken in: it is also a proactive process. The child reaches out to make contact with those around her. She increasingly acts in accord with her own, initially unconscious, intentions. To a large extent, she creates her own destiny by going out, taking on the world and then experiencing the consequences.

Why do we need to recognise individuality?

This may seem a rather unnecessary question, but the more consciously we accept our children's individuality, the more we can respect and support them in taking on their own destiny. Our destiny is sometimes very hard to understand, but it does help if we know that the challenges we meet as human beings are exactly the challenges we need to grow.

Recognising individuality is important both for the child and for us as parents and educators. This is important if we are to make hard choices in the interests of that individual's development over the time of childhood dependency. After all, these individuals do not know what is good for them for years, and they rely on us almost totally for the decisions that only a fully engaged 'I' can make while their own is developing.

It takes an 'I' to recognise an 'I'

Furthermore, the human 'I' wants to be recognised by another human 'I' if it is to gain confidence, to grow. Another way of describing the 'I' in another person is what we call a person's potential. Little of our children's potential has yet been realised. They need what life brings to reveal it. It is important to reflect that only out of true respect for this unrealised potential can we find the right balance between providing secure boundaries and giving enough free space to grow and imposing too much and leaving a child unsupported.

Learning to recognise individuality

Every newborn baby is distinctive, individuality showing itself even in the first few days of life. This later becomes somewhat clouded in the typical struggles the infant encounters when making herself at home in her new body, only to emerge more strongly once the toddler stage is well established. It may therefore seem a bit presumptuous to suggest ways in which we might recognise the individuality of our child, but let us not forget there are many inherited or acquired layers that the child needs to overcome in order to be herself.

If we want to learn to recognise individuality, we must remember that it is a riddle. It is not a question of attaching labels but of learning intuitively to sense that behind this or that character trait or quality, someone is trying to express herself. The deepest of intentions are working as hidden drives, seeking to fulfil tasks we cannot know.

Reading the message

What we outwardly see or hear of the 'I' is only a picture of what lies behind as intention. It is like looking at a painting by analysing the chemical structure of the paint itself. This would tell us nothing of the effect that the colours and shapes have on the viewer, the symbolic content or the artist's intentions, all of which are necessary to interpret the painting or form a judgement on its artistic merit.

Observing a human being is a question of taking into account not only the structure and content of the painting, its message if you like, but also the creative intentions of the artist, even if the artist is unaware of these herself. A living human being is an even greater work of art than any painting, if only in the sense that a human being's scope and potential is greater.

How individuality reveals itself

Individuality reveals itself in occurrences common to all children – when a child learns to walk and move, starts to speak or deals with a certain illness; these are the kind of activity that can reveal something of the child's 'I' and its development.

> If we look closely enough, we can see that each child takes these most archetypal of developmental steps in an individual way.

But of course individuality also reveals itself to us through the unusual and unique things that happen to a child. Even if we say it is pure chance that an individual has a major accident or suffers the early loss of a parent, this does not lessen the implications for the individual, who is affected in what may be a highly significant way. Nor is it fatalistic to dwell on such things. We naturally do our utmost to protect children from any traumatic experience, but when something happens we can try to see what meaning it has for them and their development.

The word 'biography', the story of a person's life, has an ancient Greek origin meaning both '*life*' and '*script*'. This does not have to be in book form; it can be 'written' into their life. What they do and what they are leaves traces in the world around them, and it is these and their meaning that we try to read when we seek to understand a person's biography. For individuals, whatever happens, good or bad, presents them with opportunities and challenges through which they can develop and grow, the big challenges, which we sometimes experience as disasters, providing us with the greatest opportunity to develop. So seeing the big events in a person's life, learning how they reacted, how they coped, tells us much about them.

I stress once more that we are not called upon to make any judgement about an individual, merely to see this stroke of destiny as something that in some meaningful way belongs to them. Our recognition itself may in some way help too, not because of any advice or comfort we may give, but because we can provide that individual with another perspective on her own coming to terms with it. The younger the child, the more we can help the child in a direct, non-verbal way. With older children and adolescents, having the opportunity to share such thoughts can be of huge value to them as they struggle to relate to some tragedy.

In summary then:

- human beings undergo a development that is more than mere physical growth
- each individual has an inner or higher self that is striving to develop into something more whole, more complete
- this inner self, or 'I', is not a product of our brains but a spiritual entity, this spiritual aspect of individuality revealing itself through an individual's destiny
- we can learn to recognise individuality in others and ourselves by observing biographies
- recognising the existence of the spiritual core in ourselves is an important step in being in control of our lives, which helps us to be better parents and recognise our children's needs for developmental support
- we can connect to childhood through reflection and meditation.

Different is normal

Children are all different, but we are continually challenged by the question, what is normal? In fact, difference is normal.

It is quite normal for children of the same age and gender to be quite different, so how do we know if children are developing normally? The answer is unfortunately that there is no simple answer, but most do relate to a pattern of development common to children worldwide.

It is possible to give general guidelines for children's physical, emotional and mental development, as we started to do in the previous chapter. As far as we know, however, there is actually more variation between individuals within the same culture than there is between children in different parts of the world. Important stages such as a change of teeth or a girl's first period can even vary enormously within one family. What all children have in common, however, is the actual *process* of changing teeth or entering puberty, with its shared causes and symptoms. It is the way in which a child responds to these changes that is so individual. For some, these changes can be relatively minor occurrences that just happen with little or no difficulty. For others, they may be associated with profound crisis.

But *relating* to a norm is not the same as conforming to a pattern, and, as I have stressed, one of the ways in which individuality shows itself lies in how children differ from the norm. There is a world of difference, not least in our attitudes and their effects, between seeing how a child relates to a norm and seeing some deficiency if she does not conform to it. Not conforming to statistical averages of height, stage of development or level of literacy does not mean that anything is wrong. It may simply mean that an individual has a particular area that she will need to work harder on to strengthen or adapt to. If you are very tall or short as an adult, you have to come to terms with it. If you are very fat or thin, there may be something you can do to balance things out. If you are brilliant or dreadful at maths, you will need either to improve your skill or compensate by developing the things you are good at.

If in doubt, ask

Problems with a child's growth will usually be spotted by doctors during regular consultations, but if you are worried, ask your doctor or health visitor directly. Don't be embarrassed to ask: the one who will suffer most from your worry is the child. Since there is an enormous individual variation in how children grow, most concerns undoubtedly will fall within the normal range of differences. Problems that really need medical attention are very rare, at least when a normal healthy diet and lifestyle are available.

Who defines how we should be?

Unfortunately, we live in a world that is very intolerant of difference. Society is constantly defining and redefining how we should look, what we should be. Thin may be 'in' today, but sometimes a fuller figure is cool too. It would probably be best to heed the advice of the band Jefferson Airplane – *'you're only as pretty as you feel inside'*.

> Although developing a sense of what clothing and hairstyle suits us can help, living a healthy life and finding inner happiness are the best way to look attractive.

Physical appearance is one thing, but what we can do is another. Our society has traditionally valued certain skills above others. Schools usually measure our intellectual ability by examinations, but we have known for a long time that the human being has a range of different intelligences other than plain, old-fashioned cognitive intelligence. In Chapter 15, I will describe these in more detail.

Young falling stars

Children are increasingly conscious of their appearance and susceptible to the expectations that society places upon them at an ever earlier age. This in turn leads them to put demands on us as parents, not always understanding what is sensible, healthy or even appropriate for their age. Extreme forms of unhealthy behaviour, such as eating disorders or a premature overemphasis on physical training or body-building can then result.

Some of the pressure on children comes from the well-intentioned adults around them who want them to conform to *their own* ideals of style, behaviour or achievement. It is parents who dress their daughters in high heels and lipstick and get them to parade in tiny-tot bathing beauty shows. It may be harmless fun, but are those parents also aware of what children actually need? I would ask the same question of parents who enter their children for intensive training in the fields of music, ballet and sport. None of this is necessarily harmful, but is it really necessary at an early age? We need to bear in mind the following questions:

- Are you sure it is right to impose your desire for success in a particular field on your child?
- Are you sure that the training is healthy for the child's stage of physical or emotional development?
- Do you know what a child's developmental needs are at a particular age?

My first girlfriend (a *long* time ago now) suffered because her father, also her swimming trainer, drove her to extreme levels of achievement through training. When she had an emotional collapse on the eve of some major competition – entirely understandable for an adolescent girl of her age – and had to give up, she suffered terrible guilt at having failed her father. Obviously the prizes and sheer joy to be derived from success are considerable, but how many talented young achievers find that they cannot fully enjoy their success because they have lost their childhood through training, or because the pressure to maintain their position at the peak of their profession or sport drives them into unhappiness. For every happy, well-adjusted sporting or musical star, there are many more dysfunctional individuals whose very talent becomes a kind of handicap, whose childhood may have been blighted by failure and lost time.

> One of the central messages of this book, which I will repeat again and again, is that development takes time. We must ensure we do as little as possible to reduce the opportunities for *real* development by forcing children into a type of development that does not suit them. Hot-housing always runs the risk of producing a one-sidedness that weakens the whole plant.

Some will argue that if you want to achieve pole position these days, you have to start young because that's what the competition does. If your children are blessed with a major talent, I would suggest that you take professional advice. Sport England (previously known as the English Sports Council), for example, actually offers very sensible advice about the right kind of training as they know that success should not be achieved at the wrong price. Remember though the danger of depriving children of what they need most in order to have a 'normal' childhood.

Healthy development

If we are to understand our children's development, we need to have some idea of what archetypal development is. We have to remember, however, that this is an ideal, healthy development being when an individual gets as near to this ideal as possible. But an ideal is just that; it cannot, by definition, be realised. So there can be no failure as such.

Many children's development is out of balance or somewhat out of sequence. Although the proverb tells us that we can't run before we can walk, nature or nurture sometimes leads a child to do just that. Children appear to be becoming sexually mature at an ever earlier age, although their emotional development lags far behind. We have to intervene as responsible adults to ensure as best we can that the youngsters do not get themselves into situations they are not mature enough to handle.

Readiness is a tricky concept. When is anyone really ready for anything? We would probably all agree that 13-year-olds are not ready to have their own children. But if 13 is obviously too young, when is old enough – 18, 21, 25? This depends on the individual's maturity and circumstances, on what she wants to do with her life and on her strength of character. Readiness is often the result of crisis. In crisis we take steps that enable us to develop.

> Each crisis is really an opportunity and individuals grow through crisis.

Crises may manifest bodily in the form of illness, a kind of challenge that we have to overcome in order to proceed with our lives. The more we do so out of our own inner reserves, the stronger we become. Other crises may be more emotional, but the important thing is still how we deal with it.

What is health?

Is health merely the absence of illness? What does it mean when we speak of 'healthy development', 'healthy relationships' or even a 'healthy sex life'? When we speak of health in these senses, we are clearly referring to more than might concern the Health and Safety Executive. Health here is more than bodily well-being.

Defining health is difficult: it is much easier to define ill-health. Medical books are crammed with descriptions of illness, pathologies and their gory symptoms, but do not seem to provide much information about health. One could say that 'health' means 'normal', but that only begs further questions. However, one definition of health I find very helpful is drawn from the field of developmental biology. Biologists speak of organisms having a prospective potential, referring to the regenerative and developmental capacity that an organism possesses but has not yet used. This includes not only the capacity of the organism to grow, develop and reproduce, but also its capacity, within certain limits, to replace damaged or worn out cells.

> The measure of an organism's health is its ability to regenerate. Ill-health is thus the extent to which our prospective potential is impaired.

If we apply this principle to human beings, we can see it operating at several levels. On the one hand, we know that many illnesses are the body's way of strengthening itself, perhaps by fighting off pathogens in its system. Fevers, for example, help the immune system to get rid of the virus it is fighting, but too high a fever is dangerous and needs to be controlled by other methods, such as cooling the body or taking paracetamol.

Many childhood diseases are a way of strengthening the child's constitution by building up immunity in response to illness. Children who are exposed to a reasonable amount of dust and dirt (what my grandmother called 'healthy muck') tend to have a stronger immune system than those who live in overly hygienic environments. Similarly, removing the tonsils has also been found in some cases to have a counterproductive effect since these act as an important safety valve within the immune system. This is not of course an argument for an unhygienic lifestyle or avoiding antibiotics or vaccines, but it is an argument for allowing children to build up some natural immunity before we introduce strong medicaments. Real health is not only the absence of illness; it is also *the way* we are ill; it is the measure of how we grow emotionally through illness.

Health and learning

Having an illness and overcoming it is like the process of learning and developing, encountering a problem that we have to tackle and defeat, acquiring new strengths and new abilities en route. In fact, illness can often accompany important developmental stages. One of the clearest examples is of young children cutting new teeth, which is often accompanied by pain, inflammation and general misery for child and parents alike. We can view the pain of teething as a bad evolutionary side-effect and treat it, or we can support the child through the suffering with complementary medicine rather than strong medication in the knowledge that the child will be strengthened by the experience. After all, we apply the metaphor of '*cutting one's teeth*' to situations in which we learn something new or acquire a new skill.

Facing a challenge in the realm of learning and development can lead to symptoms analogous to those indicating illness – anxiety, discomfort, tension and even physical symptoms such as headaches, nausea or weariness. Once the problem has been overcome, we feel better, maybe even filled with new energy. With an illness, the physical manifestations have to be dealt with by bodily processes that call upon our reserves of prospective potential.

The causes of the illness may be external or may in some cases be provoked by something within us. The paediatrician Dr Michaela Glöckler raises a very interesting question with regard to this latter aspect in the introduction to her book *A Guide to Child Health*. She asks:

Is it sometimes the case that illnesses also arise because something has not been learned through one's own initiative or worked through in the soul and is thus forced to be resolved at the bodily level?

Illness is a means to greater health

If the challenge of a developmental crisis or an important new stage in learning is not worked through at the emotional or cognitive level, in what Dr Glöckler calls the soul, the problem can subsequently express itself as a bodily illness. But the reverse may also be true. If an individual is able to work through new challenges in her inner development in a healthy, i.e. a *health-giving*, way, she may not need to have to go through the crisis at a physical level.

> If unresolved crisis in the soul can appear as bodily illnesses, resolving such crises ought to work in a preventative way with regard to physical health.

Body and soul are not separate, parallel realms but are wholly integrated. This highlights one of the great opportunities and tasks we have as parents and educators. If we are able to create conditions within which the child can develop in a healthy way at the right time, we may also be able to prevent the child having to experience some illnesses at the bodily level. This means that a child's upbringing should be health-giving in emotional and developmental ways, and should avoid creating conditions in which the child is hindered in healthily meeting the challenges that face her. It also means allowing that development to occur in its own healthy time and not putting the children under pressure to do things too early, when they are not yet ready to cope. Allowing a child to develop at her own pace is the best way to create health for life.

Exercise 7

This task is to try to remember what it felt like to be about 10 or 11 years old. Try to recall other children, perhaps your friends and schoolmates at that time, as well as yourself. Try especially to recall what you thought about the world around you, what interested you, what you liked doing, the places you liked to go. Write down any memories and feelings you have. If you wish, you can also try to recall what made you unhappy, although if this brings up painful memories, stop and try to find a trusted friend with whom you can talk.

6

Coming to our senses

How our senses nourish us

Children take the world in, and at the same time enter the world, through three portals: the senses, breathing and nutrition. In each case, we take something in, transform it, nourish ourselves and return something to the world. With breathing and eating, this process is familiar, yet what we perceive through our senses nourishes us in equally important ways. People who suffer sensory deprivation can vouch for how important the world of the senses is to our psychological well-being. Furthermore, the way in which we perceive the world and other people powerfully influences how we act towards them. Many problems in the world have to do with our not being able to see or hear what is really there.

The child as wholly sense organ

As Rudolf Steiner repeatedly put it, the young child is wholly sense organ. What he meant was that a very young child is fundamentally open to her environment; nothing can be filtered out. What is more, all the various sensory modalities are integrated, i.e. all sensory impressions merge into one great powerful impression that affects the whole being of the child. This is hard for an adult to understand.

We can ignore or turn away from sensory stimuli that we do not like or are too strong, too loud, too hot, but the infant cannot do this.

> Unprotected and exposed to every impression, children are at the mercy of their environment, and not all environments are merciful.

One of Rudolf Steiner's key insights was to realise how much children imitate and how deeply this imitation, especially in their early years, influences not only their behaviour, but also their whole development. Not even Jean Piaget, who did so much to map out the stages of child development, realised how important imitation is. As we shall see later, it is a crucial part of learning and developing, but, as anyone can see, it depends on being able to perceive properly. If we consider how impressionable infants are, the experiences we expose children to thus become very important in how we choose to bring them up.

What are the senses?

The sense organs are not merely windows on the world. Windows are passive, letting the light through and maybe under certain conditions filtering it out or reflecting it, but there is no activity involved. The human senses differ from cameras, microphones or other instruments to collect stimuli in that they require individuals to respond and turn their attention towards the object of perception.

> There is a difference between hearing and listening, between seeing and looking. The difference is that, in looking and listening, we direct our attention towards the object and focus on it.

That means we actively seek and create an inner relationship with what we see or hear; if we did not do this, the world we perceive would remain incomprehensible. For every sensory impression, we generate a corresponding inner activity that enables us to recognise *what* we hear or see and includes feelings generated by what we perceive. Only then can we begin to form a mental picture or a concept of what we have experienced, which can later be recalled. This is a hugely complex process requiring a phenomenal amount of activity within our nervous system before it can become useful to us, and this whole process needs time to develop.

Like any complex system in nature, the full skill of perception cannot simply be created complete at birth. The basic structures take much embryonic time to grow and then even longer to develop in terms of function, and integration with the other senses. It is like tuning a hugely complex musical instrument and adding it into an orchestra. Our hearing, for example, takes 10 or more years to be fully developed, during which time it benefits from being given relatively few primary experiences to process first before moving on to more complex and powerful sensory impressions.

Making sense of the world

In order to be able to relate to the world, we need to create a picture *in here*, as it were, of what is *out there*. For the young child, '*out there*' includes not only the world around her, but also the environment of her own body. As adults, we can learn to ignore all but the most noticeable inner impressions, such as indigestion or a painful toe, but for the infant, the *milieu interior*, as it is biologically known, is a big immediate world. Bodily discomfort, digestive processes of all kinds, even the sense of her own breathing or pulse, can assume the 'colour' and 'contour' of a whole landscape or symphony.

The objective world outside and even inside the body generates sensations, those in turn generate emotions and feelings that provide colour (texture, shape, resonance and much more besides) to the way in which we relate to the world. The environment we grow up in shapes how we think and feel about the world, which then influences how we act. In the course of our lives, the sensations and feelings that certain experiences call forth in us change, becoming deeper, richer and ever more substantial, and from this basis of experience we derive much of our sense of meaning. Only when we have formed complex feelings and concepts can we really begin to know about the world to make sense of it.

- The senses need time and protection from over stimulation in order to develop healthily, which has consequences for what we expose young children to.
- Only with fully developed sensory organs (and their corresponding neural connections) can the organism respond to the world in an integrated way. We want our children to be co-ordinated in their movements, fully capable of speaking and listening, musically capable, sensitive and responsive to other people and their environments.
- We want children to be able to perceive all the wonderful qualities of the world with fully developed senses so that they can form an open relationship with their environment.
- A child's sense of self is based upon a fully developed sense of security within her own organism and environment. This too needs fully functioning senses.
- The bodily senses provide a basis for the higher skills of understanding and using language, for the ability to think coherently and understand complex phenomena.
- The quality of our sensory experiences, together with our ability to form clear concepts, is the ultimate basis for forming meaningful judgements.

The central idea here is perhaps that the more open we are to the world and other people, they more *they* can reveal their true inner being to us. The more we limit our sensory abilities, the harder it is to relate to the world and others in it. Harder but not of course impossible. People who are limited by birth, accident or illness in one or other sense organ, can with effort overcome their limitation and detachment from the world and compensate through the pronounced development of their other senses.

Reduction in sensory sensitivity

Several long-term studies have shown that there has been a progressive reduction in children's sensory awareness of 1 per cent per year over the past 20 years, mainly as a result of sensory overstimulation. This means that children are perceiving 20 per cent less of the world than they were 20 years ago – and can you imagine the massive public outcry if someone forced children to wear glasses that cut their vision by 20 per cent? This loss of sensory perception is compounded by a breakdown of children's capacity to integrate their experiences, reducing the individual's quality of 'reality'. This desensitising of sensory experience brings with it a desensitising of the emotional life, the individual remaining more detached, less touched by her experiences. This weakens the power of empathy and leads to apathy.

> Boredom, lack of involvement and dullness all block the more sensitive side of human nature, which expresses itself in love, interest, curiosity and compassion.

The other effect of desensitisation is that the child needs ever more powerful sensory impressions to react to – louder, brighter, more violent, more dramatic experiences. It is easy to see where such a satisfaction of the need for greater thrills leads: we should not be surprised to see our children and young people drawn to activities and substances that create heightened, sensational experiences. More and more health professionals are recognising what child psychologist Joseph Chiltern Pierce calls '*the American child's need for more intense and ever greater quantity of stimuli and corresponding insensitivity to most human values*'. And the UK is never far behind America.

So what is the main cause of this loss of sensory bombardment and desensitisation?: an early exposure to TV, videos, computers, loud music and the trappings of modern urban culture. Research in Brazil has shown that children growing up in pre-literate societies in that country demonstrated 25 per cent more sensory perception and integration than urban children. But as we can't all move to the Amazon rainforest, what can be done? Let us first try to understand the nature of the child's developing senses.

How the senses develop

When babies are born, they are tiny, helpless creatures almost entirely dependent on their parents. Their limbs are totally under-developed and it is a long time before they can even support the weight of their own heads. The sensory system is, however, functional from birth and in some respects even earlier. But although the senses are sensitive from so early in life, the processing of sensory impressions, their differentiation and comprehension, takes much longer.

Although the baby's movements are uncontrolled, her eyes can focus on and perceive a face within hours. The newborn child can recognise sounds heard in the womb and can respond to her mother's voice within the first 5 or 6 days of life. After a month, babies can distinguish between the sounds 'p' and 'b'. The sense of taste can already distinguish between sweet and sour at birth, bitter tastes causing the baby to make a face. At 6 days, she can taste the difference between her mother's milk and that of another woman.

Despite the fact that babies respond to human faces, and even symbolic circles with a curve for a mouth and two dots for the eyes, within a matter of weeks, their sense of sight is limited by a kind of short-sightedness. They learn to focus at a distance of about 20 cm, which is the average distance between a baby's face and her mother's when she is being held in her mother's arms. The clue to these remarkable findings is the fact that babies gaze into people's eyes as soon as they can control their eye movements. This is one of the things that make babies so endearing: we feel as if they are looking right into us. Indeed, that black hole at the centre of our eyes reveals more of our true selves than any other part of our bodies, as the greatest painters have always known.

Active babies

It used to be thought that newborn babies were pretty passive, probably needing several months to recover from the trauma of birth, but this view has changed radically in recent years as a result of scientists making ever more accurate observations. Not only do babies have wide-awake senses, but they are also capable in their own way of significant and deliberate responses, even though they lack the bodily co-ordination and language to express themselves in ways we can more easily recognise.

They are able to direct their attention towards what interests them.

Scientists learned from breast-feeding mothers that children demonstrate their interest through the intensity of their sucking, so they rigged up dummies with sensors to measure the level of sucking to observe babies' reactions. Combined with a close monitoring of babies' eyes and head movements, researchers were able to observe how they responded to a variety of sensory impressions. It was thus possible to observe behaviour that would otherwise not have been visible in children until they were much older. Such research revealed for example that:

- babies of 3 months old realised that, by sucking, they could alter the lens of a projector and thus focus the image projected onto a screen (not very useful but showing they can focus their vision on middle distance)
- similarly aged babies could make a mobile hanging above their cots swing by moving their legs, attached by a ribbon to the mobile (showing they can deliberately cause something to happen)
- 5-month-old babies can tell the difference between a sound that is moving away from them and a sound that is coming nearer
- by responding to puppets appearing on a small stage, 5-month-old babies showed that they could appreciate numerical values up to three.

What engages babies most of course is their contact with parents or familiar family members. Babies use the limited possibilities they have to make contact and communicate with those around them. This mostly means eye contact and that very effective method known as crying.

The anthropologist Jonathan Kingdon has noted that a yelling baby coerces adults, even unrelated ones to respond. This appears to be a universal trait, which perhaps evolved when our ancestors shared savanna environments with large predators who would respond with interest to the sound of a human infant's voice.

According to Kingdon, getting the child to shut up quickly would have had immediate survival implications for a group of early humans. Whether or not this is true, it is a fact that very few people can happily ignore a screaming child for long.

The young of most animals can control their parents' behaviour and gain attention and food by squealing, wailing or shrieking. Human babies have by far the greatest repertoire of cries. Experienced mothers and child-carers can tell whether a baby's crying is serious or simply the child experimenting with her new-found voice. So babies equip themselves to engage with their environment.

What kind of environment do babies need?

After the weightless world of warmth and darkness of the womb, birth is certainly traumatic. In their first few months, babies thus need comfort, warmth, nourishment and security. They also need peace and quiet. There is so much to get used to – a body pulled down by gravity, the whole business of feeding and digesting, dressing and being changed, people to relate to – that babies benefit from as fewer other distractions as possible.

Crying and sleeping are as essential to babies as love and nourishment. In her book, *Nøkken: A Garden for Children*, Danish childcare expert Helle Heckmann says:

> At birth, which is a struggle for life and death, the infant must learn to breathe, experience pressure, feel hunger, go from darkness to light. Only sleep restores the infant to a familiar state (to the womb). That is why an infant must cry a lot and sleep a lot.

> We find this hard to accept since in our culture crying means unhappiness and we try always to avoid unhappiness.

Yet crying is the child's main means of communication, at least during her first few months. Quite apart from the benefits of crying in terms of strengthening breathing, attempting to stop a baby crying every time it does so is not necessarily the best thing to do. If the baby learns that she only needs to cry to get attention, she will quickly adopt this strategy and maybe continue to seek attention in countless ways throughout the rest of her childhood and even life. Children of course need love and security but caring does not need to mean immediate reaction and constant supervision. Here is Helle Heckmann again:

Show care and affection in situations when it is natural, such as eating and nursing, when it is natural to create a you-and-I situation, when it is natural to nurse, sing, chat and to get to know each other. The rest of the time it is important to leave the infant in peace and quiet to sleep or, when awake, to get to know herself without constant intervention from her surroundings. Often it is very difficult to show the infant this respect and leave her alone. Constantly satisfying your own need for reassurance and your need to look at your beautiful baby will often influence the infant's ability to be content with herself.

> A child who can be at peace with herself in the early months is far more likely to become a contented child, a good sleeper and the master of her own body.

This is not advice to abandon your child – she should know you are around – but judge whether it really is necessary to go in and see her. Often a quick visit to check that everything is all right will show that you care and that you are pleased she is learning to be comfortable with her body. Remember that restless, nervous parents create restless, nervous children.

What babies need in the first few months

The creation of inner peace and equilibrium at this tender early age is invaluable for a child's whole life, providing a sound foundation for all subsequent development.

To summarise what babies do (and don't) need:

- as much quiet as possible
- no sudden, loud sounds and no mechanical sounds such as radio or TV

- reassuring, friendly human voices
- the live sounds and smells of nature: birds, lapping waves, gentle wind, flowers, etc.
- being kept away from smoky places and smokers
- no unnecessary driving around in cars or buses and definitely no airplanes (not only because of stress and noise but because the change in air pressure is bad for tender little ears)
- warmth, so the child can maintain her body temperature without using too much energy
- subdued lighting, natural light (but not dazzling sunshine) and candlelight
- warm colours such as rose and violet rather than dazzling primaries, for example, a pale-coloured veil of silk over the cot to provide texture and shade from bright light
- natural materials rather than synthetics as they have a richer, more subtle range of colours, scents and textures
- clothing that provides warmth, allows the skin to breathe, is soft to the touch and is loose to permit movement, i.e. natural materials such as cotton, silk and new wool
- good-quality nourishment (mother's milk is best, then another woman's milk and thereafter the best-quality organic milk substitute), avoiding sugar
- confident, firm handling when being held, fed or changed
- time to develop without being forced or overstimulated (especially important in terms of movement, as discussed below)
- as little stress as possible.

Although this is a list of ideals, we can all do our best to fulfil as many as possible. We might not be able to prevent our babies hearing low-flying aircraft or underground trains rumbling by, but we can turn off the radio, stop people smoking in their presence and not take them to loud, brightly lit shopping malls unless there *really* is no alternative.

I would urge you not to burden your baby with the modern world until she has made a good start in life and has a strong body with fully developed senses. If people knew that loud noises *can* damage the fragile hair-like cells in a child's ear, damage that can never be repaired or healed, they wouldn't expose the child to them. If they knew how many learning difficulties and psychological problems stem from retarding the development of hearing, they wouldn't risk it.

Having said that, I have sadly come to the conclusion that some people *do* know, if not in detail at least in principle, what is harmful yet still maintain their behaviour. They still smoke, feed their children junk food and expose them to loud music – or even neurotically pamper them with piles of synthetic blankets and endless bottles of powdered milk. It's a strange thing, freedom.

Imitation

As I said above, young children are, above all, imitative creatures. This is just as well since human babies are born with huge potential but very few fully developed abilities, and there is so much to learn. Babies can already copy within a few weeks of birth: if you look at a baby and stick out your tongue, she will imitate you!

Imitation is more complex than we might think because of the very active nature of the sense organs. Rather than merely mirroring what they see, children have first to show interest by directing their attention towards something so where does this interest come from? I believe the core of individuality, the 'I' of the child, desires to make contact with similar beings around it. She assumes that everything else is a being like herself and she feels a natural empathy, at least until the world fails to respond or reacts in an unfriendly way.

The child's 'I' has boundless trust, which leads it to reach out towards anything that seems to have the same quality. Foremost, of course, this is directed towards parents and other responsive beings, but it soon extends to other people and gradually the rest of the world. When a baby looks deeply into our eyes, she is indeed fully identifying with our innermost being, doing so without judgement or even any sense that we are somehow other beings. We are all essentially familiar.

That is the secret of imitation. The child reaches out to unite herself with what is in her surroundings. Through her senses, the child reaches out, simultaneously drawing the world into herself and identifying with her impressions of it. Since the activity of perceiving and doing is practically one unified process in young children, they do what they perceive, they become what they experience. As adults, however, we can form judgements about what we perceive and choose not to respond, even though we remain imitative beings throughout our lives.

Whenever we hear someone speak, we inwardly and unconsciously imitate the gestures and movements of the sounds in minute micromovements in our muscles, perceiving these movements and interpreting them. The same is true when we hear music. In very young children, this is sometimes visible: when children listen to a story, for example, their own lips move and they begin to synchronise their breathing with that of the speaker.

Children become what they imitate

We can thus see that children imitate by internalising what they perceive. Furthermore, what they take in does not merely get reflected back in external movements: it remains with them and becomes part of the whole formative process. This is why children become stressed if regularly experiencing stress in their own environment. If they are surrounded by chaos and fear, they will absorb this into the very make-up of their constitution.

The implications of this are far-reaching, influencing their physical constitution, their habits and behaviour, even their attitudes and ways of thinking, as can be seen by their adaption of cultural traits and attitudes as they learn, essentially by imitation, their mother tongue. As we have suggested before, the moral implications of the nature of imitation are profound for an individual's whole development: if children perceive people as being generous, brave, attentive, creative – or the opposite – this will leave an unreflected but profound impression upon them.

This draws us towards understanding one of the greatest rules of parenting: it's what you do that matters. This includes every gesture and facial expression. Children observe us in detail that would astonish us, but they have no rational understanding of this. They form no judgements, taking everything, at least initially, at face value. This is the nature of their trust that the world is good and everything means what it reveals. Even if there is a contradiction between what we say and what we do, they will not judge us for it, but they will still unconsciously register that something doesn't add up. The uncertainty generated is then a great hindrance to self-esteem and confidence.

The younger children are, the more they simply absorb the influences of their environment, but as they get older, imitation changes its character as the child becomes ever more self-conscious. I will describe these changes as we proceed later through the phases of child development.

Imitation is the root of intuition

Imitation is essentially a very spiritual activity of the spirit within us, which enables us to slip behind the surface and experience the inner being of what we perceive. But we lose this ability as our intellect wakes up, as our thinking gets in the way of such direct and penetrating perception, and we increasingly add layers of mental activity between what we perceive and how we respond. This is necessary if we are to become independent thinkers and doers acting out of insight, yet it is also a kind of loss. We can retain, however, something of this quality if we cultivate the gift of empathy, which enables us to feel or inwardly imitate what another person is feeling, or if we allow a work of art or a stunning sunset to speak directly to us.

Imitation transformed becomes what we call intuition, the ability to grasp the essence of something in a way that goes beyond our rational mind. The highest form this can take is to be so in tune with a situation or another person that we can intuitively do the right thing without reflection.

Imitation is therefore a thing to be treasured in children. Recognising its nature can help us be more aware of what we are doing to our children, understanding how we act with them and how their environment works on them.

In summary, the nature of imitation in young children calls upon us to:

- respect their sense of development
- try to imagine how a particular environment feels to a child and do what is possible to make this a warm, friendly, embracing environment

- show children how to 'be' by example
- do things with children rather than merely telling them what to do
- let children discover the primary qualities in the world around before they get exposed to artificial, symbolic or virtual qualities
- let children experience as many manual experiences as possible in the home, garden and playground so that they can learn basic mechanical processes through imitation.

Exercise 8

Reflect on what I have said in the chapter about the child's relationship to her environment.

- Write down the ideal kind of environment for a child to grow up in. Try to imagine all the practical implications, and note what would be necessary. I stress I am asking for the *ideal* situation, so no expense spared! The only limitation to this vision of paradise is that you would have to be comfortable in such a place, you would have to be able to live in it.
- Write down all the things you would want to avoid at all costs, all the things you would eliminate from the child's environment if it were possible.
- Now apply these ideas to your own situation. What could you do practically to improve your own environment and make it more child-friendly. The changes need not happen all at once, but could take place over some time.

7

The twelve senses

In this chapter, I explore the nature of the five outer senses and the other, less well-known, inner senses, suggesting ways in which we can foster or protect their development. I'll start with balance because it is a sense that integrates many of the others. Then I will describe each of the other senses one by one.

Balance

If you see an experienced parent or grandparent hold a small baby, you can notice first how they support the baby's heavy head and lower back, and second how they tend to hold the baby upright facing them. This is very wise as babies need to feel safe. You can also see that babies love being held in this position, smiling and showing pleasure. They may also grace us with a remarkable display of facial imitation. They will raise their eyebrows, stick out their tongues, blink and turn their head from side to side in an imitative response to the adult.

According to recent research, it has become clear that the upright position stimulates the sense of balance and helps to provide the optimum conditions for attentiveness. Uprightness is such an archetypal human gesture that this should not really surprise us. As we shall see later, the effort needed to retain our upright posture, even as adults, requires a heightened inner activity akin to this attentiveness.

> The sense of balance plays a very important role in our whole sense development.

The organ relating to our sense of balance is located in the vestibular system of our inner ear. It now appears that the so-called vestibular system and the parts of the brain immediately connected to it have a key role in sensory integration, many senses relating directly to the inner ear because they are related to perceptions of the body in relation to gravity.

In order to move and manipulate our hands skilfully, we need to integrate many perceptions of our own body in space. This requires that we construct in our mind a kind of inner image of our body, showing its relative position in space and its overall state from moment to moment. This is known as *proprioception*, or a sense of our own movement. Even our visual perception has to relate to our sense of orientation in space. We need to know where up and down and left and right are. This too requires a sense of balance.

Balance and touch make the brain nerves grow

The sense of balance is the first sense to develop in the womb and is particularly crucial in the later stages of sitting up, crawling and walking. Between the sixth and eighth weeks of pregnancy, the future organ of balance is already forming in the embryo. The nerve connections to the brain develop between the tenth and twentieth weeks, much earlier than those of other organs. Like all the other organs, the organ of balance functions from its earliest stages of development, long before it reaches its final form and the full nervous connections have been formed. In doing this, it helps to form the nervous system via its own activity. The earliest senses, those of balance and touch, most strongly influence the development of the brain itself.

Our inner balance or equilibrium is, in a psychological sense, also related to our physical sense of balance. For the young child, the establishment and maintenance of inner and outer balance are prerequisites to the healthy development of all other senses and thus to the way in which a child relates to herself, to the world and to other people.

Even simply sitting still requires a whole symphony of senses working together: proprioception, touch, hearing, seeing, all co-ordinated by a sense of balance. Perfecting this act of inner and outer integration is a lifelong task, some achieving a greater level of perfection than others. Dancers and athletes, to say nothing of jugglers and high-wire artists, obviously have a much greater level of balance and co-ordination than most others, but it is not just such extremes that require co-ordinated sensory integration. Being able to read and write fluently also call upon good hand–eye co-ordination as well as a control of body movement, which is related to speech and listening. Poor speech skills limit our ability to think clearly too.

> The interplay between the senses is vital. Without accurate perceptions, the movements we carry out can never be skilful. The remarkable unity of activity between the sensory and motor functions of the nervous system learned over several years, and the processing of the information from the various sensory systems involves a highly complex linkage within the brain.

Finding the inner balance between sensory inputs is important to an individual's ability to protect herself from overpowerful sensory impressions, but this ability of self-regulation has its limits. Many developmental researchers are increasingly warning about the damage to sensory development, particularly integration, through strong stimulation too early in the child's life. Of most concern is the trend towards prenatal training for unborn babies, putting small loud-speakers on the mother's tummy to play the child music, speech lessons and even the voices of 'wise men'. Parents may believe that their children will become more intelligent, but considerable harm can be wrought. The same goes for the early years of child-hood. Overstimulation of the senses can dumb the individual down for life as well as rendering her insecure and possibly unco-ordinated. As the American child development specialist David Lewkowicz has stated in the German magazine, *GEO*, 1995:

> *we often have no idea what we are doing to them. Parents and child-carers would do well to respect the child's sense of balance in the early years of development. In the beginning all senses communicate contin-uously with each other in a finely tuned system. We should do nothing to disturb that system.*

This means that all the everyday things that families traditionally do are good for sensory integration of young children, but many modern practices *may not* be as helpful, for example, loud radio music or wearing headphones (damaging the hair cells of the ear and reducing the range of tones that is audible), sitting in cars rather than walking, and only walking on carpets or concrete (so there is insufficient opportunity to practise walking on different and irregular surfaces to stimulate balance).

Nurturing the individual senses

The sense of touch

Touching the walls of the womb and its own body helps the baby to develop a first unconscious sense of her bodily self. The sense of touch gives us the experience of where we stop and the rest of the world starts. Technically speaking, we feel only ourselves rather than external things we touch because what we actually perceive is the change in our skin caused by what we come into contact with.

Children have a powerful desire to touch objects – even danger-ous items such as sharp knives or electric fires – from very early on, what they touch providing them with some of their most basic experiences, on which all subsequent experiences can be based. As the first categories of tactile experience are the most lasting, they should be good quality (and safe). Natural materials have most to teach the inquisitive young child so toys and clothing made of silk, wool, cotton and wood are to be preferred from the point of view of developing 'tactile literacy', that is, the ability to distinguish a wide range of textures by touch.

To form a close tactile relationship is to feel close and familiar, which is why human touch is so important to young children. Qualities of intimacy and tenderness provide a deep sense of well-being, of emotional touch. Being gently and affectionately touched as a baby provides a basis for emotional abilities later in life as the value of relationships are learned through touch.

Touch, however, provides experiences of both closeness and separation, and it can make us recoil from some experiences, also a lesson for life. The American Indians spoke of the sacred act of 'touching the earth', the physical touch coming before a spiritual contact. Seeing alone does not make us close to the world; we need to have touched and felt it if we are to truly 'see' it.

The sense of life

This sense is unfamiliar by name but not by direct experience, especially when we feel off-colour. Our sense of well-being is based on the symphony of body processes working in harmony – what medicine calls homeostasis, the self-balancing of all our vital processes. When this functions correctly, we feel well. When it is out of balance, we feel *under the weather, out of sorts, below par*, metaphors that describe variations of feeling generated by our sense of life. Specifically, this sense also perceives the states we call hunger, pain, nausea and so on. The sense of life gives us an impression of the overall state of all our organs and highlights specific areas of disharmony and bodily need.

The sense of life teaches young children the vital process of recognising their bodily needs. This requires that we allow them to have such experiences rather than blotting them out as soon as they manifest. Without some degree of pain, for example, we would not develop, although this does not mean we should not attempt to alleviate pain when it occurs. As we *treat* a child, we need to tell her that the pain in her tummy is her body's way of telling her something is wrong. By directing children's attention to such feelings as hunger and thirst, we can help them to identify their needs and assess how urgent they are.

Another indirect way to help in the development of the life sense is through stories. Many fairy tales contain gruesome and painful consequences for wicked deeds, and learning that pain and suffering are part of life through this context helps to prepare children. Since they identify so closely with stories, their own bodily processes respond to the pain, pleasure and anticipation. In this way, they extend their own understanding of the repertoire of bodily reactions and the emotional states related to them.

Stimulating the sense of life develops a more sensitive understanding of and therefore later *control over* of children's bodily reactions. Thus, they are as adults more able to control hormonal and emotional states, or at least understand their nature.

The sense of movement

This system consists of many sensors located within the muscles that relay information about their state. In other words, it conveys a sense of our *own movement* and builds a detailed inner picture of our position. The sense of proprioception perceives very fine adjustments to our muscle tension and thus provides the basis for highly accurate fine movements and complex co-ordination.

The curious thing about this sense is that it also provides us with the basis for perceiving movement outside ourselves – a truck hurtling towards us, whether the ball bowled by Curtly Ambrose is a fast or a slow one, and other life-threatening events. How can our sense of movement do this if it basically perceives *our own* movement? Doesn't our sense of *vision* tell us whether something is moving or not?

What happens is highly complex as our senses of vision and movement work in close tandem with each other. When we see something outside our body, we unconsciously *imitate* its motion in a kind of muscular reflex, and it is these minute movements that our sense of proprioception actually perceives. This is correlated in parts of the brain with what our eyes see in the areas of visual processing. With hearing, we also judge distance, depth and other qualities such as resonance, which provides an image of things moving towards or away from us. So in forming a picture *in here* of what we perceive *out there*, a whole range of sensory experiences are integrated.

All our reactions are all related to our sense of balance, which provides a kind of basic orientation through our uprightness. Our response is equally co-ordinated by these senses. If we are walking on the sloping and moving deck of a ship, our inner equilibrium may be challenged to the point that the body rebels in nausea. We can also carry out complex sequences of movements like firing an arrow from the back of a moving horse or, more typically, driving a car in heavy traffic.

But there are other aspects of our integrated sense of movement, the main consequences of which can be summarised as follows:

- When listening, we imitate the movements of the speaker's speech organs and breathing pattern in waves of tiny micromovements, particularly in the chest and larynx. We also imitate their gross body movements, although as adults we try to suppress this. That means that how we speak to children works right into their muscular system. They are deeply and physically 'impressed' by tones of anger or loud noises which they unconsciously imitate and absorb. The effect of hearing such sounds, especially if they are frequent, is to create an underlying muscular tension.
- Learning language has much to do with imitating the sound patterns of speech through the sense of movement.
- The shapes and movements surrounding a very young child do much to condition the state of her soul, the background feeling of security, sympathy and well-being. The environment works formatively into the child's perception of the world, which is why young children should experience natural shapes, colours and movements as much as possible.
- Overloading a sense leads to its closing down rather than opening up.
- Limiting the sense of movement limits co-ordination, language perception, equilibrium, the ability to recognise form and the child's inner sense of stability and security. It may also lead to difficulties with reading, writing and maths.

So, how can we strengthen a child's sense of movement? First, parents should allow children to crawl, stand and walk at their own pace, with warm but only verbal encouragement, as the development of the sense of movement goes hand in hand with these stages. Do not force matters by using baby-bouncers (which give the child false signals about what she can do with her body) or baby-walkers.

These well-intentioned gadgets place unnecessary stress on joints, bones and muscles, quite apart from forcing the sense of movement.

Less easy to arrange is an environment in which children can explore natural shapes and encounter things moving at a 'natural' speed. This means avoiding too much motor vehicle transport, walking (even in the pushchair) as much as possible and allowing children to experience a range of various surfaces to crawl and walk on.

Avoid television because the pixels that make up the images on the screen form and dissolve too rapidly for the eye to register, imitate and perceive, which destroys the developing sense of movement. The images themselves cannot provide the child with a perception of real spatial movement. Older children and adults with a well-developed sense of movement can override this loss of reality, although this too has limits. Time spent watching TV could be better used in training higher levels of sensory integration by playing outside.

Exposing children to loud noises, especially through headphones, disrupts their sense of balance and movement.

The bottom line is to allow children to develop at their own pace.

The sense of smell

This sense reveals certain qualities in our environment in a very intimate and personal way. Although the smells and scents that plants, substances and people give off are quite objective and based on complex chemistry, we have very subjective ways of relating to them based on the fact that we remember smells (and tastes) for a very long time.

Trying to recall the smell of lavender is quite hard, but if you smell lavender, a whole host of memories come to mind. What is particularly characteristic about smell is the very personal nature of the experience, conjuring up powerful feelings of how we felt in some past situation – which is the basis of the whole perfume industry. The smell of cocoa may remind us of a beloved grandmother, the smell of olive oil of a distant holiday in Greece.

Not all scents, however, are quite as alluring. The smell of disinfectant may remind us of institutions we would rather avoid, the musty smell of an old aunt's house somehow disturbing. The smell of death may touch our deepest sense of mortality. But people can react in totally different ways to the same smell. We can tolerate and even enjoy the smell of someone we love yet feel repulsed by the body smell of a stranger, even though, objectively, there is little to choose between them.

The ability to differentiate such subtle distinctions, however, has first to develop. A child has to acquire a repertoire of smell experiences and be able correctly to associate them with their true object. Given that early sensory impressions work formatively in the young child, familiarity with smells and their origin is important to establish. Many soaps, so-called air fresheners and cleaning materials are artificially scented, produced by sophisticated chemical combinations that are designed to imitate natural scents. Children should instead get to know the far richer natural smells before the artificial ones, if only to attune their sensory system to the real association of smell and source. Artificial scents are also often less subtle and stronger than their natural equivalents, thus dulling the child's sensitivity.

Each scent produces not only an emotional reaction but, more fundamentally, a physical one too. The smell of fresh bread stimulates the digestive system to become active and prepares the child to receive food, leading to a far healthier digestion all round. Microwaved and highly processed food releases quite different smells so we are less prepared to engage in the digestive process. The high incidence of digestion-related problems may in part be related to this.

In summary, then:

- avoid using artificially scented products, synthetic fibres and heavily processed food
- allow children to experience the real world of smells and scents
- help them to develop a vocabulary to describe smells and their associations.

The sense of taste

Taste and smell are very closely related. Taste, part of our digestive process, begins to work as soon as we make direct physical contact through our mouth (smell works at a distance). The different primary qualities of taste – sweet and sour, salty and bitter – are more or less innate, babies reacting in typical ways to them soon after birth.

As with smell, children need to become familiar with natural tastes before they have their taste buds bombarded by taste enhancers or smothered by too much sugar. A healthy relationship to food depends on a discerning palate. Artificial flavourings, sweeteners and too much salt ruin the ability to differentiate tastes and lead to bad eating habits, creating an unhealthy desire for certain types of food. The artificial sweeteners and flavourings in food help to establish what amounts to food addictions. So start with natural, pure tastes, and don't overload the developing sense organs.

The sense of sight

Our eyes do not merely function like cameras, simply letting the light in. They, and the brain behind them, are active organs, looking at things that interest them, focusing on them and scanning them to determine colour, shape, size, position in relation to the onlooker, movement and many other visually determined qualities.

Those who have had cataracts removed do not automatically 'see', although their eyes are now technically capable of doing so. They first have to learn how to see or, more exactly, to identify and therefore order what they see. What starts out as a blur of colours only slowly resolves into recognisable shapes. What this shows is that we need experience to help us sort out what the lens of the eye directs onto the retina.

Most importantly, our inner activity is called upon to make the effort to adjust the various dimensions presented to us, which is why we shouldn't drive or operate dangerous machinery when tired or under the influence of alcohol or drugs. If we relax our attention, we can misjudge what we see, with disastrous consequences.

Eyes too need time to develop. They should be spared having to deal with too much light or too much brightness, as well as rapidly moving objects such as the view through a car windscreen or the flickering dots on a TV screen. Such images overstimulate the child's responses so they become hyperactive, nervous and jumpy. If a child cannot cope with the effort of trying to make sense of this flood of images streaming in, a reflex of self-protection engages: the child 'shuts off'. If this becomes habitual, the child will tend to dissociate in any stressful or challenging situation, which is just when we *want* her to get engaged.

It shouldn't really surprise us that this happens: during 2.5 million years of evolution of the human brain and the eye, the images presented were real situations and therefore responses to them were entirely appropriate. However, the *virtual* images to which children are exposed (some 5–6 thousand hours of TV before the age of 5, for example) cause the brain to cease responding as it cannot keep up.

TV programme and computer games makers know this and build startle effects, such as sudden loud noises, flashing lights or sudden shifts in light intensity, into the programmes to waken the children – so they will at least notice the advertising messages. This triggers a hormonal response, but it doesn't take long for the children to get used to this startle effect, to habituate to it, so even stronger doses are required. The medical effect is described by the researcher Keith Buzzell:

> *Our ancient survival systems react and release their shots of cortisol as they are hard-wired to do, even our higher cortical 'self-sense' expresses indifference . . . This lower brain responds with its defense-alert even before we, as recipients, are aware of the image itself . . . As the rapidity and number of startle-effects increases, the parasympathetic nervous system has no time to bring balance back into the system, shut off the cortisol [a hormone produced in response to a stimulus to prepare the body to react], reestablish the immune system, and so on. Thus the body, as its own intelligence, lives in a constant state of threat, or startle, and the brain suffers a serious over-saturation of cortisol.*

The main symptom of overload is stress, which as we all know, is a major cause of disease. (Anyone brave enough to risk the full story should read Keith Buzzell's new book *The Children of Cyclops*.)

Another aspect of visual development is the child's experience of colour. Discovering pure colours, like true smells and tastes, is important. Children's response to colours is much stronger than an adult's, each colour producing a powerful inner response that works deeply into their whole experience. The colours in a child's environment therefore need, if possible, to be pure yet rich in subtlety. We should try to ensure that spaces children spend a lot of time in have quiet, warm colours rather than dazzling, bright, multipatterned schemes.

Natural light is obviously best, but the light of candles and fire lanterns creates a friendly environment, having been part of our evolution for perhaps the last million years. Our eyes are of course very tolerant of degrees of darkness, and children should certainly be warmly encouraged to feel comfortable in reduced light, even if not total darkness, which is always threatening.

The sense of warmth

We often use metaphors of warmth to describe states of mind and behaviour that apparently have nothing to do with body temperature: *she grew cold towards him, I'm slowly warming to the idea, he's really cool* (which changes its meaning as the generations go by). This link will become clear if we think of the effect warmth has on us. We know that we tense up when we get cold and relax in the sun. Cold wakes us up and warmth lulls us to sleep. Heat after a certain point induces pain and we try to avoid its potential danger.

Being able to establish our body temperature is an important biological process that takes time to stabilise during infancy, which is why we have to ensure that babies are well wrapped up after a bath, for example. Fluctuations in our body temperature indicate states of ill-health, so doctors check our pulse and take our temperature.

As humanity evolved on the tropical savannah of Africa, infants in cooler climates need to have this temperature artificially created for them by clothing, especially clothing made from natural fibres that retain body warmth. Feeling warm and snug creates a feeling of security and comfort. It also enables children to conserve energy for other activities such as learning about the world through movement and play. A cold child using too much energy to maintain body warmth loses interest in her surroundings, becoming listless and apathetic. We might do well to learn from the comedian Billy Connelly's description of his mother sending the young Billy, dressed only in an oversized pair of swimming trunks, to stand in the ice-cold North Sea on the coast of Scotland in a chilly northerly breeze – and that as a summer holiday treat!

Our sense of warmth provides us with subtle information about our well-being and helps us to regulate it. This sense of well-being provides a basis for the *feeling* of well-being, what we might call soul warmth, which translates into social warmth. A warm-hearted person is generous, gives, welcomes, makes others feel at ease, like a warm hearth or stove. Cold-heartedness speaks for itself.

We therefore need to remember that:

- young children need to be kept warm until they can really maintain and regain their body temperature
- natural fibres retain body warmth in the best way, without producing sweat, which rapidly cools the skin temperature
- children need a physically but also emotionally warm environment to thrive in
- keeping warm does not mean being overheated or staying indoors. Being outside in cold weather is great if you are properly dressed, covering up the hands, feet and especially head from which a large proportion of the body's heat is lost. Protection from direct heat and strong sunlight is vital too.

The sense of hearing

As we touched on above, the outer, inner and middle ears contain our organs of hearing and equilibrium. Hearing is already possible in the womb but takes about 10 or 12 years to mature fully. Hearing relates to balance, to our sense of space, to our judgement of distance, direction and depth. It enables us to identify the qualities of different materials: I remember a forester once showing me how by tapping mature pine trees with a giant plastic-headed mallet, he could tell whether the wood was good enough quality for making cellos, violins or only double basses.

Hearing is obviously also crucial for our language and musical abilities. If the fine hair-like cells in the ear, which register the sound vibrations, are damaged, they can never grow again. So once damaged, hearing is impaired for life.

There are two basic aspects to the development of hearing: sound perception and the important social skill of listening to what we hear. Listening means focusing our attention on what we want to hear and then being able to understand and use the sensory information we receive. It also means filtering out what we don't want to hear, ordering complex groups of sounds, some relevant to us, others less so. Children quickly identify sounds that mean something to them, such as the voices of their parents. Familiar domestic noises, for example the washing machine, no longer disturb their sleep when they have a context. Being able to distinguish the meaningful from the meaningless is important and takes time. Background music will soon become uninteresting to children, but it still gets absorbed into their system; we should not be surprised if they later find it hard to listen to real music.

When children listen they do so with their whole being. They open right up and experience the soul quality of who or what they are listening to. The rich timbre of each individual human voice is different. The inner mood, the intentions, the personality of the person are communicated, and the child's highly sensitive organs take it all in. Electronically generated sound, no matter how high fidelity its quality, is disembodied and thus a much poorer source of information than listening to a real person singing or telling a story.

In summary then:

- loud noises can damage children's hearing because it is much more sensitive than an adult's
- noisy environments can be very disorientating for children (and adults)
- irrelevant background music makes children immune to music in the long run and stops them concentrating in the short term
- natural sounds attune the child's hearing far more effectively than electronically reproduced sounds. Using headphones cuts the child off from the world and isolates her from the integration of experience
- listening to carefully articulated speech helps linguistic development
- learning to listen to the subtleties of language, music and nature offers a much richer learning experience and basis for developing higher faculties.
- children do not need their environment to be quiet all the time – they should get used to loud noises as well – but they should have some quiet time so that they can become quiet in themselves. Loud noises stimulate inner unrest, quiet stimulates inner

quiet, and we all need both. Continuous noise produces over-stimulation, hyperactivity and, in the end, paradoxically, an inner turning off that gets progressively harder to reverse.

The sense of speech

This is an unfamiliar idea first put forward by Rudolf Steiner and later developed by the teacher and musician Peter Lutzke in his book *The Sense of Word*. A New Yorker living in Düsseldorf, he presents the case for a sense closely related to our sense of movement that enables us initially to recognise the difference between noise and spoken language. We may not understand what someone from Finland or Namibia is saying, but we recognise it as language rather than meaningless noise. Furthermore, this sense enables us to see that this person's sentences contain structure, and that this structure orders meaning in ways specific to each language. The word order in English tells us what is going on: *'man bites dog'*, is very different from *'dog bites man'*. The sense of speech also communicates to us the emotional energy of the speaker: anger, sarcasm, fear. It tells us that the famous sentence invented by the great linguist Noam Chomsky, *'Colourless green ideas sleep furiously'*, makes no actual sense, although the way in which it is delivered may convey apology or questioning.

When children learn language (see Chapter 1), they learn the values of a whole culture, their sense of speech or word being crucial to this process. The sense of speech builds on the sense of movement, so all I said about supporting the development of that sense is important here too. Beyond that, it is obvious that children need to hear the spoken word as often and as directly as possible. Since the sense of word does not depend just on the sounds of spoken language, but on body language, gesture, facial expression and context, children need to be spoken to directly. Explaining things to them, having little chats about what is happening and telling them stories is far more effective than listening to tapes, or inter-acting with a computer.

Above all, the sense of word reveals the subtle structures of conversation and dialogue, of the rhythm of listening and speaking, of taking part in real meaningful exchange. This has to be 'live' if the child is to recognise the patterns of endlessly flexible mature human conversation. Real conversation and communication involves people responding in very delicate ways through eye contact, pauses, changes of emphasis and so on. We would never expect anyone to learn to play the violin only by listening to recordings.

Children need to experience good-quality oral and verbal skills. That means enabling children to listen and participate in real conversation rather than just the snatched shorthand jargon we often use as adults in our busy lives. They also need to practise articulation, the best way of doing this being through the wonderful body of nursery rhymes and verses that we have inherited and would do well to pass onto the next generation.

So we need to remember the following points:

- speak to children often, talk about everyday events, and don't use baby talk
- tell children stories rather than letting them listen to tapes or watch TV
- let them experience adult conversations even if they don't under-stand a word (many famous writers developed their love for language through listening to articulate adults)
- regional dialects and accents are rich sources of linguistic value and contain many authentic linguistic elements that are lost in 'posher' speech
- teach your children as many nursery rhymes, verses, songs and tongue-twisters as you possibly can. Their ability to remember them will be greater than yours, so use books to acquire more; even nonsense verse contains sounds and rhythms that are a wonderful training for speech
- above all, rejoice in language with your children as they derive a deep feeling of well-being when they discover new words and sounds. Draw their attention to words: *'hey, this is called a wrench because you can wrench things with it'*. Or make something up: *'Do we want muesli, croissants or flafalops for breakfast?'* Get them to decide what 'flafalops' might be to stimulate their sense of language.

The sense of thought

Understanding what someone actually means involves our sense of (someone else's) thought. '*I have been standing here in the rain waiting for you for half an hour but now I have decided to stop waiting and go home.*' To understand this long sentence, I need to know not only the meaning of all these words strung out in a chain, but also to grasp the situation and deduce the probable reason for the speaker having gone off in a huff. All these levels of meaning are revealed to me by my sense of thought.

It is the same when we hear or read a story. We have to be able to follow the narrative, remember what happens in sequence and see how the events are linked together. This is true whether we read a story in the newspaper, hear Aunt Margery tell us about her visit to Bognor or listen to a professor's explanation of Chomsky's theory of generative grammar.

Complex ideas (which include even apparently simple ones) have to be presented in a sequence of separate sound bites (or words in a line on a page). In listening we break up the chain and put the separate parts into one whole integrated picture, the meaning of which we can grasp. This is what our sense of thought does for us. If we had to understand things as they actually happened, our understanding of the world would resemble a long telegram in semaphore.

Our sense of thought also needs time to develop, through the cultivation of conversation, dialogue and narrative, that is, through telling stories. Learning sequences of activities, as in baking bread, is also important. Putting toys or clothes away is a similar activity: things go in their place in a certain sequence. Later on, handicrafts and other manual skills are excellent preparation for developing practical thinking. The following activities strengthen our sense of thought:

- stories with a meaningful sequence of events (traditional fairy tales are classic examples since they usually have a beginning, a sequence of events, much repetition, a crisis and a resolution)
- practical tasks that involve a sequence of actions (such as baking, gardening, handicrafts); it is important that the sequence is obvious and is determined by the activities themselves
- singing songs and hearing or playing music.

The importance of the senses

All these senses are interrelated and rarely operate on their own. Separating them out as I have done here is a bit artificial, but it does help to identify them. We must, however, think of the senses as an integrated whole, providing our children with the complex picture of the world that they need. Furthermore, when the senses are all fully developed, this allows the development of the highest sense of all, that of another person as a being in his own right. When all our senses are finely tuned we can begin to perceive another's essence.

This sense is of course available to us in imperfect form as soon as we can distinguish another person from ourselves. At some point, young children become aware that they themselves are an 'I' and other people are a 'you', probably when they realise that their mother (for example) is in fact a *somebody else*. Out of our higher self we can say, 'I am there for you.' In fact my higher self really comes to expression only in being there for the other person. This moment of recognition may occur when the child realises that her mother's main concern is for her: '*My mummy loves me, cares for me, feeds me, and that makes me a me!*'

This primary feeling evolves through many stages of self-awareness until we ultimately become aware that other people are unique individuals and can develop some feeling for who they really are. What the sense of others as spiritual beings in their own right becomes in full maturity is the sense of being there for the other person. This is the central message of many of the great religious teachers. So 'Love thy neighbour as thyself' becomes 'Love thy neighbour and discover your true self.'

Furthermore, the ability to perceive and recognise the true being of another person is the same ability we need to recognise the true nature of everything else in the world, including spiritual realities. Fully developing our senses provides us with the possibility that nature can reveal itself to us. We might then not take the world so much for granted but might notice more quickly the effect of what we do on our environment. Much of the way in which we live closes down our senses and reduces our sensitivity to the world and other people; the least we can do is stop the avoidable damage.

More on TV (and video)

. . . children who have too seldom run and jumped, who have had insufficient opportunity to play on a swing or in mud, to climb and to balance, will have difficulty walking backwards. They lag behind in arithmetic and appear clumsy and stiff. These children cannot accurately judge strength, speed or distance; and thus they are more accident prone than other children.

[In Germany] . . . two thirds of all school children listen to music droning from gigantic boom boxes, walkmans and diskmans. Among elementary school age children one in three already possesses his or her own television and one in five has his or her own computer.

. . . one in ten adolescents already suffers hearing loss; 60% of children entering school have poor posture, 35% are overweight, 40% have poor circulation, 38% cannot adequately co-ordinate their arms and legs, and more than 50% lack stamina for running, jumping and swimming.

Peter Stark, *GEO magazine*, 1995

So what's wrong with TV?

First of all, TV is harmful to children's senses, especially sight: 'Television is sensory deprivation' says Jerry Mander, President of the International Forum for Globalisation. Frequent television watching, especially by young children, inhibits the development of the brain.

Television watching becomes addictive. It disrupts and replaces crucial verbal, non-verbal and emotional forms of communication, disrupting the wonderful social and linguistic glue of collaborative narrative in which Billy tells us about what he did at work and Grandpa tells us how badly his tomatoes are growing.

TV also replaces and subverts play; it entertains, but entertainment is not play.

TV inhibits language development because it is one-sided. Language development requires exchange, interaction and especially the perception and engagement of muscular responses. Real interaction creates pictures in the child's mind, images that weave the fabric of the imagination.

TV inhibits the active process of learning because its sensory input is shallow and divorced from reality. TV is unresponsive, whereas real learning is interactive. The argument that television is educational is only partly true for adults, but for children, it is ineffective because it is a passive activity. Our TV culture has contributed to the increasing difficulty in educating children because:

- their attention span and concentration are weakened
- their sensory experience is limited
- their motor co-ordination is weak as a result of inactivity
- they require ever more dramatic stimuli to respond
- they have become passive consumers of experience and are therefore resistant to the challenge of thinking or discovery through their own activity
- they tend to accept superficial explanations and do not question information
- they lack the ability to grasp metaphorical-symbolic structures such as are needed for religion, science, literature, art and philosophy
- they avoid the mental effort of understanding complex ideas such as natural phenomena, ethics, justice and human rights.

Television leads to the erosion of the cohesion upon which social structures such as family and community depend. This loss of structure is characterised by increased mental instability, alienation, depression, crime, violence, alcoholism and drug abuse. The rapidly changing, highly selected images of TV lead to false expectations and perpetual disappointment with life.

In addition, exposure to television causes children's minds to be programmed to a life-time dependency on consumption. TV literally conditions children (as in animal training) to the buying and consuming habits that keep the multibillion pound corporate world in business. The long-term strategies of marketing use TV as their prime medium. As recent US presidential candidate and consumer activist Ralph Nader put it, '*MTV doesn't just influence kids, it owns them by the age of fourteen!*' '*Watching TV creates the most vicious of cycles: It makes a person more susceptible to manufactured images by diminishing that person's ability to generate his own, a condition akin to the suppression of the immune system*', says Barry Sander in *A is for Ox*.

What to do about TV?

The most important thing we've learned,
So far as children are concerned,
Is never, NEVER, NEVER, let
Them near your television set –
Or better still, just don't install
The idiotic thing at all.

Roald Dahl, *Charlie and the Chocolate Factory*

First try taking Roald Dahl's advice and not having one. This may mean changing your habits, finding other things to do with your free time and informing yourself through other media. Or only get the TV out once young children are safely in bed, or keep it in an inaccessible room – difficult but possible. By about the age of 3 children have worked out what is going on, but if they rarely get the chance to watch it and their lives are full of other things, their interest will be spasmodic and can be usually deflected.

If you can keep the TV away from your children until they are about 11 or 12, you will have done them a major service that will benefit them for life. By then, their brain will have established the vast majority of its neural network, and they will have benefited from the best time for play and language development. If you can manage to limit the TV until they have learned to read and write and begun to find enjoyment in literacy, this will be a great help. If the best you can do is manage until they are about 5, this too will have done some good. To let under 4-year-olds watch more than occasional (by which I mean maybe 2–3 hours in total a *year*!) TV programmes will damage them. It's as real as that.

But what should we replace the TV with? This requires a totally different approach to family life, one that initially involves a much bigger input. On the other hand, once this lifestyle has been adopted, children become more independent and self-contained, so in the long run it is a time-saver. Far more importantly, it will lead to happier, healthier and more fulfilled children and almost certainly a higher quality of life for you too. The following advice is based on experience as well as on the work of the author and publisher Martin Large:

• Do the kinds of interesting activity that I have described throughout the book and can be found in the reading list. Create a culture within the family of play, seasonal and outdoor activities and celebrating festivals, involving your friends and like-minded neighbours. Create play spaces indoors and outdoors. Collect materials and tools for craft work. Put an emphasis on making things for birthdays and Christmas. Do lots of cooking and baking together.

- For children of about 6 years upwards, encourage reading, library visits, story-telling, painting, keeping pets, playing musical instruments and gardening.

- Taking your children to the circus, theatre, concerts, dance performances, story-telling sessions and craft fairs.

- Encourage regular nature walks, extending to hiking tours, fell walking and later real mountaineering. Go camping in summer. When they are old enough, encourage healthy sports. As Dr Susan Johnson MD (assistant professor of pediatrics, Stanford Health Care Centre) puts it in *Strangers in Our Homes: TV and Our Children's Minds*, 'Nature is the greatest teacher of patience, delayed gratification, reverence, awe and observation.'

- Older children need to learn to be discerning about TV viewing. Discuss the matter with them, help them to plan what they want to watch and when, and help them to limit how long they watch for. It might even help to video favourite programmes to watch at a better time. Above all, reach an agreement in advance.

Forbidden fruit is naturally more tempting then permitted fruit, so if we run against the grain of social convention by not having TV (after all, nearly everybody has TV and 99 per cent let their children of all ages watch it), we have to expect that our children will be tempted. The best way to deal with this is to put it off for as long as possible and then allow it after a certain age. If they have not acquired the habit early, they are far less likely to adopt it at 11 or 12, when their interests are expanding to other kids their own age. As is the case with all bad habits, it is early conditioning that weakens one's ability to resist.

It is important not to be too fanatical about stopping your children watching TV. Difficulties arise though when they are very young and well-intentioned grandparents, baby-sitters and child-minders like to indulge them in a little entertainment. 'It won't do them any harm.' Explaining your reasons and asking for their support is very important. Hardest to influence are neighbours, who may think that you are depriving your children of their rights and undermine you. Here lies the real test of our convictions. If what we are doing is based on insight, we will be more likely to find the strength to find a socially constructive way of dealing with the situation.

Children and computers

Children growing up today will have nearly a third fewer face-to-face interactions over the course of their lifetimes ... human conversation, so vital to children's emotional, social and intellectual development, is on the wane ... A rich diet of face-to-face oral conversations with parents, teachers and other caring adults provides the basic nourishment children need to succeed in reading, writing and many other forms of academic learning.
Colleen Cordes and Edward Miller, Fool's Gold

Most of the comments I made about TV are also relevant to children's access to computers, but there are aspects specific to computers that need to be considered. I need to stress here that I have nothing against computers: I wrote this book on one and am very grateful that it was there! Being computer literate is one of the main skills we need today, and there is no doubt that every child has a right to learn how to use this most useful tool, but when and how should children be introduced to computers?

Computers have become so much a part of life that most parents might be excused for assuming that they should be a part of childhood too. But computers assume that we already have the skills to use them meaningfully. Quite apart from the obvious desire of corporate software companies to tap into their future customers' minds as early as possible, there are some very compelling reasons to stop and reflect.

In the past, people had to learn how to acquire knowledge, a skill highly valued by society. Now it is more important to know how to manage information, which is what computers demand of us. If we can't do this, the computer floods us

> with mostly banal information. If we want to learn using a computer, we have to know how to convert quality information into knowledge.

To get the best benefit, we have first to understand how to handle information, how to select and evaluate it and, above all, how to apply the computer to gaining deeper knowledge and problem-solving. The initial stages of this process are very important if the skill is to be a genuine ability that can go on developing and adapting to changing circumstances, including changing software. I will outline here what I think are the main areas of this vast topic and ask readers to refer to the recommended literature and form their own judgements.

First, computers are (directly or indirectly) associated with a variety of health risks including repetitive stress injury, eye strain, possible harmful effects from toxic emissions and electromagnetic radiation, obesity and other side-effects of a sedentary lifestyle, social isolation and developmental retardation.

Communications and information technology undermines the need children have for direct human contact. This can lead to social isolation, a weakened bond to teachers and other adult role models, a lack of self-discipline and self-motivation and emotional detachment from the community.

Computers are no substitute for creative play. The worst aspect of computers is probably computer games, with their obsessive, high speed, push-button, visually distorted, smart-bomb appeal. These games require little motor co-ordination and reinforce the instant response mentality that breeds the bad habit of expecting things to happen at the touch of a button. The sensory illusions created by the images prevent children acquiring a healthy understanding of gravity, balance, co-ordination and visual order. The distinction between virtual and real experience remains ambiguous for the child who lacks enough real experience to make a comparison. Try to imagine what underlying attitudes are implanted in a child who spends hours zapping other beings, who then bounce back to life with no further moral consequences.

Emphasising computers in childhood can lead to a lack of creativity because the interaction is one-sided. Creativity involves the formation of original mental images in the mind of the child (or adult), which involves integrating direct sensory experiences with emotional responses. Creativity involves both playfulness in trying out ideas and the perseverance in realising them. The computer provides images generated by someone else in a virtual medium that can be modified with a mere click of the mouse; no real process of imagination has time to unfold. The ease with which images can be changed on the screen does not encourage the satisfying and rewarding hard work that is involved in developing real skill. Furthermore, direct experience generates a more lasting sense of wonder than does a virtual experience.

Good practical skills and wide-ranging hands-on experience is the basis of multiple intelligence, which is the best way of balancing the one-sidedness of computers by forming a real understanding of primary phenomena. NASAs astronaut training, for example, starts with navigation in sailing dinghies and moves on to piloting small aircraft before training astronauts to use a space shuttle.

Using a computer meaningfully first requires a good level of literacy, so literacy skills should be well established before the computer is used as a tool of literacy (for writing, reading or locating information).

In addition, access to the Internet exposes children to highly manipulated commercial pressures, to say nothing of violence, pornography, bigotry and misinformation.

The Alliance for Childhood report on computers and childhood concludes with the following recommendations (applicable really to all areas of raising children):

- refocus education at home and school to emphasise the foundations of a healthy childhood
- enable and encourage strong bonds between children and caring adults
- provide time and space for creative play
- provide children with much oral linguistic culture, story-telling, reading aloud, conversation, poetry and songs
- cultivate a musical culture with real instruments and live music
- encourage healthy movement and rhythm
- enable children to experience and participate in real work in the home and outside it, plenty of handicrafts, gardening and lots of

direct experience of nature and the physical world
- encourage and help older children to understand issues of ethics, responsibility and critical thinking in relation to computers and communications technology
- encourage older children to learn about the historical context of the computer, including the significance of the invention of writing and printing, leading up to the computer age and the impact of computers on society and economics
- encourage older children to learn about how computers work and how this relates to the history of technology.

These last three points really belong in school; if they are not part of the ICT curriculum at your school, it is reasonable to ask the school to provide them.

Exercise 9

Look back over this chapter, especially at the description of the senses. The task here is to try to describe how you might experience each of these senses. Some are obviously less familiar but try to focus on as many as you can. For each sense:

- Describe a sensation that this sense gives you (trying to distinguish it from other senses, many of which work closely together). For the sense of balance, for example, describe when you might experience a loss of balance.
- Describe what feelings each sense might give you: is a smell pleasant or unpleasant, what does a particular taste remind you of?
- Describe how you think young children can best develop this particular sense.

You can find out more about the less familiar senses by reading one of the books recommended.

8

The importance of rhythm

Dancing to the rhythm of life

Rhythm is the key signature of life. Although mechanical gadgets have repetition, this differs from rhythm in a crucial way. Machines repeat exactly the same motions. If they didn't, they would soon break down or fail to perform the functions we design them for. Living rhythm, however, is not repetition of the same but repetition of the *similar*.

> Rhythm means repetition with *variation*, and it is this which is healthy for living organisms.

The science of chronobiology studies the many aspects of rhythm in human life. It has revealed that whereas there are ideal ratios, for example between the number of heart beats and the rate of breathing (which is 4:1) these are rarely found. In fact, really we only approach them at rest, in sleep for example. Furthermore, as heart surgeons have discovered, each person has their own individual, subtly different heart rhythms.

Rhythm and health

Our bodies dance to the tune of many rhythms, all of which harmonise into one vast symphony when we are healthy. A disruption of body rhythm leads to ill-health (which is why doctors still take your pulse as a primary indicator of well-being). Each organ system within the body has its own rhythms, from the electrical activity of the brain, which can be measured in microseconds to the familiar rhythm of our breathing. Each stage of life has its own characteristic rhythms of waking, sleeping and bodily renewal, macro-rhythms that are known as our life-lines.

It is a basic fact of life that the outer rhythms of our lives influence our inner body rhythms, as seen with jet-lag and sleeplessness. This is most true for young children. Following birth, one of the things children have to do is establish their basic organic and life rhythms, including the daily rhythm of sleeping and waking.

> Children need a healthy rhythm in their lives in order to maintain their own inner rhythms.

Sudden changes of outer rhythm

We all know that children often take time to adjust to new circumstances, such as moving to a new house or school. Even more difficult for them is adapting to a new daily rhythm, such as suddenly staying up much longer than they are used to. This can happen when you go on holiday and the whole family adopts an adult bed-time (doubly worse since all the new sensory stimuli and fresh air makes everyone more than usually tired). The occasional late night can be slept off, but major changes can disorientate them and disrupt their inner equilibrium, leading to bad temper, unexplained tummy upsets, headaches and even fevers.

Traditional rhythms

Traditional societies, which are after all the ones we evolved biologically to live in, were structured by rhythms given by nature. The changing seasons and changing length of the day gave a character to the whole year, depending on each society's geographical location. People in northern regions, for example, got used to sleeping for long periods in winter, keeping warm and conserving their energy. In summer, the day was long and full. We can hardly imagine how rhythmical humanity's life was for most of our evolutionary history, everything belonging within a whole context of tasks and seasonal changes.

Most of us today would probably find such a monotonous life intolerable, except perhaps for brief therapeutic periods. Prisoners who have to follow a rigidly structured routine of prison life report this as being the hardest part of their sentence and value any diversion at all. But the ethnologists do not report such symptoms of monotony – rather the reverse.

> Unexpected events that interrupted the daily routines and rhythms in traditional societies created fear and insecurity.

Many rituals and religious ceremonies in traditional societies were created specifically to attempt to ensure that the great rhythms of nature upon which society and life depended would remain stable, or would at least return quickly to stability if the unimaginable did in fact occur. If the rains failed, if the river flooded at the wrong time, if disease struck the flocks, life's rhythms would be disrupted, leading to chaos, the very antithesis of the health-giving rhythmical order.

Freedom from natural rhythms

We modern people have a different consciousness, which has led us to free ourselves from the limitations of traditional societies. We want to be individual and to control our own lives. We are able to a great extent to dispense with external natural rhythms. Our bodies pay a high price for this, but one we are usually able and willing to pay. We can compensate in many ways through technology, medicine, high-energy foods, etc. In the end, of course, the body or mind indicates where the limits are, so we stop, take a rest and go on again. This is the very freedom our society is geared up to attain – burning the candle at both ends and in the middle too! This is of course a genuine emancipation from the gruelling work previous societies endured, but where does the happy medium lie? There is no doubt a rhythmical life is healthy, but to what extent should we be bound to this?

Rhythm and childhood

Having said this, there is one area in which imposing rhythm is highly important, requiring, however, a major sacrifice on the part of adults.

> Children thrive on rhythm in their lives. A rhythmic home life in the years of childhood and rhythms in their life of learning will give them something of inestimable value for life.

This is like giving children an inexhaustible source of renewable energy. It enables them to build up their biological being and inner self in ways that make them resilient. It makes them far more capable of coping with an arhythmic, even chaotic later life as adults. So what kind of rhythms do children need? And what implications does this have for us as adults?

First rhythms

These need to be established as early as possible. They start with sleeping and eating, and basically continue with sleeping and eating, really until they leave home, although other areas also need to be taken into account. Many doctors, midwives and mothers believe that we can start this process by establishing a regular routine of nursing newborn babies, for example feeding 4-hourly rather than on demand. But babies are highly individual: some can't wait 4 hours to be fed, and there are limits even to healthy screaming! But I am sure that if you can get this rhythm established without too much trauma on all sides, it is very helpful.

Establishing a routine of nursing, changing and sleeping can be helped by external factors such as familiar people and familiar surroundings. Have a place where you do the changing, one suitably covered, at the right height for bending over and with all the necessary equipment to hand. Moments here become focal periods of lively communication and wakefulness. The nursing chair is another focus and the cot or Moses basket a third main place in the newborn's life. Each is associated with different activities of varying intensity – one for sleeping or day-dreaming, one for focused feeding and one for all kinds of exciting eye contact, talk, handling, being washed, an exhausting but enjoyable experience. As the child's world expands, the sights and sounds of new places – the pram, the sofa – can be incorporated.

Daily rhythms

Children soon need a clear pattern of activities in the day, centring around bed-time and meal-times. These should be as constant as possible. Children soon adapt their digestion and sleep patterns to the times we establish. Most young children will wake early – often far earlier than we are used to – then needing at least one sleep in the middle of the day and an early bed-time. Young children need at least 12 hours sleep a day.

It sometimes takes a while to work out the best pattern of sleeping, which of course changes with age. The trick is to assume an attitude of flexible routine, varying times as necessary but always doing the same things.

> It is not, in my view, essential that daily rhythms run like clockwork. It is more important that the rhythm is familiar.

Once children have established a pattern of sleeping and eating, even if you have to behave as *if* they have, daily routines need to be reinforced with their own little rituals. If children get up early and want to eat, it is probably better if everyone (teenagers excepted if they can't manage it with grace) gets up and has a communal breakfast. This also teaches the social skills of meal-times through imitation, seeing us eat and drink without slopping our food or climbing under the table.

Meal-times and morality

Meal-times are also social and moral events, providing us with an opportunity to show gratitude for our food – to nature, to the farmer. We also respect the food itself, not wasting it as it is a valuable resource that takes time and effort to produce. And we are grateful to whoever made the toast and laid the table so nicely. Some families express this by saying a simple grace before meals.

> You don't have to be a highly religious person to be grateful for food and community. For me, the main purpose is to create a brief moment of inwardness so that we can appreciate and share our food and celebrate being together. The brief waiting, as in most things in life, also helps.

Setting the table and clearing up afterwards, in which the children can later participate, is all part of the overall setting, providing an element of order and even aesthetics. A well-laid table is not only a pleasure, but also a reinforcement of value. Orderly place settings, napkins and a place for the pots all help to create an atmosphere of care and respect, which is after all a basic element of ritual.

Relaxed but structured meal-times also help children to adopt a more sensible food intake, with less need for snacks between meals. I discuss eating habits more fully in Chapter 14.

Social meal-times

Meal-times are obviously one of the few times in the day when the family are together, however briefly, and if possible, families should share at least one meal a day. If this has to be breakfast, it might mean getting up earlier or setting the table the night before. Meal-times provide the opportunity for conversation, the exchange of news, making arrangements: what happened at school, who is coming to stay at the weekend, where Daddy is going to attend his conference . . .

> Visitors should always be welcome at the table. Facing each other round the table at basically the same level while sharing food helps to break down barriers and put everyone at their ease.

For small children, meal-times are a wonderful opportunity to observe how grown-ups conduct interesting conversations, as long as they too are included. They should not be allowed to dominate, but they can be given the opportunity to say their bit as well as learn that they have to listen to others. For those of us who prefer reading the newspaper or listening to the radio at meal-times, this will be challenging. I know a family of teenagers forbidden to read at the breakfast table who took to studying the minutiae written on cereal packets. They claimed it helped with their foreign languages, and they certainly all knew the words for 'sugar' and 'artificial flavouring' in at lest seven different tongues! But it shouldn't be encouraged in small children.

Bed-time and other happy moments

> Bed-time can be a melee of screaming and running, not the ideal preparation for peaceful sleep or a productive evening for the parents.

If a calming bed-time ritual and suitable time schedule can be established in the first 3 years, this will go a long way to creating good habits. The activities leading up to bed-time also play an important part in determining the mood: if the children are exhausted and crabby, it will not be a pleasant experience for all involved. A period of tidying up is a good preparation. This reflects what happens during sleep, the body and mind metaphorically tidying up, sorting out and recharging the batteries. Tidying up also redirects excess energy into calming behaviour. How we tackle this is important: *'Let's see where these bricks go, back in the basket is it?'* is better than *'I'm not telling you again, put those blasted bricks away!'* Questions engage a child more than commands. *'Where does Teddy sleep?'* will probably lead the child to show you where Teddy goes by putting him there. This of course means that belongings have to have homes in the first place, so children's rooms should have enough suitable shelving, cupboards and containers to hold everything. Restoring order is not just pedantic: caring for, remembering and categorising each object teaches both useful organisational skills and good moral attitudes.

Washing and getting changed is the next major operation. The sooner children can do most of this on their own, the better. Imitation is the best teacher, but we also need to have patience when their early efforts are slow and largely ineffective. Leaving the bathroom more or less tidy and putting dirty clothes in the washing basket belongs to the whole event. Luckily, young children have not yet developed the concept of things being *boring* or a chore, so everything can be made to have its own little challenge.

> The expectation of a story or a nice drink of milk once the child is in bed is permissible bribery that generates enthusiasm for going to bed.

The important thing is to keep the momentum of the whole process going. Don't give up and let them play for half an hour in the middle. Don't spend another half-hour on the phone or they will see that there are more important things to do than go to bed. In the end, they need the sleep, and you need the time when they are in bed.

Once in bed, a story may be in order, but not one that is too lively or frightening; I will discuss story-telling in Chapter 10. Sometimes it is good just to have a quiet chat about events of the day.

The lights then need to be dimmed and the curtains drawn. A short prayer can be said, reflecting a moment of inwardness and gratitude. Small children often respond well to this as they assume that the world has goodness and meaning in it. Elsewhere I give examples of prayers to use with children but you can make up your own if you don't have prayers that stem from your own confession or faith. It is not so much the words as the deed that is important.

The bed-time routine will of course vary as the child grows up. It can be adapted to many different situations – camping, staying with Granny, going on holiday to Ibiza, but it gives children a sense of identity, rhythm and security wherever they are. Friends and baby-sitters can also join in.

> If you use being sent to bed as a punishment or threat during the day, do not be surprised if your children start to resist going to bed.

So for a peaceful bed-time:

* establish a regular time, one that falls just before the onset of exhaustion for both parent and child
* tidy up first, which is a good calming activity that pulls the children into themselves
* encourage them to wash (properly) and change themselves as young as possible
* lead them into all these activities in a cheerful matter-of-fact manner: 'This is just what we do'
* don't use going to bed as a threat
* develop a short bed-time ritual involving perhaps a dimmed light, a short story, a prayer, tucking-in and a goodnight kiss, whatever has a calming effect
* take the ritual with you when you go away.

Rhythms of the day

The day with young children can seem very long between meal-times and sleeping. Let me start with what children need; then I'll look at the issue of who provides it.

Get them outside!

Young children need periods of play on their own, periods inside and, above all, periods outside. Infants need peace and quiet most of the time, but even before they can walk, children need to be outside, in the pram, crawling on a rug or even on the bare ground, as near nature as possible.

> The world outside has so many more sensory qualities than indoors. Wherever and whenever possible children should be outside.

Unfortunately, not everyone has a safe garden or park next to his or her house, something our politicians would do well to address. So we may have to do make do as best we can and be inventive.

But do dress them properly...

Few nations seem to be worse than the British about exposing their children to the elements!

> The British are not so reticent about getting grubby but they *are* negligent about dressing children properly for the outdoors. Whether hot or cold, the Brits often get it wrong.

Perhaps because we are so starved of sunlight, we ignore advice to protect young children from exposure to solar radiation on Mediterranean (or even British) beaches. Pink and burnt Brits are the laughing stock of Europe; Australians and white South Africans, who have been brought up to avoid skin cancer, are horrified. As for the cold, we simply don't wrap our children up well enough, instead sending them outside to freeze.

So dress children appropriately and get them outside. As the Danish childcare pioneer Helle Heckmann so wonderfully put it, *'All weather is good weather if you are dressed for it.'* If rain is a significant feature of your climate, celebrate it; there really is no need to run in the minute it starts to rain. The classic wellington boot, so easy to get on or off at the age of two and a half, is now standard equipment. Modern breathable, waterproof clothing can keep you dry both inside and out. So get out and have fun!

Collect rainwater, making water features, jump in puddles, build dams, fill and empty containers of water: with children around you never need worry about watering the garden. Running on uneven ground, clambering over logs, climbing slopes and jumping over shallow ditches are all wonderful activities for developing the kind of integrated movements and balance I talked about in Chapter 7; you can't do all this indoors nearly as easily. Sticks, logs, bark, leaves, conkers are wonderful toys. Digging around in the soil or sand is an archetypal activity for children that engages their imagination and fine-tunes their manual skills.

Children's awareness of the changing seasons is also so much more direct when they spend some time every day outside, even in a city-centre back garden. They feel the changing quality of the air at different times of the day, they see the endlessly changing sky, the different qualities of light, all experiences that develop their senses and bring them closer to the natural world than will schoolbooks or TV programmes. With such direct experience of the shapes, smells and colours of nature, they will be more able to bring real inner experience to the scientific understanding they develop later.

Celebrating the year's festivals

Traditional societies marked the turning seasons by celebrating the seasonal festivals. Anchored firmly in the religious calendar, the saints' days, carnivals and market days gave life both an inner and an outer structure. Festivals have always essentially been social and family events, however much their inner meaning derives from religion.

I think it is one of our tasks today to create a new culture of festivals, especially if we have grown apart from the roots of our cultural and religious heritage, and the traditional forms have become rather hollow, commercialised events.

Even if we belong to an active faith, there is no reason why we can't rethink and renew the old ways of celebrating what we consider to be important.

Festivals and their celebration are very important for children, whether or not we are actively religious. The essence of the round of annual festivals is that they are a *cycle*. Each year these moments reappear and remind us of something more permanent, something more meaningful than the daily grind. But repetition is not necessarily a virtue in itself. What makes a festival worth celebrating is not so much the mere repeating of certain customs, as this is probably the quickest way to their becoming meaningless events, but the re-affirmation of what it is all about. Thus, its significance deepens each time it is encountered.

Starting with nature

Most religious festivals, at least in temperate climates, relate in some way to the changing seasons. We may have lost touch with this aspect, or the festival itself may have lost touch with its climatic origin – for example celebrating Christmas' 'bleak midwinter' on Bondi Beach. But it is not sentimental to want our children to feel a connection to their natural environment. The life forces active in the developing child, the forces of growth and regeneration themselves, belong to the earth. The force that enables a tree's sap to rise against gravity is the same force that works within us to maintain our upright posture. As living organisms, we should not deny our deep connection to the natural world, even if our civilisation strives to separate us from it.

> We live and breathe in a living world that has its mysterious cycles of waxing and waning, growth and decay. We feel the spring and autumn of our lives. We even seasonally migrate – often south! The starry constellations circle above our heads whether or not we look up. With the concrete beneath our feet and the sodium streetlights blinding us to the night, we may forget that we belong to nature. But there are fewer things that feel more right than helping a young child to find wonder in the changing seasons.

To experience nature as a familiar, if not always friendly, presence is important for a child. To know that each facet of the weather has its charms as well as its downside is important too. The rain is fun though it can go on a bit; snow is great when it falls but a mess when it turns to slush. Each aspect of the weather reflects a rich pageant of moods and to recognise them in the world around us is to acknowledge them within. We can thus work with nature instead of trying to pit ourselves *against* it.

The soul as a mirror of the rhythms of nature

The secret about nature lies in its relationship to our inner nature. As modern people, our lives are barely touched by the seasons, unless we belong to the tiny community of fishermen or farmers. Nevertheless anyone who suffers from seasonally adjusted depression, which I believe includes several million people in the UK alone, will be aware that we are not immune to the changing quality of the light, to the long dark evenings, to the cold and the damp.

> The cycle of the seasons corresponds to a psychological cycle within us that works deep below the threshold of consciousness.

The seasons, which obviously vary in their character from place to place, are part of a series of cosmic cycles or rhythms; we do not need to fall prey to superstition to recognise these. There is a spiritual significance to the cycles of life and we mirror the rhythms of nature in our soul lives. If we totally remove ourselves from these rhythms, we take away one of the supports reinforcing our basic requirements for a healthy life. One of the best ways we can place our discoveries of the natural world into a meaningful context is to celebrate (and if necessary invent) seasonal festivals. Christine Fynes-Clinton says this in *All Year Round*:

When I say 'mirroring' I mean a world which 'goes to sleep' at night and 'wakes up' at dawn reflects and reinforces our own need for a sleeping and waking rhythm. When the fruiting plants and trees 'hold their breath' in autumn and winter, and 'breathe out' in spring and summer as they blossom and fruit, this also carries us as part of the creation which lives in a breathing rhythm. People are beginning to accept now that to live as though we were not intimately bound up with the whole of the natural world has its negative repercussions (quite often in terms of health) and I would include the rhythms of nature in this, too. I think you'd agree that in this sense modern life has become quite arhythmical and our children don't experience these world rhythms in life around them half as strongly as we did at their age.

Pictures of change and renewal

If we need to mirror the natural rhythms of nature in our inner life, what does it, in basic terms, involve? The cycle of the year, as the quote above hints, involves a kind of breathing in and out, expanding and contracting, only on a vastly different scale. Breathing is always about transformation: when we breathe, we take in air, use the oxygen to fuel our vital inner processes and breathe out carbon dioxide. Similarly, our soul takes in impressions via the senses and transforms them for us.

> At night, we digest the impressions of the day and transform them. The results of these transformations are all the things we produce – from good ideas and artistic creations to physical work.

This transformational aspect of the rhythm of breathing is revealed to us through the seasonal transformations. Let me try briefly to characterise what the different seasons mean in this sense, providing a summary of the drama of the seasons and human existence that can be experienced in its own way in any geographical location. Here, I will describe what we typically experience in the UK.

Spring needs least description. It is the time of new shoots, regeneration, the return of the fresh newborn green of plant growth. The days lengthen, the light bright and the weather dynamic and changeable. It is a season of quickening pace and pulse, invigorating and fresh. The mood is alert and bright.

The transition from spring to summer is perhaps the most beautiful time of the year as the plant world is at the height of its florescence. Summer itself becomes a drowsy, warm, laid-back time. Nature begins to lose her clarity of colour. The air is full of scent and buzzing insects, and we are lulled into a lazy, dreamy mood. In summer, we are less focused, less structured, more relaxed; we loosen our ties and kick off our restricting shoes.

The shock of autumn shakes us rudely awake. Things that have drifted along become heavy with significance like ripe fruit ready to drop; if we don't act swiftly, the harvest will be wasted. The leaves turn brown, the nights draw in. There is beauty in the autumn colours, but we feel nature withdrawing. It is a time for taking stock, sorting things out, preparing for the winter of life. It can be a challenging, stormy time. At best, we begin to feel a new steely resolve to awaken and face life. At worst, we lament lost opportunities, lost dreams. It is a common time for depression.

The transition into winter may be marked with a brief brightness in late autumn, but the light is cold and becoming remote. Nature outwardly sleeps, yet beneath the cold earth, the blankets of snow, seeds and bulbs are concentrating their energy and vitality. We retreat into ourselves and into the warmth of our homes. But the cold brings clarity. We tell tales around the fireside. We become inwardly active, reflecting and making plans for the coming season. It is a time of deep inner renewal. Midwinter is the moment of greatest in-breathing, just as midsummer is the moment of greatest out-breathing.

Children don't need an explanation such as the one I have attempted here: they simply need to experience these qualities, to gradually attune themselves to these great rhythms. In our busy lives filled with quick 'fixes', the long slow cycle of the seasons and their cultural celebration helps to build a deeply unconscious (but therefore more powerful) and healthy foundation for a child's inner life.

Celebrating the festivals with children

It is not my intention to list all the various ways in which our many cultures celebrate their seasonal and religious festivals, but to suggest the modest ways in which we can cultivate a sense of the inner quality of the year's rhythms while at home with our children.

We can create a simple seasonal table in our home to reflect the qualities of the changing seasons. A corner of the room is a good site because it is enclosed and provides wall space. The basic idea is to decorate this corner to reflect the inner qualities of the season, changing and evolving the scene over the year. A minimalist display at the centre of the dining-room table is another option. It is important to involve children as soon as possible in creating the seasonal table, gathering, displaying and maintaining the relevant materials, and taking responsibility for items stored until they are next used.

A coloured cloth draped over the table or pinned onto the wall helps to create the right mood. You could use deep blue for winter, green or yellow for spring, reddish-brown for autumn and orange or red for summer. Dyed muslin is light enough to be blu-tacked into folds onto the wall and can be easily folded up for storage.

There are no limits to what your imagination can come up with to display on the table, but it is important that the inner quality of the season is expressed. A good starting point is obviously seasonal plants or plant materials:

- winter – some evergreen branches, fir cones, snowdrops or willow buds on bare twigs, crystals
- spring – catkins, bulbs in pots, early sprigs of blossom and sprouting seeds or beans in a tray
- summer – fresh flowers and flowering grasses, seashells, starfish, a jar of honey
- autumn – berries, harvest fruit and vegetables, nuts and conkers.

Children can get involved in collecting leaves and branches from the hedgerows or garden, and planting bulbs or flower seeds in pots. Wheat or barley can be sprouted in trays of potting compost or even on wet kitchen roll.

Crystals, stones and shells can form a focus for the display. Stars, suns and moons made out of coloured paper or straw can be pinned onto the backdrop – the children will probably have their own ideas of what belongs on the table. Parents need to encourage the process for the first few years, but the children will soon adopt it as their own, especially at wet weekends or in the evenings.

There are, of course, other festivals to celebrate and represent too. In the UK, we can use pumpkins and lanterns at Halloween, Advent wreaths and calendars, romantic tokens on St Valentine's Day, Easter displays, Whitsun arrangements of white flowers, harvest festival fruits and Bonfire Night displays, all highlighting the cycle of the seasons.

You can also incorporate elements from other faiths. Apart from adding interesting new elements to the seasonal round, this pluralistic approach will certainly contribute to your children's appreciation of other religions.

Outdoor activities through the seasons

The family walk

The obvious outdoor activity for all four seasons is going for a walk. It is good to have several places where you can go regularly at different times through the year, and visiting the same location at different seasons helps children to get a direct sense of the year's changing mood. Depending on the children's ages, variety can be introduced by woods, meadows, water, a combination of paths and the opportunity to ramble over rough terrain. On cold days, returning home after a bracing walk to crumpets or hot soup creates a wonderful family atmosphere.

Essential things to take with you are:

- good footwear
- a small picnic, but remember to take any rubbish home with you
- lightweight raincoats
- a pocket first aid kit including adhesive plasters, antiseptic cream and wipes

- a rucksack with a plastic bag to bring home leaves, fir cones, fungi or whatever 'treasures' may be found
- old bread in case you meet any ducks!
- a penknife

Seasonal activities

What follow are a few suggestions, but many more ideas are illustrated in two books I can heartily recommend: *All Year Round* by Ann Druitt, Christine Fynes-Clinton and Marje Rowling, and *Families, Festivals and Food* by Diana Carey and Judy Large.

Spring
- Earth candles, can be lit at Candlemas or indeed at any other time. This also uses up all your old candle stubs. Dig a small hollow in the earth in a sheltered place, such as among the roots of a large tree, or in a large plant pot full of soil. Tie an old metal nut or a stone (as a weight) onto the end of a length of wick, the other end being tied to a stick placed across the top of the hollow, which holds the wick in the centre. Melt the wax in an old pan and pour it into the hole. Once the wax has cooled, cut the wick about 1 cm above the surface. The candle can be lit in the evening and allowed to burn on into the night.
- Kite flying takes advantage of spring winds.
- Egg hunts and egg rolling are fun on Easter Sunday.
- Children can help to plant bulbs and potatoes.
- Spring-cleaning in the garden, garage or shed is an activity that can involve the children.

Summer
- To maypole dance, a relatively modest height of pole can be set up in a park or garden, using bricks or pieces of wood to wedge it firmly in place. Ribbons, one for each child, are attached (by stapling or taping) evenly around the top of the pole. Many different dance patterns can be found in books on maypole dancing. The children can wear wreathes made of ivy and flowers or blossom, and music can be provided by tambourines, flutes and recorders.

- St John's Fire (sometimes called Midsummer Fire) is an old tradition of having a bonfire on the evening of 24th June, to which friends and neighbours can be invited. The event can be combined with a picnic, and potatoes baked in tin foil in the fire. Take care to choose a site where there is no risk of the fire getting out of control; branches for fire beating and a few buckets of water or sand should be kept handy. A summer fire creates a quite different mood from a winter one. Use plenty of dry twigs so that the fire will burn fast, showering sparks into the summer night sky, and then die down quickly. Tradition has it that everyone old enough can leap over the glowing embers, making a wish as they do so, and couples wishing to re-affirm their love for each other can jump holding hands. Older children and some of the adults can then perhaps spend the night in sleeping bags by the embers.
- A lovely thing to do on a summer evening is to float candles on a lake or pond. Night-lights can be set on small wooden boards, shaped at the front and back. A hole can be drilled and a piece of dowel set upright in the centre, onto which a piece of stiff paper or thin card can be folded as a sail.
- Grass mazes are patterns marked out on the grass that the children can run or dance round. The material used for marking out the pattern must obviously not harm the grass – cocoa husks, when rotted down, actually do the grass good. Sand and potting compost will also do the job. An alternative is to use coloured chalk on a large area of paving or concrete.

Autumn
- Apples can be gathered to store in boxes, press to make juice or cut to make dried rings.
- Seed heads can be collected, shaking the seeds out afterwards into paper bags to replant or display.
- Leaves, ash-keys, acorn cups, beech nuts and rose hips will make attractive mobiles and arrangements.
- Bird tables and hibernation boxes can be constructed using scrap wood.

Winter

- Lanterns for lanterns processions can be made out of paper or card (see *All Year Round* for details).
- Hang up net bags containing peanuts, and half coconuts, provide fresh water and keep the bird table well stocked.
- To make frost pictures, place watercolour paintings on boards outside in frosty weather. The frost produces wonderful patterns in the wet paint.

Indoor activities

These include baking, handicrafts, decorating the house and painting as part of a celebration of the seasonal festivals. Baking offers lots of scope – hot cross buns, pancakes, Christmas cakes. Celebratory meals can be prepared. Eggs can be blown and painted. Many suitable recipes can be found in *Families, Festivals and Food* as well as other recipe books.

Children love making things, and once you have shown them the basic skills, they can be surprisingly competent. A well-equipped handicraft basket or drawer can contain the following: children's scissors, balls of string, raffia in various colours, various adhesives, a stapler, a hole punch and awl, darning needles, assorted sheets of card, coloured tissue paper, craft knives (with retractable blades), a collection of assorted beads, crayons, paints, brushes, lengths of straw, short canes, pieces of dowelling, pipe cleaners, gardening wire, balls of different coloured wool, offcuts of shiny material and coloured felt. Depending on the age of the children, the tools may have to be stored separately and be used only under supervision.

With such equipment to hand one can make mobiles, leaf pictures, small dolls, finger puppets, paper crowns, lanterns, paper windmills and much more besides. The best ideas can be found in *All Year Round* and in *Natural Childhood* (edited by John B. Thomson, by Gaia). The further reading list contains a host of other useful references.

To summarise what we have said above:

- children need strong rhythms in their lives
- rhythm is healthy

- in the absence of traditional rhythms, we must be creative and find new, meaningful ways in which to structure our lives
- healthy rhythms begin with feeding and sleeping
- meal-times and bed-times are important moments to fill with regularity and a mood of gratitude
- the cycle of annual seasonal festivals is important to provide an inner experience of the relationship between nature and the life of the soul
- we can help the children be more connected to the seasonal rhythms through the celebration of the festivals in the family and in the community.

Exercise 10

Reflecting on what I have written in this chapter about the importance of rhythm, consider the following:

- What would make an ideal life rhythm for children of, for example, up to about 11 years of age? Describe what an ideal daily, weekly or annual rhythm might be. As in Exercise 8, this exercise is asking for the ideal, so the sky is your limit. Consider all the consequences that this might have for parents, siblings and the wider community.
- Try to list everything that would make it impossible for a child to experience a healthy rhythm. This nightmare scenario should not be science fiction but be a realistic one based on familiar, everyday situations you know or can imagine.
- Having done that, try to describe all the changes you could realistically bring about in your life to provide your children with the best possible rhythm in their lives. Again, keep to what is possible over time rather than trying to envisage any overnight revolutions.

9

Walking

Unless we have recently witnessed it, the miracle of how
children learn to walk and talk can easily be forgotten.
Perhaps it is because it happens without us having to do
very much that we tend to take it for granted. This may
be just as well since most of the problems that arise in
either development are caused by well-intentioned but
misguided attempts to speed up the process.

Walking

First let us marvel at the achievement of development. What
humankind achieved in some 4 million years, each human child
achieves in about 4. The crowning glory is actually the stage
beyond language, namely the ability to think, but although we
don't expect 4-year-olds to be able to understand everything, they
are nevertheless well on the way to having the basic equipment
they need to be able to think at the highest level. This is why the
first 3 years are the most important: all the really big steps are
taken, during these and from then on it is all about developing

the ability to use these fantastic instruments.

The biomechanics of standing and walking are a great mystery. Even adopting the human upright posture involves a permanent overcoming of gravity. Just think about it. Many four-legged animals can sleep standing up, but that is impossible for a human being. Even momentarily losing consciousness or merely getting drowsy usually causes a person to topple over.

> Staying upright requires a continuous inner effort to hold ourselves up, which is why it is so nice to lie down, relax and go to sleep.

With very young children, this effort to remain upright is even more remarkable because they are top heavy. What is more, the platform on which they are standing is merely a few centimetres of soft foot. Not even the whole foot is touching the floor – only the ball of the foot, the pads of the toes and briefly the heel. If you observe young children walking, you will notice that they tend to tiptoe around, rolling around the outside of their feet. Have a look at wet footprints on the bathroom floor and you will see the size of the supporting platform for the body during movement. This act of remaining upright depends on a powerful inner activity maintaining equilibrium.

> It is the self-activity of the child that maintains this wonderfully dynamic of being upright. As soon as this self-activity relaxes, the child goes floppy and falls asleep.

This self-activity is a strong force. It is what is so characteristic of young children, what makes them so active and light-footed, but we only really notice it when it has stopped acting. If you pick up a child who is deeply asleep, she seems heavier than at any other time of the day as her self-activity is not actively overcoming gravity.

From stretching to walking

As we saw in Chapter 4, children begin by stretching their necks and lifting their heads up. This proceeds to being able to hold their trunk upright in a sitting position. Gradually, the stretching reaches down into the legs and feet until the child can stand. The remarkable thing is that this process is driven by an inner desire to reach out, a kind of inner drive to get up.

This activity is not driven by the child's anatomy. In fact the muscles and bones necessary for standing are completely undeveloped, developing only through the actual activity of stretching and standing. At birth, for example, the child's spine has a single curve from the neck to the base of the spine. In the course of lifting and balancing the head, not only do strong neck muscles develop, but the neck bones also change shape. Furthermore, the neck region of the spinal column curves backwards. As the child raises herself up, the pressure on the vertebrae of the lower back changes and so they too change shape, getting broader where the pressure is greatest. This leads ultimately to the well-known double-S curvature of the spine. Dr Ernst-Michael Kranich, who has studied such processes in great detail, calls these transformations of the bones the signature of the child's 'I', the child's inner self.

If we were able to observe the process very closely, we would see that every child goes through this transformation in an individual way, sometimes faster, at other times more slowly. The subtle differences in the timing and the degree of difficulty encountered reveal something of the individuality of each child, something deeply personal to this individual's destiny.

A helping hand?

So what can we do to help? The answer is practically nothing. If someone really has to do something on their own, the best thing we can do is provide encouragement, praise and moral support, but *not* do it for them.

> Children should be left to undertake the trials and
> tribulations of stretching, crawling, standing and finally
> walking, on their own.

There are sound physiological reasons for doing nothing. If we continuously dangle children on their feet or put them in baby-walkers, we impose undue pressure on bones and muscles that have not yet developed to take the strain. In an organism, a change to one part, through growth for example, requires a corresponding adjustment to all the other parts, and the natural process of growth does this in an integrated way. Walking frames, however, deceive the body by providing uprightness without the organism having to take the strain. The body is being challenged to do something it is not adapted to.

Just as significant, however, is the effect on the child's inner picture of her bodily movements. As I described in Chapter 7, the sense of movement enables us to co-ordinate a large number of hugely complex muscle movements, but artificial support provides a false picture.

There is another reason too. The way in which a child takes hold of her body, masters its movements and individualises it helps her to establish her identity. Learning to walk involves a vast amount of energy – ask just anyone who has had to relearn this after a stroke or injury. How an individual marshalls this energy helps make her who she is. Our job is only to intervene to prevent accidents.

Role models for walking

> Yet, curiously, walking doesn't happen *without* us. Children
> who do not receive encouragement, who do not receive
> loving support and a safe environment, do not find it easy to
> learn how to walk.

Walking does not happen of its own accord, as many tragic cases of abandoned children demonstrate. Children need role models to observe and imitate, and they need encouragement too. Luckily, we are more in danger of offering too much rather than too little. Young children are amazingly tolerant of parental incompetence and clumsiness, and remarkably robust, but what they do need is love and interest. Knowing how children learn to crawl and walk can help us here.

Crawling is a good thing

A word about the value of crawling. Research has recently shown how important the crawling phase is. Once children have mastered the skill of moving on all fours with alternative left–right movements, they can cover ground at an alarming rate! But this is very good for them because it helps to establish laterality, that is the co-ordination of movement using the left and right sides of the body, which is essential to fine motor co-ordination.

How then can we encourage crawling? Obviously, we can't do it by commands. First, children have to have somewhere to crawl. This does not have to be sterile or indeed even clean, but does need to be free of toxins, contaminants and dangerous materials. So household floors, gardens and most beaches are good provided the child is safe from falling into holes, being trampled on or picking up broken glass!

Let them start off on the floor in their home. This means moving the cat food, the previous evening's glasses from the coffee table, the best books from the lower shelves. The space has to allow them safely to crawl, cling onto things, haul themselves up on stable furniture and finally run back and forth safely. Corridors and passages are great fun and should be well lit (and preferably not too cold).

Stairs are obviously a danger zone. Some families put up gates at the top and bottom of every staircase in the house and only take them down when the children can all run up and down stairs. Others do nothing on the principle that the sooner the child learns to deal with stairs, the better. A middle line is probably best here. Children should have the opportunity to get used to climbing and descending stairs as soon as possible, preferably under supervision. Stairs with carpets are the best as any falls will be significantly cushioned. There should also be some kind of banister (with spaces narrower than the youngest child's head of course) at a suitable height to hold on to. Try actually showing them how to crawl up and, more importantly, how to come down backwards on their hands and knees: they will undoubtedly develop their own technique. When you don't feel it is safe for them to be bombing up and down stairs or if the stairs are very steep, use a stairgate. Above all, praise them for their progress.

The child eventually proceeds from standing holding on and shuffling along holding onto the furniture, to free walking. This magical moment really is special. The little toddler, with a determined gleam in her eye, sets off – as if into free orbit – across the room with hands raised into the waiting arms of the beloved one waiting across the void to receive her! It is remarkable how often this moment is observed: the presence of an encouraging adult seems to help the child finally take the plunge.

Toddling

Once they can toddle about, life changes dramatically for both of you. You just have to go at their pace. In dangerous places, reins are useful, but don't let the child rely on them. No piece of safety equipment is a substitute for being careful. You will find that it will be necessary to go out with a pushchair or backpack for when they have run out of steam. Junior can then take a rest and walk a bit more later. The strategy also ensures that she doesn't get an early aversion to walking. A push chair or buggy helps transport the shopping.

Walking is about the healthiest thing that children (and adults) can do, so encourage it from the moment they can walk. Progressively increase the distance, and by the age of 5 or 6, a child will probably be able to keep up on walks lasting over an hour. The secret is:

- be prepared to carry them or put them in the pushchair
- enjoy walking yourself
- take the opportunity to look around at the world
- have the right equipment (footwear, clothing, rucksack, etc.)
- walk regularly in all weathers

- be purposeful in your walking (i.e. go shopping, visit friends or take a trip to the local duck pond)
- walk rather than drive whenever this is practical.

Exercise 11

This requires you to make some observations of children. If you haven't got any suitable ones to hand, go to the park or swimming pool, or even sit down in a shopping mall café and look around.

Observe how children of different ages walk. Notice how they put their feet down (whole foot, top-toeing, firmly on their heels, etc.). If you get the opportunity, look at the shape of their footprints. With very young children, look at how they hold their hands and arms. See how older ones swing their arms when walking.

Notice (if you can estimate it) at what age they can leap with one and two feet, when they can hop and skip, and when they can freely run and sprint. Notice their posture. This is particularly interesting with adolescents.

When you have made as many observations as you can and taken notes, try to characterise (in words or sketches) the main stages in the development from first steps to complete mobility. Then try to answer the following questions:

- Thinking of all the changes you have observed in how children walk, from when they are young until they are grown up, how would you describe this whole process?
- What does the whole process of learning to walk reveal to us about how children develop?
- What does the way in which children (or adults) walk reveal to us about what they feel about themselves?
- List what helps and hinders children in developing free mobility (other than accidents, injuries or physical handicaps).

10

Talking

Gone are the days (did they ever really exist?) when people thought children should be seen and not heard. Children, as we now know, need to talk and be listened to as much as possible. They also need to learn to listen, not just superficially and selectively, but in order to empathise with other people.

Language is our greatest human gift. It was probably the evolution of language that finally tipped the scales of our animal nature and made us human. Language civilises, although it does not necessarily make us humane. Much harm can be done with words, which only indicates how important it is that speaking develops hand in hand with listening. Language also provides us with the basis for our most common forms of thinking.

Speech is a kind of movement

The inner activity in the child that leads to her stretching upwards, to her maintaining an upright position, is the same activity that becomes speech. Speaking is a kind of movement that begins inside us with our breath. The movements of our larynx, a complex sleeve-shaped muscle at the back of the throat, shape the stream of air. From there, the energised stream of air is released into the space of the mouth where it is further shaped by our tongue, palate, teeth and lips. The consonants are each formed by a different combination of shapes. Some sounds are made by the lips (b, p, m), some by the teeth and lips (f, s) some by the palate, tongue and teeth (d, n) and so on. It is worth slowly pronouncing the sounds of the alphabet to identify where they are actually formed.

The stream of movement concentrates itself in the chest, throat and mouth. Interestingly, when we listen to someone speaking, we imitate the movements of the other's person's speech formation. Our own muscles, especially those of our chest, larynx, lips and face, respond in tiny micro-movements that we perceive, thus enabling us to hear what they say. We listen with our own muscles and perceive our own movements.

Many meanings

Language has many sides to it. First, there are the words, which represent the things, activities and relationships we know in the world around us. Then there is the structure that language has, the sentences that string the words together into meaningful sequences. Next, there is the emotional content. There are at least three ways of understanding any given spoken sentence, depending on the situation:

1   the literal meaning of the words the speaker speaks
2   what the listener actually hears and understands
3   what meaning the speaker actually intended.

How we say something clearly changes the meaning from neutral statement to provocative accusation. The sentence '*The bank statement has arrived*' might mean just that – but it might also mean the beginning of divorce proceedings!

Nor is language all words. There are many forms of communication that don't use words. It has been shown that approximately 80 per cent of communication between people familiar with each other is *not* based on the meaning of the words they use. Body language, facial expression, tone of voice, even pauses can say a lot in certain situations. Children have to learn to understand all these levels of communication.

What do children have to learn?

Children have to acquire all these levels of skill, but acquiring the vocabulary alone is daunting.

> From their second to their eighteenth year children learn on average 12 new words a day every day – that is, a new word every 2 hours!

Second, children have to learn to hear and understand language spoken at a rapid rate, often under acoustically difficult circumstances, for example, over the telephone. The everyday feat of understanding language while walking around eating crisps is phenomenal yet children do it all the time. The internal noise of the crunching alone would destroy any attempt to record the voice with even the most sensitive microphone. And imagine if both speaker and listener were eating crisps!

The structure of the language we speak, read and write is what is known as syntax. This orders words into meaningful combinations to express who is doing what to whom (and sometimes where, when, how and why). It seems that this part of language is in some way innate. Children appear to have an inborn ability to identify the rules of grammar of their mother tongue, and, after a short period of trial and error, they manage to speak grammatically correct language without anyone having taught them. Despite worries that children don't talk 'proper', the reality is that they speak as well as the adults around them.

The other reality is that many so-called grammatical errors are mere social convention and are, according to the actual principles of language structure, perfectly correct. Many of the least educated people in fact have the best natural grammar. If you don't believe me, try reading Steven Pinker's *The Language Instinct* and *Words and Rules* or, even more amusing, Bill Bryson's *Mother Tongue.*

What do parents have to do?

So how does all this language develop, and how can we support the process? Fortunately much of it happens with us just acting naturally. Children need role models in the form of people who speak to them. The rules they pick up without too much difficulty; the vocabulary is learned from the world around them. One of the most fascinating results of recent research highlights how parents adapt their own language to support the child's learning.

Motherese

'Motherese' is the term given by developmental linguists to what adults generally use when speaking to young children, or indeed to their lover or to animals. This is not baby talk; instead it consists mostly of highly intelligible sentences with a *bona fide* grammatical structure, the rest being well-formed isolated phrases. The sentences are shorter and clearer than those of normal speech, avoiding complex grammatical structures, but are not oversimplifications. This provides many useful examples of how language is structured:

> *Shall we have our milk now? That's a good boy. Have a good look round. What's that? Look there's your milk. Is that nice? Good boy. Yes, Mummy's got her glasses on. No, she didn't have them on before. Don't like them, do you? . . .*
>
> Mother, and baby aged 4 days, Channel 4, 1998

The great American child psychologist Jerome Bruner has called this process *scaffolding*. Just as a scaffold is a support structure put up during the construction of a building, enabling the builders securely to construct the next level, so by motherese the child is encouraged to reach beyond what she can already do until a new stage of language development has been achieved.

Typically, the main carers scaffold verbal situations until the child has mastered the essentials. So before the child can speak, her mother describes the breakfast as she prepares it: *'We're having some lovely warm milk and porridge, aren't we darling?'* The routine of the activity is reinforced with a routine patter with small variations: *'Would you like some nice warm milk and porridge?'* This is a rhetorical question because junior is getting milk and porridge anyway, but it does exemplify the question form. In this way, the child get lots of practice and correction, and the adult is continually extending the vocabulary and elaborating on the context. As the child learns to say a few words, she can add them to her mother's sentences:

Mother: What are we having for breakfast this morning?
Child: Milk.
Mother: That's right we're having milk and . . .
Child: P'ridge.
Mother: Mmm, lovely warm porridge, porridge.
Child: P'ridge.

The learning process is not always instant. Children can wait weeks and even months before coming out with the correct use of a word or its correct pronunciation. They often don't risk trying a difficult word until they are really sure, especially if a slightly heavy-handed parent makes an overt correction.

Research quoted in Cromer's *Language and Thought in Normal and Handicapped Children* has shown that what is considered to be the basic and simplest form of sentence structure in English, namely a sentence that has the subject–verb–object form, does not predominate in motherese. In conversation between adults, this type accounts for up to 87 per cent of sentences, but motherese is far more varied: only 30 per cent of sentences take this shape. Forty-four per cent being questions and 18 per cent imperatives. Furthermore, parents do not match the complexity of sentences to the developmental stage of the child, nor is there any obvious correlation between the complexity of parental language and the child's own progress in mastering the language.

This casts doubt on the assertion that learning the mother tongue or indeed any subsequent foreign languages depends upon what might be considered to be logical rules of progressing from simple to complex, introducing one new construction at a time and starting with subject–verb–object sentences. The fact that motherese does none of these things suggests that children do not learn the structure of their mother tongue by systematic imitation or systematic teaching.

Past, present and future

It was long thought that children lived in the continuous present, in the here and now, and had little memory of the past, let alone any grasp of the future, until they were about 3 years or even older. There is, however, now evidence that even before they can speak properly, they can grasp events that do not necessarily correlate with what can be immediately seen. This should not surprise us because parents are explaining the past and future to children all the time. Here is an example from the best book on the subject, Susan Engel's *The Stories Children Tell*:

> *Hello little sugar plum. You had a lousy night last night, didn't you? Yes you woke up five times. Poor little mushroom. You didn't like those strawberries, did you? They gave your tummy a bad ache, didn't they? And you couldn't sleep, could you? We had a bad night, didn't we?*

This little passage has several important features: lots of repetition, lots of friendly reinforcement and engagement, and the adult sequencing the events of the past night for the child. The adult creates a cause for the effect (tummy ache and a bad night), so the child can soon explain her own past experiences in similar vein. Similarly, the future is anticipated through descriptions of what will or might be:

> *When John comes round to play, why don't you get your shop out and play shops with him? I'm sure he will like that, and then maybe we can have a snack time with honey bread and some juice. Would you like that?*

Quite apart from preparing the child to imagine something that has not yet happened, the child is also having a positive outcome suggested to her. This may help to overcome a certain feeling of threat if John turns up apparently out of the blue. Whatever does eventually happen, at least a mood of welcome and friendly expectation has been created.

As well as adopting the motherese pattern of speaking, there are other ways to support early language development (see also Chapter 4):

- Talking (or singing) to children and talking in their presence is the best way for them to learn. Use natural language, correct words and sentences, and give them plenty of opportunity to join in.
- Be honest. Children have to learn the meaning of words and assume everything you tell them is true.
- Don't force things. Children will learn at their own pace.
- Let children hear the human voice live in order to identify its full range of nuances. Recorded or electronically produced sounds lack especially the overtones.
- Too much background noise makes it harder for children to distinguish the sounds they need to hear. The natural sounds of domestic life are important, but distraction from the radio or TV uses up considerable energy that could be usefully applied to learning and growing.

Story-telling

> I would venture to claim that as soon as human beings acquired language, they began to tell stories, because we continue to seek to understand the world, and above all we make sense of who we are and what happens to us, through story. Story-telling is the oldest art form, at the very heart of human culture.

Homo Fabula: *We are story-telling beings.*

Ben Okri

Once we tell about things in the form of stories, we create the possibility of having an inner life. Events we may have experienced acquire new meaning when we hear about them in stories because they then become objects of thought, which allows us to reflect on them. In other words things, people and events acquire a level of reality other than their immediate physical sense-perceptible presence. They become images of reality in our minds. As Jerome Bruner put it, making experience meaningful involves interpreting it. Stories are interpretations, a version of experience. Furthermore, they are collaborative. Even if I only listen to a story, I am imagining what I am told and therefore I participate in the telling. In fact, most young children do far more than just listen: they actively participate.

How it starts

Once children can talk, usually between 14 and 24 months of age, they tend to refer to what they are doing, or what things look or feel like, unless prompted to recall events by adults. Between the ages of 2 and 4 years, they begin to refer to things not present. At first, the child requires a contextual clue, something present that has an obvious connection to a recent event – a piece of broken vase recalls the breakage, for example. The greater the amount of interaction in terms of discussing things that have happened or will happen, the more easily the child is able to learn the correct linguistic forms and visualise absent things or situations.

In order to be able to refer to the past or present the child needs to expand her repertoire of place and time words: for nearly a year, my daughter used '*yesterday*' to refer to almost any day in the past or future. Meanwhile, the young child's general memory develops, but it remains strongly associated with sensory impressions up until she is about 6 years old. Stimuli have to be strong to awaken memories of things from more than hours or at most a day ago.

Perhaps the most significant aspect of memory and language development is that it benefits from social or interpersonal exchange. It has long been recognised that societies and communities build up their cultural identity by telling and retelling their common tales. It is the same with children. Through the dialogue of telling and retelling commonly shared (or imaginative) experiences, parents and young children together not only build up a family identity, but also enable the child to place herself in an ever-expanding context. Taking turns to tell parts of the story, parent and child recreate all manner of situations. Collaborative story-telling (which may seem more like a conversational exchange between adult and child) is very important not only for children's language development, but for their whole social, emotional and psychological development as well. Through story-telling, they learn to define who they are in relation to the rest of us.

> Stories provide young children with the scaffolding to help them to attain the next stage of their development, to proceed from being babies to toddlers, from toddlers to young children and so on.

Furthermore, story-telling provides children with a way of dealing with crisis, anxiety and uncertainty. It enables them to digest and relate to their experiences in a healthy way, helping them to extend and feel secure in their social environment, to become whole people.

Stories are the secret reservoir of values: change the stories individuals or nations live by and tell themselves and you change the individuals and nations.

Ben Okri

The phases of story-telling in young children

The child psychologist Susan Engel has identified five important phases in children's collaborative story-telling.

Phase 1

Parents tell their children stories about everyday life from the very beginning, the children participating at around 18 months of age. The most important aspect of this phase is that parents direct the child's attention to the child's own self by describing it. The child acquires a first sense of self through the reference of the parents: *'Jenny's a happy girl who likes to go bouncy-bouncy'*, *'That's where you sleep when you stay over at Gran's, isn't it?'* The child learns that she has a past, likes and dislikes, that things happen to her and that we all love her.

Phase 2

From about the age of 3, children can hold their own in conversation. In fact, it is sometimes hard to get a word in! They now use language to say how they feel and what they want. As Susan Engel puts it with admirable academic clarity:

> *At the same time they are engaged in a dramatic exploration of their uniqueness. This exploration builds on their surer sense of themselves as having a cohesive and interesting extended self.*

This playgroup age is delightful in its loud egotism: 'Me, me, me!' Dialogue and shared story-telling are now vital to support the child's sense of herself over time as this example of a 3-year-old in story-telling mode with her father shows:

Child: Daddy, when I was a tiny weeny baby, did I sleep in a tiny weeny bed?

Father: Yes sweetheart. When you were a baby, you slept in the cot.

Child: When I was teeny weeny, I slept in a cot.

Father: Do remember what your cot was like?

Child: Yes I 'member what my cot was like when I was a teeny weeny baby. Daddy, was I teeny weeny?

Father: You were about this big. I could put you in my arms like this.

Child: I'm a big girl now. I'm right up to here. I'm too big for my cot. Daddy, where is my cot?

Father: Don't you remember? We took it down and gave it a good clean and packed it away in the loft . . .

Children at this age love to hear stories about themselves told to others (and even to themselves). Even hearing the same tale again seems to bring a deep satisfaction. If the story is of a painful experience, they will listen sympathetically. They are taking in the version of themselves that you are telling and identifying with it, so alterations in terms of praise, reinforcement or assurance are possible. Children need so many positive images of themselves that we should take every opportunity to stress the positive, especially when their view of other people is incorporated in the story. Attitudes towards other children or strangers can be subtly supported.

Such stories have to be heard. They need a listener. Since we spend so much time sitting in the car, this is a place where stories can be told at length.

Phase 3

Children from the age of 3 or 4 onwards share their sense of self not only with their parents and trusted adults, but also with friends their own age. This becomes a means of building relationships. After all, our closest friends are those to whom we can tell our stories. If the baby formed her sense of identity around the parent–child relationship, the 3 or 4-year-old begins to establish her identity in relationship to other children. That means she gets a different kind of feedback, one that may be far less sympathetic. Children begin to get a new sense of identity through those who annoy, frighten or compete with them.

This leads to the increasing use of fantasy in the story-telling process. Children will exaggerate to impress their friends or even totally invent situations, but this should not be judged too harshly. It is also an attempt to measure parameters and establish a bond of imagination with other children. It in fact leads into true creative play in which children make-believe all manner of situations and roles: '*You be the horse and I be the man who feeds you hay and brushes your coat.*'

By the age of 5, children spend as much time talking to each other as they spend playing, the two activities often going hand in hand. The planning of the game may take up the whole playtime, and carrying out the plan may have to be put off. By 6 or 7, children tell each other long stories about what they like and don't like. They also greatly enjoy recalling shared experiences, which strengthens their intimacy and in turn their sense of self. Stories begin to feel like personal possessions. When an older brother challenges your version of the story, this is taken as an affront to your very existence. If your version of the story is confirmed, the sense of pride is profound.

That is why daily news time is so important. Children should have the opportunity to tell what they think is important, what has happened to them, what they have seen, heard, thought or felt. It is important that this is done in an atmosphere of total acceptance. Different versions should be allowed to stand in their own right. I know school classes in which this has been practised every day over 7 or 8 years. The preoccupations, topics, style and main contributors change over the months and years, but by the age of 13 these children have the most astonishing ability freely to describe even the most intimate experiences in the knowledge that they will be listened to but not judged (at least not unjustifiably). And this at an age when most 13-year-olds become increasingly inarticulate and secretive about their innermost feelings.

The power of talk is immense, but the situation has to be right and the rules adhered to. There are many adults, who cannot articulate their thoughts and feelings, in whom the tension bottles up and comes out as anger, depression, self-denial and an inability to face the truth.

Phase 4

By the time children are 6, they have a wide repertoire of stories about themselves, which can extend from oral to written versions. By now, they have heard all manner of other story-telling genres from parents, friends and teachers. They can choose the story-lines, themes and plots that suit them and adopt them in their play (i.e. in their inner life). Powerful stories with real archetypes can nourish a child's inner life in ways we as adults can barely imagine.

Children will now increasingly seek and respond to stories that reflect their own inner developmental challenges. This is obviously individual but there are general themes that appear to each developmental stage, which I shall summarise later.

Phase 5

Collaborative story-telling dwindles in the school years. There is a phase when children talk to themselves, especially when they are trying to master complex matters: '*I have to do this, then I do that, then I look out for those . . .*'. This gradually becomes internalised and we continue these dialogues with ourselves in thought. The story-telling mode gradually transforms into, on the one hand, the ability to reflect on one's life and relationships, and on the other hand, creativity, not least literature itself, the ability to create a story within a range of aesthetic rules we call style.

The desire to hear and read stories does not of course fade. In fact, those who have developed an ear for a good story, those who, perhaps unconsciously, recognise the stages of narrative development, will be the most avid readers, the most interested in going to the theatre. So what are these stages of narrative development? In most stories, a situation is presented, the main players are introduced, something happens, a crisis ensues, perhaps followed by more crisis, and then there is some kind of ultimate resolution. In classical drama, the plot unfolds in the following stages:

- Act One: Exposition, the problem is portrayed
- Act Two: Intensification, the main tension, the drama, becomes apparent
- Act Three: Reversal, something happens to worsen the crisis
- Act Four: Retardation, a reflective element delays the resolution
- Act Five: Resolution, transformation occurs.

Even the simplest parent–child stories have something of this classical structure. It is a universal theme and something that has a deeply therapeutic (perhaps even cathartic) effect.

People are as healthy and confident as the stories they tell themselves.
Ben Okri

How to foster narrative development

First of all, **listen**. It is often said that children need to be watched to grow. They need to be listened to as if what they say is meaningful, interesting and informative. Listening means reacting and responding with smiles, frowns, looks of surprise, disbelief and so on. The active listener participates in the story and helps the teller to be more motivated and supported. Children soon sense if adults are not really listening so set aside a time and place when you can listen to them.

Then **respond**. Don't listen to children's stories with a view to correcting them. Accept them as they come and ask questions that lead them to elaborate. A good way to respond is to tell them a story.

Don't forget to **collaborate**. Enter into the world of the story and participate accordingly, which means adopting the same story conventions as the child. Don't ask logical questions if the story is not at the logical level: if the child tells you that a fairy flew down the chimney, don't say, she couldn't have, we have a gas fire.

When telling children stories, choose stories from a wide range of **different sources**. Children are very receptive to interesting phrases, different styles and unusual sounds. They do not have to understand everything they hear: even if a story is beyond them, they will appreciate the structure and what little they can visualise. This generates an interest in and respect for the as-yet-unknown and stimulates the desire to learn.

Choose the **best stories** you can find. The main benefit of traditional tales is that they have stood the test of time and probably stem from cultures that contained far more wisdom in their story-telling traditions than we do. Authentic traditional stories (as opposed to modern or Victorian sentimental versions) contain archetypes in both the characters and the plot. Many traditional folk and fairy tales were once teaching stories that have come 'down' to the level of children's tales. They contain great wisdom that we can no longer access with our intellect. Obviously, many traditional folk tales contain sexist or racist stereotypes, usually acquired in more recent historical times, but these can be replaced with more appropriate characters while staying true to the plot.

Suggestions about story material

There are two kinds of story:

- collaborative stories, those we tell with our children every day as part of being together, tell of us and them directly
- stories that belong to the wider culture, those we hear from story-tellers or read in books.

There are also stories that have something of both of these types.

Without doubt, listening to stories well told from memory is more engaging than listening to stories read from a book or heard on a tape. Story-telling is essentially an oral art form that has literature as a branch of its development. Listening to a story is an activity that invites participation as well as one that lets the child witness the unfolding of thought and the use of language.

> Listening to stories strengthens the child's memory by showing how complex events can be strung together. Story-telling is one of the best ways of cultivating the imagination. Finally, it provides the strongest basis of all for literacy, which is more than just reading and writing, and involves us in being able to make sense of the world.

The following guidelines seek to characterise the kind of story that meet the developmental needs of the child. Story-telling is going through a major revival these days. There are many professional story-tellers around – try hiring one for a children's party. There are also many story-telling courses available. If someone wants to give you a treat, let them pay for you to attend one (and look after the kids too, naturally).

Babies and toddlers

Very young children need collaborative story-telling throughout the whole period from birth until their language is established, which means until it is possible for the child to hold conversations with people like Granny or friendly neighbours. Such stories can involve fictional characters that do all kinds of familiar things, going over familiar ground again and again, while gradually incorporating new episodes. You can embroider elements from your own childhood and adult experiences into the endless story – when the hamster escaped, the time Daddy burnt the toast, the day Auntie lost the car keys. A basic 'family' similar to the child's own can help the child to identify with it as well as teach elementary moral strategies for future life. This genre can change to suit the age of the child and works right up until she is about 8 years old.

Young children also enjoy looking at picture stories that have no text but require the adult to describe what the pictures show. Such books can be 'read' countless times with the stories getting progressively more complex at each telling:

Look, the little girl is in her bed,
Can you see who else is in the bed?
Yes, there's a teddy.
The little girl's in bed with her teddy. Look, the sun is peeping through
the curtains . . .

The images in these books should portray real things in a clear and uncluttered way, without too much detail. Cartoons and other artistic distortions should be avoided until later as they do not match the child's actual experience and will appear 'untrue'.

Conversely, images in a story that can be assimilated will be experienced as true. Images that reflect an inner reality, perhaps the psychological reality of an archetype in a fairy tale, will be experienced by young children as valid – even though our rational minds find Jack's beanstalk 'unreal'.

From 3 to 5 years old

Collaborative story-telling continues in age-appropriate ways. A wider range of 'family' stories can continue. These have the wonderful advantage that they can be told whenever they are needed: in a traffic jam, at the doctors and of course at bed-time. Picture books continue to be useful too. Even books with text play a part: since the children cannot read, they will not mind or notice if you take liberties to edit the printed story. Sometimes it is necessary to leave out parts. Some Eastern European books have beautiful illustrations, even if the text is equally incomprehensible to both child and adult. Pop-up books with strings and tabs to manipulate the figures are a great source of fun.

In the UK we are blessed with some of the best children's books available: take a hunt through titles at the local library. Kim Lewis and Shirley Hughes are favourite authors, and Floris Books publish a series of textless picture books and, for slightly older children, a range of folk tales.

Fairy tales

Children at this age love fairy tales, the authentic versions from collections of folk and fairy tales being more suitable than modern film versions. There are many collections from around the world: as we live in such a multicultural society, children should be involved in a multicultural story world. Start with the simpler, shorter tales before gradually moving on to longer ones. The children's attention span will probably be the best guide as to length and suitability.

Some such tales contain grim and gruesome imagery, albeit described in a very matter of fact way, without the kind of physical detail that might shock a child. It is the visualising that causes the problem. Fairy tales contain real human drama clothed in unrealistic settings, often in far away lands with forests, mountains and wells. The events portrayed involve birth, death, leaving home, meeting challenges, making mistakes, encountering danger, trickery, loss, joyous reunion, magical events, wise men and women, fools, con artists, heroes and heroines, craftsmen, spirits, witches and so on – in other words, human psychological archetypes. The only types that hardly ever appear are fairies! The plots often involve challenge, trial, deceit, love, jealousy, transformation, redemption and damnation – *real* real life – which is why children have an infinite hunger for such tales. It is also why fantasy literature and movies are so popular with adults too.

So if real life contains pain, death and destruction, isn't it right that children should first learn of these things in the context of fairy story, in which good usually triumphs and bad gets, in the end, what it deserves? I feel that it might be best to avoid the darkest tales until the children are older, say 7 or 8. Read the stories beforehand, leave out the worst, most graphic parts, but don't change the drift of the story. Follow your child's response: if she is very sensitive and becomes frightened, change to a happier story instead.

From 6 to 8 years old

Throughout this age range, fairy stories remain a staple part of the diet. There are many classic tales that are so long and complex they need to be told in several sittings, for example the classical Russian tales – The Firebird, Wassilisa the Beautiful and Puskin's retelling of The Tale of The Dead Princess and the Seven Knights. Older children will love the tales of Hans Christian Andersen and Oscar Wilde.

Around the ages of 7 and 8, the children live very strongly in their imaginations and love to feel a close connection to the natural world around them. They enjoy stories that tell about the changing seasons and animals, about rivers, hills, forests and the spirits that inhabit them. Many of these stories relate to the origins of local features, such as rivers, caves or hills, English and Welsh fairy tales often having a strongly geographical content. I recommend a few collections in the bibliography.

Children around the age of 8 begin to appreciate short fables, such as those of Aesop and la Fontaine. In these, animals assume human character and portray moral lessons in pithy and often enigmatic form. Such fables lead to interesting discussions about personality types: Am I a hare or a tortoise? A fox or a crow? To these animal fables belong the wonderful genre of Native American teaching stories, of which Jumping Mouse is the classical quest story. There are many similar genres in the Asian Indian and Chinese traditions. In fact, many of the stories surrounding the life of the Buddha have the character of fables too. I can recommend all the Oxford Myths and Legends series (Oxford University Press), which collects the best from around the world.

At around the age of 8 or 9, children often want to hear about heroes who have shown how to overcome their weaker nature. The stories of many saints both in the Christian and Hindu traditions are full of excellent examples. The classical story for this age is the life of St Francis of Assisi. All the legends of his youth and the later stories of addressing the birds and taming the wolf of Bobbio show how animal nature can be both respected and redeemed through human consciousness. These have, in many ways, a more effective ecological message than do modern forms of preaching. Similar examples can be found in various African traditions.

Many Celtic legends have a distinctive fairy tale mood and a strong connection to nature. One of the best stories for this age is a wonderful book by the Irish novelist and poet Padraic Colum, who was inspired to write the wonderful book *The King of Ireland's Son*.

Age 9–11

Obviously the older children get, the more individual they become in their tastes. Once they can read on their own, and with the right kind of encouragement, they will find their own story material. There are, however, some guidelines about themes. At around the age of 9, children become much more demanding in their sense of self, needing and challenging authority. It is also a time of great insecurity. They want to know that the world has order and structure, that things have their place and that there is justice. They want to know how things come about and about how the world works, questioning things they previously took for granted. It is as if they had suddenly awoken from an enchanted golden glow of childhood into the cold, clear light of dawn.

The best approach we can take is to describe how basic things work – where food comes from, how we build houses, how people work together, how relationships work. If ever there is an age at which children need an image of a paternalistic god-father, it is at this stage of their lives. This need, once satisfied, will soon give way to a more pluralistic expression of authority. In Steiner Waldorf schools all over the world, children hear the stories from Christianity's Old Testament, starting from the Creation, the Fall of Adam and Eve from the Garden of Eden and the subsequent trials and sufferings of the Hebrew people. Whatever your religious persuasion, it is hard to find a better source of wonderful and varied stories. When we consider how much art has been inspired by this text (and many of the associated texts that we no longer have in our Bible but which were once part of the body of story material often portrayed by Rembrandt and other great artists), we can see that we have a cultural goldmine of stories here.

Other literature too is valuable. At around the age of 10, children's perception of people has matured to the point at which they can appreciate more of the subtleties between good and bad. Evil, for example, comes in many shades. The legends of Norse mythology provide a wonderful source of powerful, mysterious images as well as gods and heroes behaving in an-all-too human way. The great figures of Loki the trickster with a different face for every situation, Thor with his great hammer and lack of finesse, beautiful yet tragic Baldur, all make a deep impression in children's imaginations. The stories are racy, humorous, full of tricks yet overshadowed by a deep melancholy as the battle of Ragnarok awaits the heroes at the end of time. Beowulf's battles (now in magnificent translation by Seamus Heaney) and the Sagas of

Harrald Hardrada are available in fine well-written translations by Kevin Crossley-Holland or retold by Rosemary Sutcliffe.

Between the ages of 10 and 12, children can enter into the world of mythology in a way that only adults with a specialist interest can match. The legends of Finn McCool and the Fianna, Cuchulain and the Cattle Raids of Celtic Ireland, are marvellous, moving stories that roam from the fairy tale-like mood of magic and mystery to real psychological drama of love, betrayal, loyalty and sacrifice. The story of Finn McCool's betrayal by his beautiful and much younger wife, the red-haired Grania, who falls in love with Finn's first warrior Diarmid, introduces children to real adult emotion within the context of a myth. These stories are heart-rending yet mysterious, enough to engage the imagination of any 11-year-old.

The same can be said for the great Greek myths and the stories of the Odyssey and the Iliad, all of which are available in readable versions. These stories really belong to everyone's heritage. If they are not made available at school, parents should make an effort to provide them at home. One can also sweep through the great myths of ancient Egypt, the epic of Gilgamesh, the tales of the Incas and Maya, the maori legends, the Mahabarata and other Hindu epics. Try too the stories of Alexander the Great and the Romans. The legends of King Arthur and other medieval romances introduce a wonderful range of human types as well as the whole concept of chivalry in the form of the quest for the Holy Grail, the search for spiritual truth, at a time when the children are just entering puberty. Arthurian legends are full of complex morality and moral dilemmas with which youngsters this age can readily identify.

So why all this myth and legend? The main reason is the sheer quality of the stories. Second, they express something of the essence of the civilisations that created them, allowing children to find an inner connection to some of the great themes with which humankind has concerned itself through the ages. Finally, if we are really to understand our heritage and where we have come from, mythology and legend reveal the path that humanity has trodden down to the present. It represents in imaginative form the chief concerns that have preoccupied people since time immemorial and which our culture is in danger of losing: what myths of our own age are likely to be read in a thousand years' time?

Finally, I would put in a plea for the reading (and writing) of poetry with children. It is very sad when children grow up and inherit adult prejudices against poetry; poetry really is for everyone. It can be a wonderful fulfilment for children and adolescents to discover this realm, in which the world is filled with meaning in ways that cannot be rationally explained but remain all the more meaningful for that. Make poetry special and you will have given your children a gift for life.

This long list of recommendations highlights only aspects that may not occur to most parents, but I have not even begun to mention the wealth of books we have available for our children. Just go to your local library with your children and browse around. They are bound to find something. The reading habit is one that I wish for all children. Happy story-hunting!

Exercise 12

Practise reading stories out loud

Now you have to practise being a story-teller. Find yourself a good book of stories (see my recommended list), choose one that is not too long and read it through a few times. Then practise retelling it in your own words. If you have a listener willing to listen to your attempts that is wonderful, but you can do it on your own, as actors and musicians do. Speaking into a tape recorder and playing it back can also help (but don't be surprised at how unfamiliar your voice sounds). If you have trouble remembering the details, try breaking the story down and writing down a few key words on a crib sheet. Telling a story in your own words is important because it means you can respond better to your listener.

If there is dialogue in the story, decide what kind of voice you are going to use for each character, but don't ham it up. Bear in mind that traditional fairy and folk tales do not benefit from dramatic telling; let the story tell itself. An audiocassette of an actor reading folk tales or stories will provide some hints.

Making up your own stories

This is especially good for very young children, who really benefit from having their everyday experiences reflected back in story form. You can write the stories down or tape record them to help. With children of above 5 onwards, you have to be pretty imaginative to make up suitable stories, so why not go on a story-telling course?

If you have children, get them to tell you what they did one day and then restructure what they have told you into a story form. Find a good beginning such as, '*There was once a little girl called Rosemary who lived in a . . .*' Weave in the other events (not too many), tie up the loose ends and then bring the whole thing to a happy conclusion – '*and so they all went happily home and told their Mummies all about it*' or '*and when whey had finished, they brushed their teeth, said their prayers and were soon all tucked up fast asleep*'. Keeping the same characters in your stories allows you to develop them.

Try writing and telling a range of different simple stories and imagine what age of child you would tell them to. If you have children, try them out. Keep notes both on the stories and on how you progress, and jot down the bones of good stories you find.

11

Child's play

Young children are active learners. They use their bodies to explore and experiment. Activities requiring total body involvement are likely to encourage problem solving. In addition to using their bodies to find solutions, children who are challenged with objects, obstacles and props, are using their bodies to learn about themselves. During early childhood, what a child feels about himself is largely dependent upon what he thinks he can or cannot do with his body. Therefore, to foster positive self-concepts, children need to experience challenges, equipment and activities that will promote feelings of success, safety and fun.

Linda M. Carson, quoted in *Fools Gold*
edited by Colleen Cordes and Edward Miller

The phrase 'child's play' suggests something simple and easy, something effortless, yet this should not blind us to the face that children's play is a very serious business. Indeed, play is the serious work of childhood. In the past, play was regarded as a childish pastime, something insignificant except in the sense that it kept children occupied and therefore out from under a busy mother's feet. Now we know that play is crucial to the whole business of growing up and becoming competent adults.

Animal play

From an evolutionary perspective, play is common to the young of all the higher evolved animals. That is what makes young animals so endearing to us. Whether they are lambs frolicking, piglets squealing or puppies or kittens playing chase, all are that their most interesting to us when they are young. As soon as they grow out of this phase, they become far less endearing to most of us.

Play is something that is apparently unnecessary, is not essential to survival. Yet closer observation makes it obvious that, in play, animals practise skills that they need as adults. Young wolf cubs play at hunting and fighting. But this does not explain all of their behaviour. What is happening here?

> Animals that have the longest period of childhood, and therefore of playfulness, are also the most intelligent of animals.

Intelligence in an animal means not only that it can learn more, but also, more significantly, that it has greater flexibility in its behaviour. An intelligent animal has greater scope for expressing itself, for freedom. This usually also means that it has a far greater complexity of experience and a much richer emotional life. In short, animals with a longer childhood have a greater potential for freedom from biologically determined behaviour, and this is of great significance for human beings since we have the longest known childhood.

Play is about spiritual nourishment

The games children play, the way in which they play and what they play reveals what is going on in them at the deepest level. Play reveals to us their deepest, and therefore spiritual, intentions. If we observe their play with truly open eyes and minds, we can begin to sense what mighty forces are at work shaping the individual, at the same time getting a glimpse of their intentions to shape the world. Play both nourishes the developing individual and reveals something of who she is struggling to become.

> The faculty of play becomes the origin and source of the
> most important skills and abilities we can develop in life.
> Childhood play becomes the highest form of creativity.

In play, the child imbues the activity or the toys with a greater meaning than they inherently have. A piece of wood may become a magic wand, a game of tig the ability to reach out and touch another person. Play is all about transformation, about filling life with greater value and meaning.

Play, with its ability to transform, is also the source of great art, as can be seen if we consider the religious icons of the Orthodox Christian Church. These are not merely paintings of a mother and child. The mother and child in question are *the* Holy Mother and Child. Furthermore, the icon is believed to have the ability to transform the individual who gazes upon it in reverence or even to perform miracles. The icon painters of the monastery on Mount Athos in Crete had to follow a path of meditation for 20 years before being allowed to paint such pictures. The icon is thus not merely a painting; it is an object that has been transformed with significance.

Modern artists have again revealed this mystery to us, teaching us to see the significance and beauty of everyday objects, even things we turn our heads away from, such as garbage or dead animals. As the artist Joseph Beuys has shown us, ritual can imbue ordinary objects with spiritual significance. Interestingly, the oldest forms of art known, from the Ice Age, had the same significance. The human ability to play means creating meaning, making things and relationships sacred. Both the activity and the objects are imbued with higher meaning through play. In art, elements of colour and shape are imbued with high meaning too.

It is important to bear this perspective in mind, not least when we go into a toy shop. What has this to do with our highest human ability, that of bringing meaning into the world? We should encourage our children to be creative in the highest sense of the word.

Play begins with touching

A baby explores the world through touch, reaching out to discover the world through her senses. She touches the skin of her mother, or feels the texture of the fabric under her, repeating the movement. In reaching out and repeating the process, we have the two primary gesture of play.

> Play is always an interaction with the world and with other people, and we need to do it again and again.

Throughout the first 2 years or so of life, the child will explore the world of objects and sensations within her reach, often repeating the experience over and over again. Among her first playthings will be her own fingers and later toes, these initially discovered by accident. The child also plays with her own ability to make sounds. Soon other objects become her 'toys'. The child 'gets in touch' with what is around her, through this beginning to distinguish herself from the world outside.

Getting in touch with yourself

If we remove something from a child's hand, her sense of loss will be momentary, since she has little object memory. Out of sight, or rather out of touch, is out of mind. Yet at any particular time, the young child desires very much to get in touch with what is around her. It is astonishing how our language retains the significance of these primary experiences. What does it mean to be 'out of touch' as an adult? It may mean that we cannot identify with or understand what is around us, or that we are too preoccupied with ourselves to open up to what is outside us. This distance is paradoxically also a distance from ourselves, especially the inner, essential aspects of ourselves.

> We speak of getting in touch with the 'child within' or 'our sensitive self' or even (for a man) of getting in touch with 'the feminine side' of ourselves. The origins of this ability lie in the deep time of early childhood.

What can we do to help the very young child get 'in touch'? Should we just let her get on with it, discovering whatever comes to hand, as long as it isn't dangerous or toxic? Or should we choose what we want our babies to take and hold? What kind of 'toys' should we give them? Let us consider for a moment what it means to children for a beloved adult to bend down and offer something to their eager little hands. The very gesture of giving is almost sacred in its significance. A gift, a blessing, a grace is freely given. The love-filled gesture of giving already imbues the object with meaning. But does the object itself deserve such significance?

Suitable toys must be small enough to hold but large enough to be easily grasped. They need to be firm yet not too heavy, and obviously not sharp, toxic or easily choked on. For the reasons outlined in Chapter 7, natural materials are better than synthetics. Toys will also need to survive being put in the child's mouth and chewed on. Even as adults, we retain this primary interest in holding and touching things for the sheer pleasure they give us. Greek men play with worry beads. Samburu men like to carry short carved sticks. Many walkers like to hold the carved handles of staffs. Even mobile phones have to feel good in the hand!

Playmates

Children soon want to add another dimension to their play. They want playmates.

The sheer delight young children derive from peek-a-boo activities is remarkable, beginning early and, in transformed way, remaining for a long time. The art of the game lies in the timing. Just how long a child can hold out before needing the reassurance of the familiar face is highly individual and requires fine judgement. When children are old enough to play hide and seek, it is interesting to observe how long they can hide or keep quiet in the cupboard. It has a lot to do with courage, confidence and self-control.

The basic principle of these games involves a voluntary denial of an experience on the part of both players. This creates a kind of expectation, a kind of longing for affirmation. When this is finally given, it is a cause for celebration and, inevitably, for repeating. In this exchange, the child strengthens her interest in life and the quest for grasping it.

A related game that develops in the first 2 years is that of dropping objects, often from the high chair, with the expectation that someone else will pick them up again. As in the activity of taking things apart and putting them back together, the child is engaging in the active process of analysing and reintegrating the elements that make up the world. This is an important part of developing the child's understanding of the world as well the rules of social engagement with other people, even if it is somewhat tiresome for the adults involved!

Dolls

An important stage in child development is reached when children begin to play with dolls, which usually occurs around the end of their second year. The doll differs from other toys and people in that it is both inanimate yet has the shape of a human being. The child experiences the doll as an extension of herself. As she gradually constructs her inner picture of the world, the doll becomes a representative of herself, a format on which she can project her self-image. Everything the child discovers is played out by and with the doll, which helps to reinforce the child's sense of herself.

I seriously considered my use of the pronoun 'she' for the child at this point. Is it only girls who play with dolls? Unless they have been encouraged not to, boys do in fact play with dolls, puppets or teddy bears. It is true, however, that girls spend more time in such play than boys. Nevertheless, the boys who don't get involved in the kind of role play that dolls involve often end up charging about getting into trouble because they need a focus for their play and usually look to the nearest adult to provide it. There can be highly beneficial effects from encouraging boys to play with dolls.

It is quite astonishing to observe how children play with dolls. Their dolls not only get dressed up, washed, fed, put to bed and cuddled, but they have complex feelings and reactions too. The child carries out a dialogue with her (to our ears silent) doll:

Poppy has a tummy ache and a bit of a headache and needs to lie down quietly.

This is my little baby. She doesn't like going out in the wind. It's too cold for her.

The value of this imaginative play is immense, which can perhaps be made clear by taking an extreme example. It is known that traumatised children (such as those of war-torn Sarajevo) can come to terms with the horrors they have experienced by playing with dolls. Such a re-enactment enables the child to re-experience yet also relate to what she has been through.

In terms of which doll to choose, the more that is left to exercise the child's imagination, the better. A doll that is complete and finished down to the eye-lashes leaves little to stimulate the child's imagination. Quite apart from imposing certain stereotypes of style, such dolls prevent the child projecting a real – and for the very young child that means a physical – image onto the doll. Later on, of course, children can get into the delight of dressing up their more fashion-orientated dolls. By then, however, the activity has moved to a different level, one that is far less fundamental to the child's emergent self-image.

From ages 2 to 4, children's imagination is unconsciously much more bound to their image of themselves. The best dolls for this age are the simplest, with barely any features, having soft, yielding body forms filled with warm wool or cotton wool. A plastic doll will never have the same plasticity of moulding itself to the child's imagination, of providing a medium for the child to become herself.

Creative play

From the age of about 3, children begin to be able to develop their imagination. They have outgrown what is known as the sensory-motor phase during which the primary senses are established and the child can establish a comprehensive picture *in here* of what is *out there* in relation to her body. Once this inner picture, or at least the broad outline, has been created, the child is free to let her mind roam and play. This is another way of describing the imagination.

> This is the age at which early learning begins to become an issue, but there is no need for it to do so because children will naturally learn through creative play. They direct their own play and therefore their own learning.

The carer's primary role is to create a warm, friendly, encouraging environment free of harmful influences, which is easier said than done. Children who are free to play do so, but what makes them free? Children need to be freed of the pressures of survival, which means reducing their stress level and increasing their sense of security. Children under stress lack confidence, which inhibits their imagination. That the emergence of a sense of self-identity, some-time between 2½ and 3 years of age, coincides with the birth of the imagination is no coincidence.

What children need above all is encouragement and praise. We can make a few modest suggestions for what they might do – *'What have you got in your shop today?'*, *'Does Dolly need to go for a walk?'* – but these are really more in the nature of reminders. Our appreciation of their endeavours is much more appropriate.

From imitation to imagination

Imitation is the key to imaginative play. Whatever we do, our children will want to join in with it or parallel it. This is not always possible, although even when it is necessary to paint the kitchen, they can be happy painting an outside wall with water, as long as they use a real brush! So we have to set up opportunities for them to work alongside us. Although this reduces our productivity, the long-term benefits of having capable, self-assured children are priceless.

Once they have observed real actions, children will internalise them and re-create them using whatever comes to hand. Adult interaction and compliance is important, however. *'Would you like a piece of cake?'*, *'Yes pease, that would be nice'* is sufficient to send a child off to bake some sand in an 'oven' in the sandpit and to return within seconds with a full birthday cake with candles for you to blow out. *'Can I help blow them out for you, Daddy?'*

Notice the subtle levels and dynamic shifting of focus in such an exchange. The child thinks of cake, knows it needs baking (or buying from the shop), returns with one (carefully carried of course), thinks of a reason for having a cake, comes up with birthday cake, which leads to the thought of birthday candles, which leads to the idea of blowing them out, which naturally the child wants to do herself, but wanting to be polite to the birthday boy, she asks whether he needs help. All the elements of a mini soap opera.

With imagination, memory is also born. The ability to imagine something is related to remembering what has happened. For a child, memories spark off the imagination and lead to play. In addition, the process of re-creating requires that she has experienced something at least once. As imagination and memory are both very closely bound up with sensory impressions, play is closely related to real-life experience.

4–5 year olds at play

With 4–5-year-old children, creative play becomes ever more elaborate, the children ever more skilful and capable. They need to supplement their play with real work in the house and garden – really cooking, baking, peeling apples, sewing, weeding and sweeping leaves. If children are carefully shown what to do and are supervised, they can do these tasks properly and safely.

Once this age has been reached, children are less stimulated by outer experience. They no longer need to see the kitchen utensils to think of baking; they can now be motivated by the idea of helping or making food.

Children are now able to generate their own imagination and then follow their impulses. They have an inner mental picture of what they want to do, or even of what needs doing. At this age, they are much more able to work together with other children, preparing something in secret and surprising the adults with what they have done. They are capable of turning the play corner into a café or hospital, a complex situation with a whole range of equipment and roles that have to be played. Whatever simple props are to hand are transformed into the required vehicles, tools and equipment, and the more this requires imagination, the better. Real objects are not as good as they are invariably the wrong size or shape, or in the wrong place at the wrong time, for the flow of activity. Children's imagination is so much more efficient and faster.

Healthy children whose imaginations have been free to develop have no difficulty solving the logistical problems created by such imaginative demands. Children who have become prematurely bound to real equipment get bogged down and frustrated when they haven't got the real thing: *'But we need a real telephone/ submarine/aeroplane!'* Free imagination, however, knows no limits. One can only imagine what such attitudes translate into in adult life – which children will grow up into people who can come up with unexpected creative solutions; which ones will freak out if their luggage gets lost or their ideal plan can't be realised?

A recent study carried out at Emerson College, East Sussex, showed that, in 17 hours of kindergarten time observed, the group of children played out some 64 different real-life situations. All human life was there – violence, families splitting up, falling in love, having a bad back, everything they had really experienced in daily life. The only differences between play and real life are the bewildering pace at which one situation mutates into the next, and the fact that no one gets permanently hurt!

Help or hinder?

So what stops or limits this activity? Children need the right kind of environment to develop creative play, a safe one that gives them time, space and energy. If they are exhausted by stress, they need time to relax and regenerate.

Imaginative play requires energy, although the beauty of it is that it generates energy too. But children first need to be relaxed. They cannot have the energy to find calm and creativity if they are under pressure to learn things, to conform to inappropriate expectations, to be more grown up than they are really ready to be.

This kind of play needs quality time. It needs to be a main activity of the day, not something tacked on to the end of a busy day in school. And children need plenty of sleep during which they can digest the events of the previous day and re-energise themselves.

Creative play needs to be bedded into a strong rhythm of activities that help children to feel part of a group, perhaps a community, gently opening themselves up to other children. They also need to experience an environment in which adult role models are engaged in meaningful activity with which the children can join in. In today's fast-living world, a kindergarten provides an ideal environment in which to encounter this, not shutting the world out but creating a space into which children can bring the world and, through play, digest it, stimulating their creative imaginations in the process.

Play and work

Here are some ideas about creating a play environment for young children and a few hints about enjoyable activities.

A children's garden

Such a garden can be situated on your own land behind your house or it can be a communal garden for several families or an apartment block. The space needs to be completely safe, with a secure perimeter fence so that children cannot run out onto the road and uninvited visitors cannot simply wander in. A combination of hedges and fencing is a good balance. The hedges attract birds and provide berries and sticks; the fencing keeps out dogs who might foul the play space.

The area needs to be used primarily by young children. Older children, with their bikes, playground games and occasional bad habits, should be encouraged to set up their own space. If the older ones can also be involved constructing and maintaining the garden for the little ones, this gives them a sense of participation and reduces vandalism.

Trees are ideal, the more mature the better, although one can plant one's own. The ideal children's garden is actually, like the

Garden of Eden, an orchard with running water. A mix of fruit trees providing apples, pears, plums and cherry blossom is good. Trees that spread and have low, supple branches for climbing and swinging on, such as chestnut, beech or willow, are useful. Avoid too many conifers as they create too much shade and the needles do not allow much undergrowth. Bushes and shrubs to hide under and climb between are helpful. Mature rhododendrons are perfect, but avoid too many sharp thorns and prickles.

In the absence of suitably shaped trees, small, low climbing frames can be made – young children tend not to have the arm strength for hanging from high bars or rails. They prefer clambering on and over broad, rounded shapes.

An area of bare ground is useful, perhaps one naturally occurring under a large tree or created using bark chips, which tend not to get too muddy and can be dug in.

A sandpit with broad retaining walls, for sitting on and using as a play surface as well as retaining the sand, is ideal. Cats are a problem, so sandpits need to be designed with some form of cover, preferably one that is not so heavy it cannot be lifted or so flimsy that it blows away. Heavy duty plastic mesh is also good as it allows rain water to drain through but isn't too popular with cats. The pit can be lined with a permeable membrane to drain the sand but keep weeds out. Play sand is best ordered in bulk to reduce the cost.

Also consider a lawn (optional since it has to be quite robust) and flower and vegetable beds to grow sturdy colourful flowers, hardy perennials and herbs that will stand regular plucking and give off interesting aromas.

Some robust but low swings that small children can get on and off by themselves provide great fun.

A shed or playhouse is essential, ideally with a small veranda and overhanging eves for storage in bad weather. It also needs to be fairly robust so shop carefully. Stable doors and shutters are better than glass or perspex windows. Inside there should be storage boxes with lids (e.g. for sitting on), some benches, a table, stools and a supply of blankets and rugs for multipurpose use (stored in a wooden box).

Permanent equipment can include child-sized brooms and sweeping brushes, buckets, wheelbarrows (excellent for balance and co-ordination), watering cans, robust spades and digging sticks, rakes and some bowls, plates and cutlery for picnics and use in the play house. Various lengths of timber can be available, some sawn but smooth enough not to give splinters, others slab wood with the bark on and some nice knotted branches of interesting shapes. The pieces can be as large as is manageable by two small children. Tree stumps can be used for sitting on or rolling around. Baskets of various sizes are always needed for collecting fir cones, pebbles, feathers and conkers. Not on this list are manufactured toys, bouncy castles, bikes: the emphasis in here is creative play, experiencing nature and encouraging sensory and movement development.

Additional equipment for supervised use can encompass gardening tools and pots, ropes for skipping, an open hearth or fireplace, and cooking and eating utensils for picnics.

The children's room

Not everyone has what the Victorians called the playroom, complete with large rocking horse, dolls house and governess. Nevertheless, children are going to have to play somewhere indoors. The following suggestions for such an area cover only the basics for stimulating children's imagination.

- If a playroom is not available, a designated play corner needs to have an enclosed feel to it, plenty of child-height shelving for displaying toys and treasures, and lots of baskets and boxes of various sizes to store things. The key element here is that *everything has its place*. Things can then be tidied away and found again.
- Some space needs to be set aside for displaying treasures – seasonal offerings, flowers, pretty stones and shells, special postcards.
- An old fashioned clothes-horse or similar free-standing wooden frame can serve as a screen with cloth draped around it or can be used to make the frame a tent.
- A basket of pieces of cloth can be used for dressing up, covering the clothes-horse or making fields, rivers and hills. The cloth can be dyed in a range of primary colours.
- Pieces of wood of different sizes and shapes, dried and oiled,

some squared off so they can be stacked, others left rounded like logs or half logs, are far more versatile than regular building blocks. Ideal for this purpose are branches of silver birch or beech up to 10 cm in diameter, sawn into lengths of 2–20 cm and dried. A few forked pieces can be included.

- Collections of stones, pebbles, fir cones, conkers and nuts are ideal for props.
- A low table has countless functions and some stools or small wicker chairs need to be available. These need to be robust and portable as they may be turned into all kinds of things.

Children love the following too:

- some simple dolls and finger puppets
- a collection of wooden toys, including farm animals, houses, trains, cars and boats etc.; most well made wooden toys last for several childhoods!
- small pans, baking trays, cutlery, plates, cups and wooden spoons, not forgetting a cupboard to put them away in. A simple box with rings painted on top for a hob and a door for the oven is very helpful. A small washing-up bowl, dishcloths and dusters
- a wooden iron, ironing board and drier
- screw-top jars full of pasta, beans, nuts and cornflakes, with a good supply of paper bags and shopping baskets, will be used to play shop
- wax crayons, large-format paper or drawing pads, and a drawing board (such as a large piece of hardboard) to protect tables and carpets
- beeswax for modelling
- safe scissors for cutting, a small roll of sticky tape and an adhesive stick (all housed in a drawer for supervised use until the children are competent to use them on their own).

The balcony or patio children's garden

If you cannot set up a children's garden, either on your own or with your neighbours, a balcony can provide an alternative.

If the balcony has railings, it is best to enclose it – with tarpaulin, groundsheeting, grass mats or bamboo – so it is not too exposed and so that toys do not get dropped onto passers-by. Leave a window for peeping out. If the balcony has a wall, how about painting it a warm colour. If you are artistically gifted, you could paint a mural. If possible, fix hooks and pulleys to the overhang so that children can join in with hanging out the washing. Baskets containing toys can also be hung from the roof.

As children need as much space as possible, be creative with shelving along the side walls. Try to avoid too many chairs and tables that can be dragged to the edge and climbed on; sawing off part of their legs can be a good compromise.

Pots or flower boxes with trailing foliage can be positioned low enough for children to water them. A large pot of bamboo or a dwarf conifer or azalea is another option: the plants need to be hardy, evergreen and happy in a confined space. Vegetables such as carrots, peas and climbing beans can be grown in soil 30–40 cm deep with compost at the bottom to retain moisture (and withstand overwatering). This is better than a grow bag, which dries out very quickly. And boxes have sides toddlers can hold on to.

Create a sand box, however small, but try to reduce the amount of sand that gets carried into the house.

A rain barrel to collect water for watering and play can be set up if there is enough drainage, collecting water either directly or via a diverted downpipe. If necessary, top the barrel up with a hose when the children are in bed. This is far less stressful for them than playing with water in the house or carrying it outside from the bathroom or kitchen.

A bird table and hanging bird feeders will bring wildlife into even the most urban setting, but place them out of reach of cats. If you are very keen, you can fix the feeders to a simple pulley so that they can be lowered to child level for refilling.

Modelling

Children love modelling, and it is extremely good for their fine motor co-ordination and for cultivating their sense of form and shape. If you observe children modelling, you can see what a calming effect it has on them, focusing their attention and causing them to breathe more deeply and slowly.

The question is, what material should be used? This, of course, depends on what you want to make. The key factors are that the material should be pleasant to handle, reusable and inexpensive. Plasticine and commercial play-dough are usually oil based, give off an unpleasant smell and feel tacky, so these are best avoided if possible.

Beeswax

This wonderful natural material has all the advantages of being organic, being very responsive to human warmth and having a pleasant colour and scent. It can be purchased (the firm Stockmar make excellent modelling wax for children) in various colours, including its natural golden yellow. The wax has to be warmed before it can be modelled; this can be done by pressing it in the hands until their warmth makes the wax soft (the hands must obviously be clean or the wax will soon look grubby). This is in itself a calming and warming activity for children, although very young children, find the wax simply too hard. One can also place it in a plastic bag and immerse it in warm water, or place it in a bowl on a radiator or stove.

Beeswax has the advantage of retaining the modelled form once it has hardened. In addition, the translucent surface of the wax gives a very pleasing effect, which softens the outlines and thus stimulates the imagination. Children cannot make exact copies of real objects but it is anyway far more artistic to allow the shapes to arise out of the activity and retain an indistinct form, which can be filled out by the child's inner eye. Start with simple shapes, like small balls, which can then be pressed into cup shapes, flattened out into saucers or rolled into long thin sausages. Older children could be given the stimulating task of turning these into sheep, cattle, shepherds, Mary and Joseph in time for Christmas.

The wax does not keep its pure colour for ever, but it can be recycled by being melted together in a bowl over a pan of hot water. Add a few drops of lavender or rosemary oil to give the finished product a lovely smell when it is warmed up by the children's hands, or a few drops of food colouring to give it a more homogeneous colour for further modelling. Finally, the used wax can be added to all the candle stubs that go to make the earth candles I described in Chapter 8.

Salt dough

This is wonderful material, used since ancient times, has recently been elevated to the level of a full-blown craft material, and coffee-table books with a thousand ideas for home craftwork have now been produced. Salt dough is great for children too. It is inexpensive and harmless if accidentally eaten. Once made it can be used as a modelling medium, pressed into a mould or cut into shapes with biscuit cutters. Then it can be baked and painted. The basic recipe is as follows:

- a cup of the cheapest plain white flour available
- 2 teaspoons of cream of tartar
- half a cup of salt
- two tablespoons of cooking oil
- a cup of water
- several drops of food colouring, preferably one that does not look too edible.

Mix the ingredients into a fine paste. Stir this in a pan over a low heat until the mixture peels away from the side of the pan. Remove the pan from the heat. When the dough is cool enough to handle, take it out of the pan and knead it on a board as you would bread. The texture you are aiming for is like a very good biscuit or pastry mix, firm but pliable. It is then ready to use.

This dough will last for many sessions of modelling if it is squashed back into a ball shape again and kept in a plastic bag or airtight plastic box. The modelling surface needs to be smooth, *dry* and clean. Afterwards, the children need to wash their hands as they can get rather salty.

For readers who wish to explore the craft of salt dough with their children, I can recommend *The Dough Craft Sourcebook* by Sophie-Jane Tilley and Susan Welby.

Play ideas

These few ideas of play and play/work activities with children are only meant as an example. The sky really is the limit to your imagination once you start to think in terms of helping children do things. There is something of the Blue Peter presenter in all of us.

Making shops rather than shopping

Young children, say between 3 and 5 years old, love to have little shops full of items that they can collect, display, weigh out, put in packets, mix and above all offer their customers. Older children will play more advanced and complex versions of this right up to 11 and beyond. As children nowadays are limited in their experience of old-fashion shopkeepers serving customers by weighing out goods into paper bags, it appears that collecting, categorising and handling are archetypal human activities that underlie much meaningful and necessary human behaviour. I believe that children need very little prompting to set up shop because it is an activity that they want and need.

You can find many ways of incorporating this into everyday life. My daughter's third birthday party was based on the shopping theme – complete with empty honey jars full of pasta shapes, conkers, beans and beads, a wooden sugar shovel, coffee filters for paper bags and a wooden cash register as a birthday present from Granny. (This also shows how other family members and friends can be encouraged to give gifts that stimulate the child's imagination in suitable ways.) Our daughter took to this in such a big way that we eventually had to 'buy' back the family supply of tea bags!

Such an activity costs very little and provides hours of activity and pleasure. You can of course expand the business into clothes shops, with rails and changing rooms, hardware stores with screws and useful bits of wood, or even, if the living room has become plagued with cars, a garage. Shops can also, with only a little imagination, become restaurants, doctors' surgeries, post offices and aeroplanes.

Wrapping presents

I am sure we have all observed the amount of entertainment that children can get from the packaging as opposed to the present. Boxes and similar reusable containers are fascinating, but even more interesting is, of course, the wrapping itself.

Tissue paper, pieces of ribbon, raffia, string and even a few small boxes can be recycled and kept and this does wonders for a child's awareness of reusing paper and not just throwing it into the dustbin. Once a child has wrapped a present herself, she will take more care unwrapping one. Additional skills that can be learnt are tying ribbons and string, cutting out, illustrating and writing on labels and cards. This enhances the gift, goes some way to counteracting the throw-away culture that comes with consumerism and develops their thought and creativity.

Recycling

Save all those old vests and T-shirts that really can't be passed on to other children or Oxfam and get the children to cut them into something resembling a square, to be used for countless mopping up and cleaning operations. It's a wet Saturday afternoon job and encourages a recycling habit.

Shoe boxes can be used for store painting, drawing and craft materials and equipment, reusable wrapping paper, cards, string, marbles, toys, CDs or cassettes and anything else you need to keep in one place. The boxes can be livened up with a covering of wrapping paper, magazine pages, water colour paintings or even home-made paper. Hand-made and individually designed labels will enable you to identify the contents.

Toys can be made out of all sorts of junk, endowing the materials with greater value. Cover a screw-top jar by glueing on coloured paper, tissue paper or tin foil. Cut an oval slot in the lid, being careful to round off any jagged edges. The lids can be rubbed round with a little cooking oil to make sure they open and close smoothly. Then cut out card or plastic discs (e.g. from the bottom of yoghurt cartons). Small children love dropping these discs into the slot, rattling them around and then unscrewing the lid and emptying them out. This may not sound very exciting but it will occupy children for lengthy periods of time in activities that school their fine motor control and their wrist action.

Or what about night-light lanterns made from glass jars covered in tissue paper? Or houses made from empty cereal packets? Or spy-glasses fashioned from the inside of kitchen rolls? Use your imagination to create something out of the junk we produce daily.

Saving useful materials as you go along creates the possibility for creative practical activities.

Easy bubbles

Blowing bubbles is fun, and you don't have to have one of those bubble-blowing rings. Take some disposable paper cups, as many as you have children to entertain, and punch a hole about an inch below the rim with a hole punch. Insert a drinking straw. Take a piece of T-shirt (from the store established above!), wet it and tie it over the top of the cup with string or a rubber band. Add a couple of drops of (preferably ecological) washing detergent onto the cloth. The children can produce cascades of bubbles by blowing into the straw. The detergent can easily be replenished and there is no water to spill or bubble mix to lose.

Marble painting

Put a sheet of paper on the bottom of a shallow pan and then splash a few drops of watercolour paint on the paper. Quickly put four or five marbles on top of the paper, roll the pan around and watch the marbles make beautiful patterns on the paper. Then dry the paper. The finished product can be used for wrapping presents or covering boxes, as described above.

Exercise 13

This is quite a complex task to explain, and you will need to adapt it yourself as seems appropriate. It consists of two parts. The first considers planning activities with a child or a couple of children of different ages. The second looks at planning special events.

First, choose an age group (toddlers, 3-year-olds, 6-year-olds) and plan a series of activities you could do with them over the course of a morning or (for advanced players!) a whole day. Imagine you are a child-minder and have to keep them meaningfully occupied for this period of time.

- Define the number and age of the children.
- Decide on your location (e.g. house with garden, on holiday near the beach – choose a different location and try the exercise again).
- Draw up an overall plan for the time (time in free play with toys, going to the shops, having a meal, making biscuits).
- Draw up a list of things needed for the various activities.

Next draw up a plan for the following situations:

- a birthday party with about 12 other children (varying the ages)
- an outing to the woods/country with a group of young children
- a very wet, cold day in the holidays.

12

Ready for school?

Getting children ready for school in the morning, seeing that they get out of bed, are washed, suitably dressed, breakfasted and equipped with what they need, to be delivered to school in time for them to have a chat with their friends before the bell rings is a major achievement. But almost more important is determining the age at which children are ready to start the formal learning that comes with going to school.

Too soon?

The problem is that, in the UK and the USA at least, formal schooling begins ever earlier, and the old transition from early years learning to infant school is rapidly disappearing. Children tend to go straight into formal learning at an ever earlier age, and such is the panic created by this that parents are queueing up to enrol their children at the earliest age possible.

> There is absolutely no evidence that starting children with formal academic learning earlier gives them any advantage over children who start later.

On the contrary, there is much evidence that the early start can increase the problems. Back in November 1998, a Channel 4 *Dispatches* documentary should have shocked the nation into street protests. It was made by David and Clare Mills, respected documentary makers, who spent several years researching the background to early years education in the UK and several other countries. They called their film *Too Much Too Soon*. This was not a sensationalist title, just a factual description.

The film, however, did not go unnoticed and the UK government began to lean towards the broad alliance of early years organisations who are unified around the idea of providing child-friendly early years education. The *Dispatches* documentary, and the large amount of research that backed it up, established that the UK principle of the *sooner you start you sooner you get there* is actually wrong and that the later start may in fact get you there more quickly. This depends of course, on what you mean by '*there*'. If the desired outcome of education is able, well-adjusted, creative, healthy individuals, starting earlier does not necessarily get you '*there*' faster, or even at all.

In most countries around the world, formal schooling begins at age 6 or 7. That does not mean that just because children are not formally taught reading, writing or numbers until that age, they are doing or learning nothing up until then. They are indeed usually doing all the things that are the necessary preparation for the tricky tasks of becoming literate and numerate, scientific and able to use information and communications technology and all that modern education has to offer. Even a paper prepared at the request of the government's school inspectors, for the National Foundation for Educational Research's Annual Conference in October 1998 reported:

> *What we can say is that a later start appears not to be a disadvantage to children's progress (although it is important not to forget the important contribution made by children's experiences at home and in pre-school). Certainly, there would appear to be no compelling educational rationale for a statutory school age of five or for the practice of admitting four-year-olds to school reception classes.*

When asked why the British government favours starting children on this path at 3 or 4, the reply is that it wishes to ensure that no child is disadvantaged and that all are empowered to succeed in life. These are indeed laudable aims, and the government is rightly haunted by the spectre of failing schools, failing children, social exclusion and the social costs generated by this massive problem. The ever growing number of people who are excluded from the opportunities we all expect because their education has failed them is not only morally wrong, but also socially dangerous and expensive to deal with.

There is no evidence that the path of starting children early leads to the promised land. Indeed, many of us in the early years alliance believe that taking away children's right to be children, which early learning pressure does, will lead to an ever greater drop-out rate, alienation, social dysfunction and sheer human misery. So what are the issues involved here?

There are four key questions that need addressing:

1. What current symptoms advise caution?
2. What do children need to develop before they start formal learning?
3. What are the potential dangers of starting too early?
4. What can we do?

The symptoms

I have mentioned above the government's concern for education and listed the factors behind why it promised to put education at the top of its agenda. The general issue of failure does not, however, take specific issues such as the marked increase in nervousness, anxiety, stress-related disorders, hyperactivity, autism and Asperger's syndrome among children over the past 20 years into account. A whole generation of children is being given drugs such as Ritalin to suppress their hyperactivity, a medication that does not treat the condition but only suppresses it. And no one yet knows the long-term effects of giving children these drugs, which so powerfully affect their behaviour. There has also been a significant increase in learning disorders such as dyslexia, despite a far greater awareness of the problem and the widespread availability of methods of dealing with the problem. Schools themselves have great difficulties dealing with disruptive children.

As well as these behavioural problems, there has been a great increase in allergies and chronic illnesses such as eczema and asthma. Eating disorders (mostly among teenage girls) have multiplied, as has violence (mostly among boys) and the widespread use of drugs of all kinds among children and adolescents. The UK has the highest rate of teenage pregnancy in Europe and one of the highest rates of homeless young people.

Obviously, no one can blame all this on starting school at 4 or 5, but what it reveals is that children are under pressure and increasingly lack the resistance to counter these attacks on their very development. So what can we do to strengthen them, to make them resilient? Solving the problems is one thing but preventing them occurring, or at least reducing their prevalence, is another. Prevention is always better than cure.

What has to develop?

Readiness for school has both a developmental aspect and a chronological aspect. In my view, children who are introduced to formal learning too early, that is around 4 or 5 years of age, are deprived of the opportunity fully to develop the foundation they need for bodily, constitutional, emotional and intellectual health. Being put under pressure to start formal learning can cause stress.

> However kind and friendly the teachers are, early formal learning generates stress in many children because they are not ready for it and so feel like failures if they cannot keep up, which may lead to other behavioural problems. This is especially true of boys, who are late starters by nature.

First, children have to feel at home in their bodies, to develop control over them, to develop and fine-tune their sense apparatus, brain systems and gross and fine motor control, to establish their individualised immunity (through, for example, minor childhood illnesses and an increasing range of nutrition). This process of healthy bodily development takes up to 5 or 6 years. If the child

211

lacks the opportunity for creative play or is simply deprived of enough healthy movement and practical activities (because she spends too long in front of the TV because she rarely walks any-where, because she has nowhere safe to play), this will take much longer.

If the energy that the child needs to develop, control and master her physical processes, growth and life rhythms is deflected into abstract and intellectual learning, something has to give. Reading, writing and mathematics are abstractions for the young child and, being highly complex activities, take up far more energy than we might suppose. Stress, of course, causes the greatest consumption of energy. A child who is bored, lacking in initiative, lacking in imagina-tion and lacking colour in her cheeks is lacking in energy. Inner energy is what drives children, but where does this energy come from? It comes from healthy food, a healthy lifestyle, enough deep sleep and enough soul nourishment that can be digested, such as play and stories. Abstract concepts lie like indigestible stones in the memory.

Real vitality comes from enthusiasm and the sense of being at one with yourself and the world. The sense of being at *odds* with your own body, with your social situation or at school depresses that vitality. A child lacking in vitality becomes pale, sickly and prone to infection. Obviously happy children get colds and runny noses too, but they get over them more quickly and are stronger afterwards. Body and soul really are one in the young child, so we shouldn't be surprised if stressed children are more prone to illness and insecurity.

Second, children have to acquire and master their mother tongue and be able to communicate more or less fluently before they add the skills of reading and writing. A child who cannot form the sounds of her mother tongue clearly because of a lack of muscle tone and who is not yet speaking fluently will struggle to recognise the link between sound, letter combinations and words, let alone spelling, and will find learning to read and write demoralising. Many of today's children have, for varied and increasingly common reasons, not acquired full spoken language skills by the age of 7 or 8, let alone 4 or 5! Literacy has to be carefully built on a rich and sound basis of oral culture, this oral culture and the imaginative consciousness that goes with it taking longer than four years to develop.

Cognitive development too needs its developmental time. The ability to form abstract images (needed to understand written language and mathematical symbols) begins only around the age of 6 or 7, and in some children even later. The child's ability to recall things at will and to be able to form mental images of items not present begins at 6 or 7 at the earliest. Children should have lots of direct hands-on experience before they start with abstractions, especially if we want them to have a living connection to the natural world.

As I describe below, there are many kinds of ability that develop side by side in children. If we place too much emphasis on one or two at too early an age, the others may remain undeveloped. Musical skills, motor co-ordination (which lies behind many practical and sporting skills), emotional and social skills may all suffer if we promote academic skills too early and too intensively.

Third, children have to be socially comfortable before they can happily cope with the social demands of large institutions, and even small schools are large for young children. In their natural development, children only begin to be able to play *with*, as opposed to *alongside*, other children between the ages of 3 and 4. The ability to interact socially involves a rhythm of giving and taking, sharing, accepting and allowing other children to be themselves. Children can't do this until they feel confident in themselves, until they have developed their first real sense of self.

The best environment for this skill to develop is one that provides a safe space and an opportunity for free play, children choosing to be together and learning to negotiate the forms they need. They don't want to be overorganised into groups and hurried along. Around the age of 5 or 6, children who have acquired social skills in such an environment can learn to help others less socially competent than themselves, such as younger children. They can do this by playing with them, helping them get dressed or looking after them when they get hurt. The devotion that 6-year-olds can show to other children is astonishing. These social skills will serve individuals (not to mention the people they come into contact with) well for life.

Children need time to get to attain these vital social skills through doing rather than being simply asked or *told* to behave in a certain way. They do it best by imitation, which has far more lasting effects.

What are the dangers of starting too early?

Many children appear to cope with starting early, but they may in fact be left with specific deficits in their development. The long-term effects are impossible to prove, but intuition suggests that they might lie in a certain one-sidedness and lack of emotional competence. They may also result in a premature loss of vitality. What children establish in their first 6 or 7 years is an inner constitution that is part physical, part constitutional, part attitude, part ability to retain the best qualities of childhood in transformed ways.

If this inner source of renewable energy, life force or vitality is healthily established in those first years, an individual can draw on this fount of inner renewal for another 70 or more years. If the powerhouse is constructed with flaws or simply not allowed to develop fully, the energy source will not last as long.

In the short term

In the short term, the consequences of starting children too early at school may be:

- a loss of enthusiasm for school and learning
- an increase in worry and anxiety
- repeated naughty behaviour (often a sign that a child is trying to hide some insecurity)
- mysterious tummy aches
- an inability to sleep

- clingy behaviour
- overtiredness and depression.

It is easy to see how some of these symptoms can themselves become problematic, leading to a downward spiral of ill-health, trouble at school, bullying and other worrying social behaviour, which even if it were to affect only 20 per cent of children, would still account for a very high number of unhappy children.

Some children, for many reasons, have learning difficulties *however* and *whenever* they are taught. These children will greatly benefit from a later start because they need all the help and strength they can get. Since up to 70 per cent of children with difficulties are boys, it is obviously boys who benefit most from a later start (see Chapter 13).

Pressure points

Even what we might consider very slight pressure can make children clam up. I know of a case in which an off-hand remark by a (perhaps himself stressed-out) father to a boy along the lines of '*Haven't you learned that* [*one of the letters of his name*] *yet?*' had the consequence that the boy became a school-refuser at the age of 7. That small remark was, however, probably the tip of the iceberg of unspoken parental expectations.

Another example was noted by chance during a study of foreign language teaching, when transcripts were made of tape-recordings of the lessons. It was noticed that a child who could not pronounce '*th*' properly was corrected by the teacher. The researchers monitoring the language development of the children noticed that this boy avoided saying any word with '*th*' in it for a long time afterwards. The remarkable aspect was the skill the pupil showed in managing to avoid the sound '*th*'.

> Learners, of any age, have to learn for themselves.

The best we can do is provide the right context, the right experiences, the right support and the right responses; the actual learning is done by the individual. Mother nature has provided human beings with an innate learning method, which ideally suits the purposes to which it has evolved. We can see this best in the way in which children learn to speak and use language. We don't teach our children to speak their mother tongue, though we offer (also instinctively) useful support (as I have described in Chapter 10). How children go about it follows what we might call a natural pattern, which varies in timing from individual to individual. Any method of learning that we apply to them at school or home needs to work with the nature of the child, with their natural way of learning.

> When we apply pressure at the wrong time or in the wrong way, we inhibit the natural learning process.

It is very helpful to understand at least the basics of how children learn in order to support, and especially avoid hindering, the process.

Life does not proceed in straight lines

What is this natural learning process, and where can I get hold of it? Unfortunately this is not simple to explain. If it were, every school in the world would have cottoned on by now.

> The main thing that gets in the way of our understanding is that it has taken a very long time for us to get to grips with what *holistic* really means.

Holistic learning means that everything happens in a totally integrated way. Children learn in a holistic way, which also means that they progress – if allowed to – in a way that enables them to adopt everything they know and can do to the next challenges they meet. If we try to channel this learning down pathways we think make sense and are logical, rational or linear, children resist. Learning proceeds via its own holistic rhythms that integrate experiences as they go along. If we apply pressure, we can block the natural unfolding of ability.

What does this mean in practice? To take the examples quoted above, the children described became inhibited when they felt that their parents or teachers were not respecting the natural learning process. In both cases, they were in a particular phase of learning sometimes known as the receptive phase, which occurs in the following learning sequence.

The stages of learning

Stage 1

The child has a new experience; in the case of the first boy described above, this was a letter of the alphabet. The child has to realise that the symbol represents a sound but also has a name that is different from the sound. We write T, we say '*tuh*', we call it '*tee*'. Confusing isn't it?

Stage 2

The child has to fit this new complex of experiences – symbol, name and sound – to what she already knows about language. The child *consciously* knows very little about language but has *unconsciously* learned a great deal. She already knows how to hear it, understand it and produce it, but practically none of this helps immediately to prepare the child to link all this to a printed letter. This is further complicated by the fact that the letter looks different depending on how the teacher writes it, the child herself writes it, Dad writes it, the sign-writer writes it. What constitutes '*T-ness*' in all these cases?

Stage 3

The child has to experiment with this new concept to see how it can be applied in different circumstances, and also how it can be varied. The child knows that here is something she can't yet do, at least not with great confidence that it will work out, so she is cautious. She waits until she thinks she's got it right before using this new thing called the letter T in front of everybody. This is the receptive phase. Outwardly, the child appears not to be doing anything: doesn't answer when asked, doesn't write the letter of her own volition. Although the child appears not to know, she does, but she's not yet certain.

So when a parent, whom she loves and respects, says, '*Can't you do that yet?*' the child is offended or made to feel inadequate. She is doing her best. She is in fact very busy. Only father doesn't know this, and his implied criticism undermines the child's confidence and results in her being held back in his development by refusing to continue learning to read at all, or at least refusing to be seen to be learning to read.

In the meantime, the child becomes labelled a slow learner, becomes the focus of worry, more pressure and expensive, time-consuming remedial lessons, experiences the social stigma of being considered a failure (through refusing to read in the tests and thus scoring a very low mark) and so on. The boy in our example above was, in the end, discovered reading from the back of a cereal packet to his little sister with a competence equal to that of his expected reading age. Shortly afterwards, he declared himself ready to admit that he could read.

Stage 4

The child now integrates this new knowledge into everything else she knows and therefore in a sense no longer needs to be conscious of it. We only really need consciousness when there is a problem: if there is no problem with something we have to do, we don't have to think about it, thank goodness. So the knowledge becomes unconscious but active, allowing the mind to focus on the next thing that has to be learned. This stage of forgetting usually needs to happen frequently. That means things have to be activated, exercised then allowed to sleep, then picked up again until real ability gets established.

Stage 5

The child has become competent at this activity and has now moved on to the next stage of learning, which repeats the stages above.

In reality, the process is far more complex and individual than this, but my summary gives a useful overview. Learning proceeds from an initial encounter, via the adoption of the new skill or activity, into a chaotic period, in which there is much trial and error. During this phase, the child has to adopt the new knowledge to all she already knows, and the new knowledge has to be tried out and experimented with. The mistakes that arise are crucially important in the adopting/adapting phase.

What can we do to help?

If you have the option, send your child to a good early years setting, nursery or kindergarten that provides her with structure, form, security and creative play. Children should be encouraged to learn a wide range of practical skills, including painting, modelling, handicrafts, baking, gardening, singing, story-telling and dancing. They should have plenty of time outdoors in all weathers through-out the seasons. They should experience a strongly rhythmical day, week and year, with seasonal songs and activities as well as community celebrations. There should be oral story-telling and a culture of talking and listening. The early years setting should have a strong emphasis on cultivating the social skills of being together, listening when necessary and caring for each other.

> The nursery setting should be cared for, ordered and full of natural materials, providing a warm, friendly, child-sized environment. Above all, there should be a policy of encouraging imaginative, creative play.

Children should if possible remain in such a setting until they are ready for school (see below), ideally at the age of 6. I realise this is not always possible since most schools in the UK start with 5-year-olds and admit 4-year-olds into the transition class. Schools such as Steiner Waldorf schools that start primary school at 6 years are unfortunately few and far between.

So what can parents do if they want to protect their children from the potential pressures of early schooling yet have little real choice of local schools? Short of lobbying your local MP or Local Education Authority to protest, the following may help in easing your child's path:

- Provide the best possible child-friendly environment at home (in the ways I have suggested throughout the book).
- Help your children gain good oral language skills through collaborative story-telling and regular stories, lots of conversations and singing, so that their language skills become as good as they can be.
- Avoid the TV, stereo and computer as much as possible until children get well into school age.
- Once they have started at school, ensure that children have plenty of rest during schools terms (early to bed with a good story).
- Ensure that there is plenty of time for creative play (as this can help children to work through problems that may be brought home).
- Have regular talks about school. Don't be too nosy, but ask what they enjoyed, whom they talked too and so on. Make it light and stress the positive. Give positive feedback on the teachers and help the children to feel good about them.
- Make early contact with your child's teachers and tell them you are concerned about early pressure and emphasise that you will be happier if your child feels good about school rather than progress quickly. Ask how you can help at home, but don't get into home coaching until children are at least 10 or 11: there are too many examples of natural later starters to start panicking if little Jim can't read at the age of 8. Work with your children's teachers in the most supportive way you can. Schools are under such pressure to identify so-called failing teachers, that the last thing teachers (and therefore your children) need is parents putting pressure on them.

Exercise 14

Reflect on what you want in the way of education for your children. Consider your answers to the following questions:

- What do you think are the most important values and qualities in school education (e.g. that the children be respected)?
- What do you want your children to have gained from their education? Prioritise your ideas.
- What do you want from early years education (i.e. up until they go to school)?
- What age do you think they should start formal education?
- What do you think are the most important things about primary education (up to the age of 11)?
- What do you think children should get out of secondary education?

Then reflect on your own education by answering the following questions:

- What do you think you got out of your own education?
- Do you think your own education prepared you for the life you have so far had?
- What were the best aspects of your education?
- What were the worst parts?

13

Boys and other problems

This section looks at some of the problems children may encounter. It deals with the special aspects of boys, girls and some other difficulties that have to do with learning at school.

Boys will be boys

It used to be politically incorrect to say that boys had special needs. The special needs of girls have been ignored for so long that the backlash of feminism was a necessary corrective, but some people feel the pendulum has swung too far the other way. Whatever one's personal view, there is no denying that boys (and men) have problems that are often ignored yet need to be addressed. Before describing the problems and their possible solutions, it is worth briefly summarising the symptoms we all have to deal with.

> There is no doubt that men cause wars, commit most crimes (or at least make up 80% of the prison population), drive recklessly and drunkenly more often than women and are more violent, especially towards women they know. Most violence (excluding war) is domestic, and most of that

is carried out by men on women. Boys also have the most problems at school, problems that often lead to bad behaviour or dropping out.

As a number of authors have recently pointed out, this depressing statistic hides a far wider problem. Many of the wider population of troubled boys and men don't behave in a violent way, become criminals or start wars, but they do lose their way, become depressed and fail to cope with the demands of modern life.

The wrong kinds of hero

We live with a number of paradoxical images of men in our society. We constantly see the Hollywood hero, the man of action and sometimes of charm. We see the sporting hero, who may or may not be a good guy. Among these, we have the really bad guys (violent, aggressive, macho, often sexist). Then there are the crazy guys (often rock stars and daredevils, glamorous but doomed) and the loners (antisocial figures who in real life may be dysfunctional and incapable of real relationships). Although the entertainment media has generally cleaned up its act, it is still not showing many suitable role models for boys to emulate.

How often do we see the hero as faithful, supportive family father, a caring, emotionally strong man in touch with his feminine side who happily works for his female boss and knows both how to cook and how to tell bed-time stories?

Well maybe that would be asking too much, but some of those qualities wouldn't go amiss to provide boys with positive role models. If we want boys to grow up caring and responsible, emotionally and socially capable *as well as* strong and manly, they need caring for as children. So what is it with boys?

How boys grow up

In general, baby boys grow faster and become stronger and more active than baby girls, but their fine motor co-ordination and language development actually lags behind. In fact, boys' brains develop more slowly altogether. It is unclear whether it is a basic physical difference that is genetically predetermined, the result of different experiences in their upbringing or an effect of both.

There is considerable evidence that the brains of boys and girls mature in subtly different ways, largely because of the higher levels of the hormones testosterone and oestrogen respectively in the bloodstreams of boys and girls. Girls have a high proportion of oestrogen, which stimulates the growth of nerve cells in the brain. The hemispheres of the brain grow at different rates in all babies, but in boys the left side grows even more slowly, which leads to an imbalance in the connections between the left and right sides of the brain.

Lopsided brains

The human brain has a distinctive lateralisation, and while the brain functions as an integrated whole, the different hemispheres are related to distinct abilities. In relation to literacy skills and early development, complex skills such as those involved in reading and writing require good communication pathways between the linguistic skills of the left hemisphere and the spatial and movement skills of the right. The ability to co-ordinate the perception of letters and words effectively, as well as the motor control to write them, needs to be well connected to the perception of the flow of verbal language. Since girls' brains grow with fewer lateral differences than boys', the connections between the hemispheres are more comprehensive and the integration of the different cognitive skills therefore greater.

Boys, with their somewhat lopsided hemisphere development, have fewer direct connections between the two halves of the brain. Thus, the right side tends to have a greater wealth of internal connections, which may later express itself in a greater capacity for mathematical and spatial-geometrical thinking. The overall integration may, however, be weaker.

In short, boys frequently have difficulties with learning to read and write, communicating their feelings and expressing themselves.

In children of both sexes the lateralisation of the brain takes its final form only around the fourth year of life. That means that if one half of the brain is damaged before 4 years of age, the other half can take over the function. After the fourth year, this is much more difficult. Women's brains, being better integrated, have a better chance of compensating for damage, as shown by the fact that women recover from strokes better than men.

All this argues for giving boys not only more time before teaching them to read and write, certainly beyond the age of six, but also a different method of teaching.

It's the way we treat them too

Whatever genetic factors there are, boys definitely become *more* different because of the way they are treated by adults. Many people mistakenly assume that boys are more robust emotionally as well as physically and tend to treat them with less affection. They receive fewer cuddles. Fathers, especially, tend to treat them as if they were older than they actually are and tend to wind them up more through rough play. Many fathers can't wait to engage their sons in manly pursuits such as wrestling, throwing and kicking balls (often half the size of the child himself), all this accompanied by boisterous and raucous calling, as on the training field.

As Steve Biddulph wryly points out, if fathers had as little sleep as mothers, they might seek to calm boys down more than overexcite them before departing for the day to the office, leaving mum to deal with the wreckage.

Boys may appear to be less sensitive, but they can be more upset by changes of circumstance such as being separated from one or another parent. They can become very anxious and clingy. Steve

Biddulph, the child psychologist and author of *Raising Boys*, advises against sending boys to day care or nursery before the age of 3 for this very reason. If their parents have to leave them to go to work, boys do much better if left with a relative or regular carer.

Sadly, boys also tend to get treated more harshly by stressed-out parents. They get smacked more frequently than girls for misbehaving. By systematically treating boys in this way, parents are unwittingly reinforcing behaviour patterns than manifest later in adolescence as antisocial behaviour, aggression and overdefensive attitudes. Boys need to be treated with the same gentleness and nurturing care as girls.

> Furthermore, boys need to experience when they are young that men can be gentle and caring as well as strong and heroic, that men not only go out to work but can also cook, do the housework and gardening, read books, help children get dressed, do the shopping and offer comfort to those in need.

To be honest, don't we actually expect men to be less tactful, less thoughtful of other people's feelings, less nurturing? Do they lack these graces because they simply can't develop them or because everyone tolerates less tactful men or men who forget other people's birthdays?

Late starters

As I stated above, one highly significant difference between boys and girls is that, because of the slower rate of brain and linguistic development, boys are at a disadvantage if they are introduced to formal learning before the age of 6 or 7. In fact, even at that age, they are still at a disadvantage and it is crucial for parents and teachers to be aware of this fact. Considerable misery can be created for all concerned if boys are treated not as *different* but as in some way *deficient*. Boys who take longer to grasp the rudiments of literacy and formal numeracy can be psychologically scarred for life if they lose their self-respect and think of themselves as failures at the age of just 6, 7 or 8.

In addition, let us remember that, as beings with a 4 million year path of evolution behind us, the activities of reading and writing, sitting still in desks and so on, are very recent and very unnatural ones. The fact that many girls can adapt to these challenges more easily than boys because of how their brains develop is not necessarily an argument that girls themselves should be introduced to literacy earlier.

> Learning difficulties need to be understood, respected and taken into account.

There are thus powerful arguments (and no one has marshalled them better than Steve Biddulph) for boys not starting formal schooling until the age of 6 or 7, and even then going through school a year older than girls in their class. That means they would spend an extra year in kindergarten, where they would have time to develop the social skills they need and the fine motor co-ordination. This will be a difficult piece of advice for many parents and teachers because of the fear of being left behind in our highly competitive society.

But the flipside is also worrying. Boys who have difficulties feel bad about their failure. They notice that they are less competent and seek to compensate by refusing to take part, hoping to cover up their inadequacy. Their motor nerves are still growing, and so they are continuously stimulated to move; in a classroom situation, this looks like disruptive behaviour. Stressed teachers trying to cope under pressure of attainment from parents and external expectations have no choice but to transfer the pressure to the child, thus escalating the downward spiral that leads to serious problems of demotivation and alienation. There is much one can do to ameliorate the situation and give boys the support they need, giving them more time to develop being the key. As Diona Hinds put in the *Independent* on 14 September 2000:

> *some boys fall behind at school at an early age, not through lack of ability but because the government's drive for high test scores at seven means children get pushed into formalised reading and writing at age*

four or five – before they are ready. Those that struggle in these early stages, and they tend to be more boys than girls, quickly become demoralised and, by seven many have decided that school is not for them.

If, however, the start of formal reading and writing was delayed, say until six, these children . . . like their counterparts in other European countries, would get off to a better start and we would not see such a worrying gender gap in achievement at seven and eleven.

Don't separate, appreciate

I doubt, however, that separating girls and boys is really the answer. The social benefits of learning together, even with their differences, is valuable enough in itself to justify the challenges that it brings. Co-ed may at times be harder, and the different genders may need a different approach from time to time, but the social interaction between the able and differently able, between genders and social groups, is vitally essential to the development of real social competence. Single-sex schools prevent us growing up in sufficient proximity that we can learn about the other gender in guided situations in which each can learn to appreciate the other and live with each other in later life.

> Throughout their whole schooling, boys and girls take the lead at different times and in different ways, and both are essential.

Learning differences

There are many kinds of learning differences other than those of gender. Integrating rather than separating children with learning differences is certainly harder for schools to cope with and requires great flexibility on the part of the teachers.

> In the end, however, I believe that the benefits of mixed-ability learning groups in terms of social perception, mutual encounters and problem-solving, as well as the cultivation of empathy through direct experience and the aspect of learning through the (different) eyes of the other, outweigh the disadvantages.

Whole-class teaching with undifferentiated groups of children has many social advantages, not least in providing children with a central role model of authority in the form of a teacher with overall and long-term responsibility for them. A class of children who have learned to appreciate the gifts of others in a direct and intuitive way will also not need to be taught tolerance and respect at a later, more conscious age. Tolerance is not learned theoretically but through guided experience.

What helps everyone learn

What greatly helps is having a method of teaching literacy skills that benefits all children, boys and girls, dyslexics and those with or without linguistic or motor disabilities. Such a method would stress the following pre-school preparation:

- developing oral and verbal skills and listening through conversation, dialogue, story-telling, developing communication skills and in short exposing children regularly to good-quality spoken language
- cultivating balance and fine motor skills through many practical activities, including domestic activities such as gardening, craft skills and finger games
- creative play with other children so that real social interaction can take place, especially from the age of 5 onwards
- helping children, especially boys, deal with problems such as anger and frustration, not least by showing a good example; avoid punishment that frightens children or makes them feel resentful or misunderstood
- sharing many meaningful experiences such as birthdays and seasonal festivals, with others.

Once children have started to read and write the following guide-lines can help dyslexics and children with other learning differences access books and reading.

- choose exciting stories with lots of action
- choose books with a simple and direct style
- find out which authors your child likes and then encourage her to read several of their books as the vocabulary and style may be familiar; librarians or teachers can often advise on this
- read to your child and get her used to literary convention: choose books you *both* enjoy because your enthusiasm can be catching
- when choosing a book, decide in advance whether the child is to read it independently or with help from you, or whether you will be reading it aloud, varying the level of difficulty accordingly
- look for clear, decent-sized print, an uncluttered page and attractive illustrations.

Girl trouble

As we all know, girls are not always angels, especially not to each other. Girl–girl relationships can be far more trouble to those concerned than anything boys get up to, and this is one of the main causes for girls becoming unhappy, losing interest in school, becoming disenchanted with their lives and losing motivation.

Once girls start to become conscious of their identity in relation to people outside their family and immediate familiar social circle, which occurs from about 7 years of age onwards, they become very susceptible to the opinions of others, especially girls of the same age. Girls can have special girl friends (or indeed friends who are boys, depending more on parental attitudes than actual gender choice) from the age of 3 or 4, but at this age their level of self-consciousness is less focused. From about 7 onwards, however, a child's friendships can be very important in defining her social and personal sense of self.

From here on, children's relationships begin to give them feed-back on what kind of person they are perceived as being – easy-going, generous, a bit possessive, aggressive, dreamy or very alert, even pretty or not pretty, fat or 'normal'. At this tender age, such experiences are highly formative. Later on, relationships become more habitual: '*With my friend Susy I am like this and we play with dolls*', '*With Grandma I am busy and helping.*' Although this also applies to relationships with boys and men, it can become very intense with girls because both sides are uncertain and searching for a stable identity.

> I suspect that girls and women establish their identities largely through relationships, boys through activities.

Thus, for girls, losing a friend or being rejected can be very painful and a major source of anxiety and insecurity. And when children (or indeed adults!) become insecure, they bite back, projecting this onto other children and hurt them. This is closely related to the symptoms of bullying, victims often bullying others as a reaction.

Among girls between 7 and 12 years of age, relationships can often contain a strong element of role-playing. Their games, which mimic complex real-life dramas, can involve elaborate protocol governing who does what, how and when. If there is any disagreement, things can turn very nasty. It usually takes more than three to cause real grief, since the jealousy aspect of taking sides is the most hurtful part of it. When two fall out, both are uncertain who is right (or wrong), but if it is two against one, there is greater support for the majority. And the situation is often accompanied by those painful little darts – '*Oh, she's stupid anyway*' (even though we happily played round at her house for weeks up until now) or '*She's got goofy teeth*' (says the one with the huge brace!). Once girls approach puberty, the added dimension of sexual awareness is added to the already potent brew.

The right gear

Children are generally under great pressure to conform to group norms, and this has a particular intensity with girls. The social dynamic that naturally arises between groups of girls is one thing, another factor being the added pressure of commercial advertising, which plays on their natural tendency towards group identification.

This happens especially at the so-called '*tweens*' age, between 10 and 13. Being in the in-crowd demands wearing the right clothes, buying the right brands, reading the right magazines and listening to the right music.

> Girls can get obsessive about having the 'in' gear, usually the more expensive brands. To resist this pressure requires great strength of character and independence of mind, rare at such an age.

With regard to peer pressure to dress in a certain way, this is obviously not a simple issue but requires the long-term establishment of a value system, which is based on the following principles.

First, we need to reinforce the child's sense that she can choose how she wishes to present herself and that this is a right that needs to be respected in others too. We establish this initially through imitation. If the child experiences her parents making conscious choices about the appropriateness of dress for the circumstances or about aesthetic choices, they will be able to learn how to make these judgements themselves: '*Oh, I think that colour of jumper really suits Daddy, don't you?*' '*It's really cold and windy today; I'm going to wrap up warmly and make sure I don't get an earache, aren't you?*', '*It's a very special occasion today at school/church/home, so I'm going to put on my smartest clothes.*' The questions may be rhetorical, but the child is made to feel involved by a format of dialogue, choice and agreement.

The criteria for dress codes are primarily practical and secondly aesthetic. Children simply need to learn at a very early age what kind of clothing or footwear is necessary and appropriate for different circumstances – wellies for outside, slippers for the house. It is like using the right tools for the job. The aethetic side is based as much as possible on objective judgement based on the colour, material, shape or style itself. There are no absolutes here, but there is experience. Children can learn to develop a feeling for what they like and what suits them. This involves much trial and error, from the days of dressing up in different hats, footwear and robes while playing.

Clothing care is important for developing a consciousness for style and aesthetics, which is why dress designers first have to learn about the manufacture, handling, qualities and care of all the various materials they use. Children need to understand how to look after clothes, where they go when they are dirty, how they get washed and ironed, and how they are repaired. Shoes need looking after. There are winter clothes and summer clothes, smart clothes for best, school clothes, clothes to play in, sleep in, go swimming in, play football in. Children who never learn this and merely dump their clothes in a heap, expecting an endless supply of clean or new ones, will never really be able to make an informed judgement.

Caring for possessions generally is an important value to establish. This includes the idea of care and maintenance, tidying up, storage, re-use and re-cycling.

A sense of economic reality is important to establish quite early on. Explaining how the family budget has to be spent on a wide range of essentials can be done in an age-appropriate way. Children need to know in a matter of fact way (i.e. not with a deep regret, frustration or sense of injustice) what we can or cannot afford. That's it folks, we have to make a choice so this month we will not be buying new coats/shoes/watches etc. It won't stop them complaining, but as objective fact, it is easier to accept in the end.

Being prudent is not only necessary on a limited budget, but also a value in itself. Even if you have a lot of money, you do not have to be a miser or puritan to see that waste is unhealthy both morally and for the planet. Like the old saying, *to know the price of everything and the value of nothing*, one can see that understanding value has many dimensions, many of which are material and practical. Everyone wants quality these days but what we are offered is *value for money*, usually meaning cheap and nasty. The artificial prices put on many products today bear no relation to their economic value anyway. The same pair of jeans can cost £40 or £400 depending on the label only because the clothing industry has persuaded us that other values such as image, identity and emotional state (wear this label and feel happy, or confident, or attractive) are more important.

As Johann Arnold puts it in his powerful book *Endangered*, remember that having £200 trainers doesn't buy lasting happiness. *Never use the power of your credit card to buy the love of your child.* First, it does not work and second, it sends all the wrong messages with regard to values. That does not mean you shouldn't treat your child to nice things. Do so within what you can afford and in relation to what they really need, while teaching them to value what they have and get the best use out of it. Give them the love they need first; *then* buy them treats.

If children can learn early on to understand the value of consumer products, they will be in a better position to deal with the commercial pressures they are exposed to later in life. After this, they can learn to develop a sense of style based on their evolving self-awareness and sense of personality.

Respect their choice, when they make it, if it really is their choice. Learn to appreciate what is an experiment and give feedback at the right moment and in the right way: *'Well, that is an interesting combination, very original'* or *'That will certainly make an impact at the party; do you think you'll be able to bend over?'* is more helpful than *'My God, what do you look like?!'*

General tips for dealing with girl trouble

For parents:

- Be aware of the problem and watch your daughter's relationships, whom she plays with and whom she likes to spend time with.
- Offer help but wait for her to react. If you are too heavy-handed, she will hide her feelings or avoid the issue. Let her feel able to come to you for help and advice, a quiet chat, perhaps just a few words of encouragement and a cuddle.
- Don't try too hard to analyse what your daughter tells you and don't offer judgements that may reinforce her prejudices. It is more important to listen sympathetically.
- Look out for symptoms such as a sudden lack of interest in going to school, a bad mood on coming home from school or from visits to friends, tears at bed-time and not wanting to go out.
- Mothers are more effective than fathers at dealing with these problems.
- Mothers should counsel their daughters to make friends again, telling them that these things happen, are normal and can often be easily patched up if you try. Girls and boys need to be regularly

counselled that relationships have their ups and downs, crises and resolutions, and that people and friendships grow through such cycles.

- Encourage girls to establish a network of friends rather than get fixed in single relationships. Having different groups of friends, perhaps in different contexts (school, hobbies, neighbours, etc.), is a good way of avoiding the intensity, even dependency, of one-to-one relationships.
- Encourage girls to include boys in their circle of friends, which is not the same as having boyfriends, who bring a whole new range of problems (and pleasures) with them. Having boys as friends can be a very healthy balance for girl–girl relationships.
- For schools and situations in which larger groups of children gather, adult supervision is important to observe bullying, children being excluded and children who are upset or distraught. Coming to their help in time, with tact, sensitivity, fairness and lots of common sense, can often be crucial.

Advice to girls who are having problems with their friends

A leaflet available from *Childline* advises that if you fall out with your best friend:

- Don't keep it to yourself, tell your mother or someone you really trust.
- If someone in a group is being nasty to you or ignoring you, speak to another member of your group and try to find out why your friend is unhappy or upset by you.
- Try not to respond to hurtful comments by retaliating, try joking about it or just go away.
- If more than one person in your group of friends are being unpleasant towards you, see if you can make friends with another group of children at your school or neighbourhood.
- Remember that if people are going to be unfriendly, they are probably not the people you should be with. Find other friends.
- Take up other activities, do something you always wanted to do. There are lots of other things to do than hanging around with

people who only go around being horrid to others.
- Think what you would do to help someone who was being left out.

Bullying and victimisation

Bullying is the kind of problem that gives us nightmares. It brings up the worst kind of suppressed memories from our own childhood and without doubt can scar a child for life. Fortunately, bullying (the Germans have a very appropriate term for it – '*mobbing*') is now a widely acknowledged problem in schools, and most teachers are sent on training programmes to learn to recognise and deal with it.

Bullying comes in many forms, not all of which conform to the image of a small child being cornered in some dank corner of a Victorian schoolyard by big boys with crew cuts. Sheer physical threat is only a part of the picture, one that can be dealt with most quickly because it is most visible. Bullying is often hidden, or *covert*, protected by the kind of silence of conspiracy that can strengthen antisocial groups in their identity.

What is bullying?

There are many approaches to bullying, all of which have something to offer. In my school, we define bullying as follows:

Bullying is persistent, intentionally hurtful behaviour towards someone who is younger, weaker, smaller or less powerful in some other way. It is always painful and distressing to the victim. Bullying is always relative to individual sensitivities: what one person can happily ignore, another finds hurtful. If it hurts, it is bullying.

This kind of behaviour includes:

- physical bullying: pushing, kicking, hitting, pinching and other forms of violence and interfering with someone else's property or possessions, such as taking someone's school bag and throwing it in a puddle

- verbal bullying: including name-calling, persistent teasing, taunting and threatening
- emotional bullying: excluding individuals from the social group or activities, tormenting, ridiculing, humiliating, intimidating and inciting others to bully
- racist bullying: racial taunts, graffiti or gestures
- sexual bullying: unwanted physical contact, abusive comments and stalking.

This list obviously includes behaviour sadly also common to adults. Indeed, children's propensity to imitate adult role models is certainly a factor in bullying. It can start when children are very young, although it obviously has a very different character when 4-year-olds snatch toys from each other. Little children need strong role models of kind, considerate behaviour. They need to observe adults and older children showing consideration and respect for others. They need regular examples in story form of people being mindful of each other's feelings, and images showing that it is bad to be destructive.

The reasons why children (or indeed adults) become bullies are complex and individual, but it is fair to say that anyone who has a need to bully is themselves insecure, lacking in social skills and inadequate in some way. Bullies have often been victimised themselves, although that is never an excuse.

The key to dealing with bullying is empathy, the ability to feel what someone else is feeling. Young children need to be shown what this means. They need to observe adults feeling what others, be they children or adults, are feeling, but without sentimentality. That means pain and emotional suffering need to be recognised as objective facts and met with an attitude of compassion. This leads to the no-blame approach to bullying.

The no-blame approach

This does not mean that no one is culpable; children should be held accountable in age-appropriate ways for their behaviour. However, punishment without understanding for the victim or the wider consequences can lead to a reinforcement of the reasons why children become bullies in the first place.

Experience has shown that children punished in conventional ways for bullying may gain status in the eyes of their friends, go out and punish the victim at the first opportunity, become even more socially alienated than they already were and in some cases feel themselves to be the victim of a higher power, which reinforces their tendency to bully. Bullies often crave attention. Even the negative attention of being in trouble and having adults focusing on them is in a curious way welcome to them. By making an example of bullies, we can succeed in making them martyrs in the eyes of their friends, which then leads to a spiral of violence. The group then defend the bully as 'one of us'.

In addition, punishing or exposing the bully can lead to further risk for the original victim.

The aim of the no-blame approach is to defuse rather than inflame the situation, to deflect rather than polarise and above all to make everyone involved as conscious as possible of what has happened.

Seek help

Parents can rarely deal with bullying on their own. As soon as you her about it, make contact with the relevant professionals, at school, in the playground or wherever. Tell them that you want the problem addressing but not necessarily through punishment of the bullies. As parents, our role is to offer support and advice, and to help to liaise with professionals such as police, social workers and teachers.

Help the victim of bullying by:

- looking out for the signs of bullying (general unhappiness, loneliness, wanting to be alone, refusing to go out or go to school, anxiety, bed-wetting or signs of physical injury)
- encouraging them to speak about it to you or another adult of their choice. This means having a family culture in which active listening can be practised, listening with empathy but without getting immediately aggressive ('He did what to you? Just let him wait till I get hold of him . . .')
- taking the matter seriously rather than saying 'Oh, never mind dear; I'm sure she didn't mean it'
- not jumping to hasty conclusions about fault but allowing your child to tell you the full details

- reassuring her that it was not her fault: many children feel guilty if they are bullied
- telling them that it will be dealt with and that no one need get into trouble
- helping them to talk about and learn social skills and how to react if they are bullied in future. Teachers can help here.

The bully

The key elements of our approach are sharing responsibility, addressing the problems factually and involving all parties in finding constructive solutions. Parents can help considerably if their children are either victims or bullies, and the children involved have to have the opportunity of owning the problem and suggesting ways of redressing it. They often have remarkable insight and are above all pragmatic. They want to find solutions. The role of parents is to facilitate this while ensuring that limits and boundaries are respected and that the process is seen through. That means reminding the children concerned of what has been said and agreed. Fairness is the key.

The professionals involved will tell the bully that bullying is unacceptable and that violence is no way to deal with conflict. They will try to determine whether the bullies are anxious or upset about something in their lives, which is causing them to bully, working with them to find any possible resolution to those problems. The effects of their behaviour on the victim will be quietly and undramatically described.

The bullies will then be asked to suggest ways in which they can resolve the situation and how they might change their behaviour. They will be set limits, and efforts will be made to teach them strategies for better social skills and how to resist being drawn back into bullying by other children. Finally, the task of the school or institution is to provide opportunities for the bullies to feel more confident and fulfilled in their own lives.

None of this is the task of the parents, even if they wanted to take it on, but it is helpful to know how bullying can be successfully dealt with, if only to share this with your own children so that they can better understand the process of social healing. The victim will need to know that the bully is in need of help too.

Exercise 15

This exercise asks you to think of ways in which you could encourage your children's self-esteem and help them to cope with their difficulties.

First, look at your own experiences. Can you remember how your parents and teachers dealt with you when you were badly behaved or had difficulties?

- Picture a specific situation and write down what people said to you.
- Note how you felt at the time.
- How did you react or respond?
- Did it help you?

Then look at your child's experiences. If you have children of school age, can you recall any situation in which difficulties have arisen?

- How did you first discover these difficulties? Did you notice them and bring them to the attention of the teachers, or did they tell you?
- How did you feel when you found out?
- How did you talk to your child about it?
- What do you think helped or hindered the situation?
- What would you have done, or hoped to have seen done, differently?

Finally, if you have children, consider the future. This may help to set out a kind of manifesto for yourself. Life may turn out differently, but at least you have started with some ideas!

- What do you think you would do specifically to help your son become a well-adjusted individual? What do you think is particularly important?
- What do you think would generally help your children to become well-balanced individuals able to fulfil their potential?

14

Thought for food

'*Ugh! I'm not eating that*' is one of the most demoralising things a parent has to listen to, especially if he or she has slaved over a hot stove for hours: the parent who is committed to offering his or her children a high quality of nutrition has the extra challenge of getting them to eat it! Providing children with healthy, well-balanced food is becoming an increasingly challenging part of our agenda, ironic when you consider that for most of human history just *getting* food was difficult enough.

Now that we have greater access to food than ever before, we have an almost equally great difficulty getting our children to eat what is good for them.

As in so many areas of bringing up children, we find ourselves up against massive commercial (and carefully stimulated peer) pressure, the insecurity of not knowing what actually is right for growing children and the educational challenge of establishing the right attitudes and habits. There are several key issues here:

- What is good for children?
- How do we protect them from the worst?

- How do we get them to eat what is good for them?
- How do we establish healthy lifelong eating habits?

The problems

Let me summarise the main problems related to food and eating. First, children are suffering from an unprecedented level of obesity caused by the combined effects of a sedentary lifestyle and the temptations of unhealthy food. According to the National Diet and Nutrition Survey of Young People aged 4 to 18 years, published by the Department of Health and Food Standards Agency in July 2000, children eat far too few vegetables and far too much salt.

The Food Commission found that 9 out of 10 food products aimed at children were '*nutritionally disastrous*', because of high levels of fats, sugars or additives. Children's diets can be very one-sided, with too much saturated fat and too little roughage and natural minerals and vitamins. Above all, too many foodstuffs have too much sugar in them. Children today tend to choose a very limited diet, crisps, chocolate, white bread and sugar-based soft drinks providing many children with their staple intake. Even Stone Age people had a more varied diet than modern people, including 30–40 different wild seeds and grains, as well as dozens of herbs and roots, and a wide range of seafood and fish, not to mention the fresh organic meat, all of which contained a wide variety of trace minerals and other nutritional elements. And how do we know what is healthy and what is unhealthy? Which authority do we believe?

Modern farming methods and highly processed foods bring nutritional problems. It is not just the risk of BSE that concerns us: the use of hormones and antibiotics in animal feeds, the insecticides and herbicides sprayed on food for human consumption and the level of lead contamination in plants and water are all serious causes for concern.

Eating disorders, of which bulimia and anorexia are the best known, although not strictly to do with food, are related to an adolescent's relationship to eating, to food and health and to the values associated with health and food. Related to eating disorders are of course substance abuse issues, which are aspects of a consumer attitude. A child used to instant gratification through pre-processed high sugar foods has a deep physical and psychological need for instant gratification through the consumption of drugs, starting with nicotine and alcohol and going on to illegal substances.

Caries and dental problems are related not only to the consumption of sugar, but also to generally unhealthy eating habits. In addition, the incidence of bowel and intestinal problems in the adult population is related to the dietary patterns established in childhood. There has also been a dramatic increase in food allergies, some of which can be very serious.

There is a general problem of children's increasing lack of relationship to the natural origin of food, namely to nature and the environment. It may be an urban myth that there are children who don't know that milk comes from cows, but there are certainly children who don't know that yoghurt comes from milk or who don't know that chicken pieces are made of reconstituted 'food matter', which if presented in the form of the raw material, no one in their right mind would eat.

The Co-op food chain recently produced an enlightened report highlighting the powerful effect that TV advertising has on children, who then blackmail their parents into buying the products.

What can be done?

> The most important thing is to establish healthy eating habits at a very early age and sustain them for as long as possible. After that, education can do some damage limitation.

The experts, nutritionists, child psychologists and food professionals all agree that setting and maintaining a good example is the most effective thing parents can do. That means inform yourself first. Change your own eating habits in order to create a healthy food culture at home, provide access to healthy food and try to limit access to unhealthy foods.

Weaning

Weaning is a very important stage of development in which the child emancipates herself from the maternal influence. It is like becoming upright, a kind of *grounding*, in the sense that the child takes on (and *in*) the material world in a stronger way than before. The temptation to prolong breast-feeding after 6 months in many ways holds the child back from individualising her own organism.

Start with simple but healthy food

Start simply is another basic piece of advice. It seems to be the case that what children eat during the first 3 years strongly influences what they prefer later. Once children are weaned from breast milk (or an organic, simply formulated milk substitute), we should allow their palates, sense of taste and texture, as well as their digestions, to adapt slowly to simple, natural foods such as blended, grated or pulped apple, carrot or banana. Other soft fruits – raspberries, strawberries and peaches – can be servd with natural yoghurt or quark. Citrus and exotic fruits like kiwi, pineapple and lychees can be added later. Vegetables such as fennel, spinach, cauliflower and beetroot (beware the powerful colouring effect on everything from lips to nappies!) can be cooked until soft and served in semi-liquid form with a spoon. A little honey can help to add taste.

Children should be introduced to the various grains in ground form (ground rice, millet, barley, etc.), cooked with either water or a blend of water and milk. They can gnaw on bread crusts as soon as they want to, both to strengthen their gums and to introduce them to bread. Offer water (and cold herb teas) rather than soft drinks full of sugar and flavourings. Give fresh fruit or muesli bars rather than sweets when they are hungry.

Putting on the beef

Highly concentrated foods such as meat, especially red meat, potatoes, eggs, fish, nuts, oils and sugar, stimulate growth, especially muscle development. This will be important later when the children start growing physically and need to be much stronger. The balance of protein, carbohydrates and fat that mother's milk provides is, however, the best model for the first 3–4 years, when the development of the nervous system is of prime importance. That does not of course mean feeding them only milk, suggesting instead a diet of milk products, grains, vegetables and fruit. As a substitute for meat, soya protein is very healthy. Once the children start to do physically demanding activities and when their muscles naturally start growing, as they do in puberty, concentrated foods are more suitable. Stimulating muscle growth in the early years can actually lead to medical problems.

We should perhaps reflect on the fact that the larger mammals that have to grow very quickly have a very high level of protein in their mother's milk. The faster they grow physically, the sooner their development comes to an end. We humans want to grow slowly so that we can grow for longer and never stop developing.

Meal-times

Regular meal-times during which good food is eaten in a thoughtful way help children to develop good eating habits. Although meal-times change as the children get older, we should always value the time together, the food itself, the people who produced it and the rhythm it brings into our lives.

The alternative is chaos, what my grandmother used to call the 'smash and grab' culture. A culture of fast food, instant gratification and eating on the run goes together with stress and indigestion. Compare that with the (albeit relatively rare) opportunity to sit down in a favourite restaurant with special people at a quiet, beautifully laid table to good food and no rush. It is the latter we should try to emulate at our family meal-times.

When and how each family chooses to eat is up to them. The important thing is '*to bring your consciousness to seeing your situation and working towards what feels best*', as Rahima Baldwin Dancy describes in her book *Special Delivery*. Rahima gives the example of a family in which the father and children breakfast together on workdays while her mother enjoys a lie in. It is a special time because Dad is often away, and Mum undoubtedly appreciates a chance to catch up on sleep that she misses while he is away.

Social nourishment

Meals provide the day with a focus during which the family literally see each other face to face across the table. The social contact can be as nourishing as the meal itself. If the table is simply but thoughtfully decorated with flowers, a small seasonal display, a candle this creates a special mood. Neatly laid places, with napkins and table-mats, bring a festive element to the situation. Of course you *can* eat on a table crowded with books, toys and clothing, but does it add any value to the occasion?

As I said in Chapter 8, the atmosphere contributes to the digestion. Small children benefit from calm and the ability to focus on what they are doing. TV or radio in the background distracts them. For addicted Radio 4 *Today* listeners like me, this is a hard one, but I get round it by being *allowed* to listen in the kitchen while preparing the meal. What we talk about at the table also creates the mood, and everyone, even the smallest, should take turns at talking and listening.

> The table is one of the central meeting places for the family and should be treated with the respect it deserves.

Grace

You don't have to be religious to say grace before a meal. Beginning a meal with a grace adds a profound element of gratitude and reverence to a well-prepared meal. We are in effect saying thank you to the world (divine or otherwise depending on your perspective) for the miracle of life and nourishment. The graces below can help provide this focus:

Earth, who gives to us this food,
Sun, who makes it ripe and good,
Dear Sun, dear Earth, by you we live,
Our loving thanks to you we give.

For the dark earth that cradles the seed,
For the rain that brings forth the green leaves,
For the warm sun that ripens the fruit
For all this goodness and beauty, our heavenly Father, we thank you.

> Giving the meal an ending, maybe with a closing grace, rather than simply letting everyone drift away is a good way to round off the occasion. It is not just a hollow informality for the children to ask if they may leave the table: it is a real question that needs to be given individual consideration.

There is a moment when each individual is ready to leave (because she has finished, feels unwell or has to go somewhere in a hurry). The reasons are relevant only to those concerned. The important thing is that there is a conscious moment to close the proceedings. We hold hands around the table and say, 'May the meal be blessed.'

Home helps

Within this context of thoughtful, social meals, good food has a better chance of being eaten, but what also helps is if the children have grown up helping in the kitchen. From the earliest age babies have been propped up in bouncy seats, sat in their high chairs, and stood on chairs. They have risked being sliced with sharp knives, scalded with boiling water and soaked in washing up water so that they can get a grandstand view of the great magician's cave that we call *'the kitchen'*.

> As soon as parents can cope with these active and busy helpers, children *help*! This *'help'*, of course, helps them more than it helps us.

They witness and ultimately take part in all those wonderful manual skills of washing, scrubbing, peeling, grating, rubbing, rolling, picking and scraping. They taste and feel and smell fresh vegetables, fruit and herbs, they crumble and squeeze pastry and dough, they sip yoghurt and juice . . . In short they enter an intimate relationship with a whole world of culinary delights, all of which stimulates rather than stifles their appetite.

Real versus junk

At an older age (certainly by 9 years old, they can do it mostly on their own), real cooking is a great activity for getting children involved in good food. Being able to bake cakes, flapjacks, bread, pizzas, popcorn and even home-made chips and crisps offers not only useful contributions to parties and celebrations, but also a great antidote to fast food and junk food.

> Children will always be drawn to fast food outlets for all kinds of sociological rather than nutritional reasons, but they are unlikely to become obsessed by what is on offer there if they know through direct and regular experience what good food is, where it comes from and how it is prepared.

What counts in the long run is whether or not children's constitution, digestion and sensory responses as well as their habitual behaviour predisposes them to eating well. Set the right patterns early on and they will return in adulthood to good food even if the adolescent years of rebellion led them from the wise nutritional path. Adolescents seem to have been granted by evolution an almost indestructible digestive system between the ages of about 15 and 25, but before and after this the human being really needs good food, and the adolescent too will only survive if a robust and healthy constitution has been established in the first place.

In summary then:

- set an example: eat and enjoy good food yourself
- start with simple foods and progressively increase the variety. Children need lots of variation as they grow up so that their digestions and taste can evolve to meet a wide range of food
- neither animals nor children instinctively know what is harmful

so show them what they can and can't eat, reinforcing this with matter of fact but exaggerated facial expressions. 'We don't eat that, baah!'

- hold back on high-protein foods until children are about 4 or 5 years old. Grains are better than meat even if you are not a vegetarian
- choose your food carefully. Place a value (including sometimes paying more) on high-quality, organic, unsprayed and if possible free-range food. Buy fresh rather than frozen or processed food, food that has undergone the least mechanical or chemical processing and that comes from humane animal husbandry. Supporting those who produce quality food will help to keep their produce on our shelves.
- keep salt, sugar, fats and saturated oils to a minimum
- choose fruit and vegetables, whenever possible in season, and preferably local rather than exotic
- provide a good variety of foods. Inform yourself about balanced diets and nutritional value. Collect recipes for good (and where possible easy and quick) meals
- accustom your children to regular meal-times and make those occasions sociable and structured events
- avoid too many sweets and snacks between meals.

Exercise 16

Confession time! First of all note down all your beliefs, if you have any, about what constitutes a good diet for children. Then write down what you actually experienced as a child in terms of food and food culture. Can you see any connection?

Create a worst and best case dietary scenario using the following questions:

- What do you think would be the worst possible way to bring children up with regard to food and nutrition (including what they see other people doing, such as smoking or drinking)?

- What do you think would be the ideal food culture? What would children eat? How would meal-times be? How would they relate to food?
- What food culture do you think you could actually create in your family?

15

More than one kind
of intelligence

One of the great and liberating discoveries of recent times is the recognition that traditional ways of valuing (and measuring) intelligence are too one-sided. The Harvard psychologist Howard Gardiner was the first to articulate what many researchers had felt, progressively increasing the number of different kinds of intelligence that meet his rigorous scientific criteria. His mould-breaking work on different kinds of human intelligence has led to re-thinking how we value people's skills and abilities and allowed us to value those other kinds of ability.

We still have some way to go before the pre-eminence of the rational, logical mind is challenged by social intelligence, but the other intelligences are in reality equally valuable. The world has suffered much from brainy, powerful people with one-sided intelligence who are socially or morally incompetent. The well-balanced, healthy person has instead a harmonious range of these abilities.

There is no doubt that we are all born with stronger inclinations towards certain kinds of intelligence and less towards others. Quite apart from natural genius, all intelligences can be developed to some extent through careful upbringing, a holistic education and the right opportunities. We need to realise that many children's potential is hindered from developing either by a lack of opportunity or through harmful influences that hinder healthy development.

> Remember, intelligence is always only potential. It needs to be developed if it is to become a real ability. Even Mozart still needed to learn how to play the piano. Potential has to be recognised, fostered and cared for – without pressure.

What is as important, however, is that these abilities can develop in harmony with each other. There is a theory that the human mind evolved over thousands of years with a range of specific and separate skills co-existing as modules within the brain. These modules form the basis of what we now recognise as a range of intelligences. Originally, these capacities related to things like making tools, observing the behaviour of the other members of the group, dealing with relationships, orientation around one's environment and so on. The modular theory of mind accounts for evolution of the higher faculties of the human mind by suggesting that the breakthrough came when the separate modules began to network with each other, this integration leading to higher faculties. Thus, the more an individual can develop a range of abilities and integrate them, the greater her overall competence will be. This is one of the strongest arguments for a truly holistic education as opposed to one that stresses only certain abilities.

In this chapter I briefly describe the nature of these intelligences and suggest how each needs fostering. Since 'intelligence' is in many ways a value-loaded word, one could also say 'potential', since they are no more than a precondition for certain types of development. This approach is most useful as a diagnostic tool to identify a child's abilities and weaknesses so that we can strengthen them by offering more opportunity.

Linguistic potential

Linguistic potential is characterised by the ability to communicate with others through language. This is one of the abilities that is usually taken as an indication that someone is particularly bright, but there are people who have the gift of the gab but on closer examination have little of meaning to say. Some politicians seem able only to deliver what the speechwriters write.

Indeed, in some pathological cases, individuals can talk with great fluency, even using elaborate phrases and unusual words, but are in fact speaking gibberish. This can best be seen in enthusiastic young children at the age of around 3 or 4 when the language stream is flowing faster than the vocabulary can keep up with. Another example is when young children chatter away on a pretend telephone. At a distance, this sounds like an animated conversation, but closer listening reveals that the child is repeating only the tone of voice and the cadence of imitated speech patterns, the vocabulary itself being replaced by speech-like sounds. Don't worry; this is a sign of linguistic potential.

The linguistically gifted person will enjoy word-play, often in verbal humour. They will invent words and collect others that appeal to them for idiosyncratic reasons. As children, they will speak more than others, perhaps almost continually! The language gift leads people towards poetry, drama, literature, story-telling, arguing (a good skill for lawyers, trades union negotiators and politicians), journalism and publishing.

Smooth-talking types

In adolescence and adulthood, linguistic potential, if allowed to develop in a one-sided way, may lead to the individual becoming 'bookish', more at ease in the company of books than people. In extreme cases, this can lead to a kind of literate autism, in which the individual becomes obsessed with certain types of books: romance, science fiction or academic tomes, for example. The other danger is the extrovert demonstrator of linguistic potential, the compelling talker, the charmer, the conman.

Dumbing up during adolescence

One worrying and common phenomenon is the apparent loss of language skills during puberty. It is very often the case that children who have been fluent and enthusiastic speakers with an excellent use of words become seemingly inarticulate mumblers. They grunt and stutter, hardly managing to string more than a few words together. Their good English is increasingly replaced by slang and, if they get away with it in your presence, swear words. Don't worry; this too is normal.

There are very sound reasons why this happens to adolescents. First, some major physical changes occur when boys' voices break. Added to the increased self-awareness that comes with puberty, this can lead to a loss of confidence in speaking in public. Boys can go from having a very pleasant tenor or soprano voice to a growling bass in a few months, which is very disturbing when you consider how much a person's voice reflects his or her personality. Girls' voices change too, although not as dramatically.

Finding their own voice

Puberty essentially sees a major new stage of development, a kind of new birth. The major physical changes are accompanied by subtle yet equally dramatic psychological changes. The forces children have used to build up their inner life, their memories and their thought patterns become less accessible. Things learned easily in context now have to be relearned with conscious effort. The young person has to individualise her inner life through conscious effort, make it her own. This is particularly true of language. Each young person really has to acquire her own voice, both literally in terms of gaining adult vocal characteristics and also figuratively. The process of developing personality means developing your own way of saying things, your distinctive way of thinking and expressing yourself and much of adolescence is spent experimenting with finding one's own personality and voice.

As in many such developmental processes, while the new form is being prepared, during what we might call its embryonic phase, it is well hidden. Outwardly nothing is visible of the new while the old is deteriorating. Teenagers should wear badges saying, 'Temporarily closed for reconstruction'. Their whole personality seems to resemble a building site, shrouded in scaffolding and dust-sheets.

Teenagers go on adding to their vocabulary throughout adolescence, at the phenomenal rate of many new words a day. Many of these words come from school of course, new historical terms, foreign languages, scientific words, many come from literature, but some belong to the murky but linguistically interesting world of slang and teenager jargon. Bad is good, cool is hot, hot is illegal and so on. But what marks out linguistic intelligence is originality. Anyone can adopt the latest in-words, but it is a sign of talent if the individual crates his or her own, or starts writing a diary or even poetry. Encourage this!

Once children have learned to read and write, linguistic potential will show itself in the following ways:

- the child will be able to explain quite complex experiences and ideas and be able to engage people in what they are saying
- the child will pick up interesting vocabulary unprompted
- the child will love listening to and telling stories
- the child will enjoy reading and may prefer reading to other activities
- the child will enjoy and be good at word games, word-play, verbal jokes, riddles and tongue twisters
- linguistic ability usually shows itself in an interest in and ability for learning other languages
- they will start writing diaries and poetry.

How to encourage linguistic potential to develop

First, try to follow the advice I gave in Chapter 10. The best encouragement for language skills is exposure to a wide variety of quality language in all forms – spoken, written or sung.

A love of language in the child's environment also helps. Show an interest in words and their sounds and uses. Take time to discuss unusual words with your children. When they are busily learning between the ages of 3 and 7, help them to appreciate the sounds of words:

- In your own speaking, start to relish the literalness of words like '*whisk*', '*swish*', '*fizz*' and '*bubble*' by speaking them like the sounds they describe.
- If the word allows, try to form a clear picture of the link between the name and the item, such as '*sunflower*' or '*rocking horse*'. This helps the child to see that you value words not merely as labels but as something intrinsically connecting object and name.

- Pronounce new words carefully, especially if they accompany some special event, for example '*Advent wreath*'.

Read quality literature out loud. When abroad, discuss road signs, menus and the way in which people speak to you, showing an interested respect for their language (one of the most important lessons in a multicultural world).

As I have said several times before, live language and real text are far more effective at cultivating real language than are TV, tapes or the computer screen.

Musical potential

Musical ability is closely linked to linguistic ability, although it is obviously an ability in its own right as not all musicians are necessarily good speakers or particularly articulate. We hear music and language with different parts of our sense of hearing and use different parts of the brain when working musically. In a way, musical ability is even more internalised than language, which makes it even harder to understand.

Music often seems an inspirational thing, which highlights an important aspect of these different intelligences. Each requires specific skills that have a basis in a combination of sensory and mental capacities, but it they are to become a true gift, more is needed. First, these abilities have to be schooled, refined and integrated with others. Above all, however, the individual must have something original to say. Many people possess the right balance of skills and mental capacities, to control and co-ordinate their fingers or their breathing, but they don't all become a Bach.

> Genius, even talent, is a factor not of intelligence but of individuality. Intelligence serves talent, but an underlying intelligence is pretty essential.

Recognising musical ability

Musical ability reveals itself to us in familiar ways, in the child's interest in singing, playing and listening to music. Later, it will show itself in the ability to play and appreciate music. Children who are musical can hear when others are singing off-key. They can keep time when singing or playing and have a good sense of rhythm. They often have excellent memories for tunes.

Musicians can often recognise that, among musically gifted children, particular children have an aptitude for percussion, or piano or strings, and then among the strings, the cello, the violin and so on. Such judgements are best made from about the age of 8 or 9 years. Some people promote the idea that a good violin player can only reach the highest level if one starts at 4 or 5, and from a certain technical point of view, this concept of training is probably true. There is, however, more to playing the violin than pure technique.

A great violinist first has to be a great musician. That means having good all-round musical skills as well as the kind of sensibilities that enable a musician to have 'something to say'. This ability to convey musical insight comes not only from musical ability, but also from life experience and individuality.

Many music teachers believe that children should have a good general musical experience before specialising, and that specialisation should proceed in stages. Children should first have an introduction to stringed instruments and only after a year or so progress to cello or viola. A number of instruments require breathing control that is only really possible after the children are about 10 years old.

What musical ability itself is based on is actually quite hard to describe. First, a musical perception of the world involves experiencing something of tonal values. Spaces have their qualities, such as dark and gloomy, lofty and elevating. This quality becomes clearest to us when a tone from a flute or voice resounds in the space. We call this the space's resonance. The same is true when we strike, for example, a metal plate with a hammer. Different materials resonate in different ways, and the ability to perceive these qualities is akin to musical ability.

Another related aspect is that in order to grasp a piece of music, we need to grasp it as a whole, or at least the parts of it that need to be grasped in their entirety. It would be nonsense to listen to each succeeding note in a melody. We have to string together what we hear into a meaningful sequence and anticipate what will come.

We must also possess the ability to identify the mood of a piece of music. Composers do this in reverse, translating the mood of a situation, a thought or feeling into a musical form that gives it expression. Music has something that expresses higher qualities, often beyond words, over a period of time, and perceiving this is another aspect of musical ability.

How to foster musical ability

> Endlessly linking fragments of disconnected music from different periods, genres and moods that bear no relation to the situation or context (as on the radio) deprives real music of its magical, transformative and civilising function. Music should elevate the soul because its source is the elevated soul. If we allow it to become mechanical and repetitive we render it incapable of lifting our children's souls.

Good musical ability obviously requires good hearing. As I stated in Chapter 7, anything, including music that is too loud, that damages the child's sensitive nerve cells, which cannot be repaired once damaged, will limit her musical ability. Headphones are not advisable since the child does not know how loud to set them. Real musical appreciation depends on developing a fine sense for real sounds in different spatial contexts, which means listening to live music on a variety of instruments in different spaces.

All music starts with the human voice so children should start their musical education singing, and singing should accompany all subsequent musical training. Sing to your child as infants, even if your voice is not as good as you would like. Sing with them as soon as they can join in. If you really feel you are totally incapable of singing, join up with other people who *can* sing. Arrange regular sessions when four or five toddlers and parents can join together in singing nursery rhymes and songs. Why not attend a singing class yourself, or learn to play a simple instrument like the recorder. You will never regret it.

Make music part of your family life by singing, playing and listening to music together, going to concerts and discussing music in terms children can understand.

Up until about the age of 9 years, the child's inner emotional experiences are very much bound up with her overall experience of life, but after this, her inner life becomes increasingly differentiated. Emotions and feelings begin to separate from thoughts and reflections, and logic and abstract thinking become possible. That means that musical appreciation can become increasingly differentiated too, and the child's musical experience should reflect this. The young child lives much closer in consciousness to the simple tunes of traditional melodies and to music that has a less rigidly structured character with the melody in the foreground. Music for young children often involves movement and gesture; only later does music become more formal and structured.

If music is important to you, it should not be made banal by simply having it playing away in the background. The whole concept of piped music in shops, arcades and restaurants serves to debase musical experience, reducing it to aural wallpaper. In the past, music – such as sea shanties or marching songs – was a part of work, not because it created a calming or stimulating background but because it enhanced the rhythm of the work.

Encourage your children to learn a musical instrument, but seek a music teacher's advice about when and which instrument. Paying for lessons and instruments is a costly business, but will give a child far more in the long run than too many expensive holidays or visits to theme parks.

Once they start learning an instrument, keep them at it, especially when they reach puberty, when most children give up. At this age, they lack the willpower, find it time-consuming and unrewarding and may feel under peer pressure to do other things. The best one can do is be kind but firm and use all one's dwindling powers of persuasiveness and authority to see them through the worst phase, between 13 and 15. Encourage them to befriend other children who play instruments. Be prepared to drive them around to practices and concerts. Create time within the home routine for instrument practice and help them to establish this. Once they can play, they will have endless hours of happiness playing and appreciating music and sharing the art with their friends. Who knows, if they get famous, they might buy you a nice retirement home in Dorset!

Logical–mathematical intelligence

This is characterised by the ability to calculate, apply logic and reason to situations, as well as be good at all aspects of maths. In young children, this ability will show itself if the child can recognise patterns and perhaps find solutions to jigsaw puzzles (although fitting the pieces the first time is a matter of visual-spatial intelligence). Most obviously, she will have a strong sense for order and sequence. All children like to collect things – conkers, marbles, coins – but only certain children will sort them out into piles or order them on a shelf. Children with this kind of intelligence are able to deduce what a series of different objects have in common.

Once children have been introduced to numbers, this intelligence shows itself in a delight in number sequences such as times tables, number combinations (that add up to 10, for example) and odd and even. They will be very quick at mental arithmetic and are always finding out curious things about numbers. Many children find mental arithmetic a challenge unless they feel very sure about the processes, but mathematical children tend to grasp number relationships almost intuitively, without any apparent conscious thought. The numbers just seem to belong together. The more mathematics develops, the more they enjoy it.

This intelligence is however, not only about mathematics. It also enables the individual to follow precise instructions and complex arguments. Her logical deduction will quickly recognise logical inconsistencies in other people's arguments. She is drawn to logical and systematic procedures such as those used in computer software. This gift can even express itself as the ability to produce order and structure, as in keeping a garden neat and tidy.

On its own, this is a very one-sided ability with a tendency to inflexibility, abstraction and that annoying trait of being *too logical*. There is a pedantic risk and there is a risk of becoming a '*nerd*' or '*anorak*'.

How to cultivate logical–mathematical intelligence

Mathematical–logical intelligence, especially the ability to think in abstractions takes time to develop. It is one of the intelligences that tends to get hurried because it has long been thought of as *the* most important kind of intelligence. Mathematicians are often considered more intelligent than artists or people who are socially gifted, so little children are pushed too hard through their paces. But there is much that one can do to allow its potential to grow in healthy ways, also ensuring that it does not develop into a premature one-sidedness. How do we do this?

Many children get off to a bad start with sums. Arithmetic is very abstract once the symbols are introduced, even for children with this ability, so they need to have a great deal of concrete practical experience of numbers before they have to write them down. That means they should be handling things that come in natural quantities and exploring the qualities before the quantities. This starts with concepts such as *more than, less than, bigger than, smaller than*. Cutting cakes, sharing biscuits, folding paper napkins into quarters and pouring liquids into differently sized containers are typical examples.

Numbers themselves will be introduced to children soon enough at school (often before they have formed a living relationship to them), but one can help to make numbers more real and also more magical if you show children how each number has a different character (which they may not learn at school). Take '*one*' for example. What is there only one of in the world? The sun and the moon are the most familiar unique things. Sooner or later, children also discover that 'There is only one me and there is only one you!' They then discover that wholeness can be divided into halves, quarters and so on.

'*Twoness*' is about pairs, twins, things we have two of – hands, eyes and ears. It is about things that go together, like brother and sister, and it is about things that are opposites but go together, like day and night, summer and winter, hot and cold. 'Duality' is not a term to discuss with children but it is an archetype, a philosophical property that they will one day understand. Discovering dualities in the world is the start of understanding how life is made up of polarities.

'*Threeness*' is a trinity, as in the family constellation of parents and child, two opposites and a uniting factor. '*Fourness*' is reflected in the seasons, the points of the compass, and the division of the clock into quarter and half hours. The other numbers up to 10 also have their correspondences (five fingers and toes, the six-sided honeycomb, the seven stars in the constellation of the Plough).

In this way, the numbers begin to have reality for the children, especially through shapes that they find on their own bodies or in the world around them. Number and geometrical shape is hidden everywhere. Discovering this helps children to realise that the world has intrinsic shape, structure and patterns, and this is especially apparent to children with mathematical intelligence.

There are too few people with real mathematical skills, and too many children get put off too early. Recognising the special character of mathematical-logical intelligence and fostering it in our children can help. We don't all have to become Einsteins, but the world of logic and mathematical thinking is a fascinating one, and being able to think quickly in numbers is a very useful skill in this age of computers and calculators.

Visual-spatial intelligence

This intelligence reveals itself in the ability to use pictures to convey meaning. Images can communicate ideas both to ourselves and to others in ways that differ from ideas represented in words.

> Sometimes it *is* the case that a single picture says more than a thousand words.

Having visual-spatial intelligence enables one to envisage things in three-dimensional mental pictures. Most of us are pretty two-dimensional in our thinking. We tend to visualise things as maps. If you can think three-dimensionally, it helps enormously if you have to orientate yourself in space. It is a skill that is essential for architects, engineers, cartographers, graphic artists, navigators and sculptors. It is also useful to the rest of us who simply use spaces or need to move around in them.

Visual intelligence shows itself in young children in the following ways:

- They like drawing and progress quickly from the universal scribbles that all children do to drawing houses, people and landscapes in recognisable shapes. This would normally show itself by around the age of 6 in children with the skill, in others a year or so later.
- They enjoy drawing generally and often doodle when working.
- These children have a good sense of direction and find their way around the house and neighbourhood well before other children of the same age; they can even tell you how to get there or even draw you a simple plan. This does not normally occur before the age of 9 or 10.
- From about the age of 6 onwards, children with this gift can draw what things look like from different angles.
- They will often arrange their furniture or toys artistically. They may also have a sense for which clothes suit them at a much earlier age than other children, independent of any external fashion influences.
- They will make lovely arrangements with flowers or natural materials on a nature table.
- They like puzzles and jigsaws and can often solve them quickly.
- They can build elaborate shapes with Lego and Meccano, and later like to build things in wood or model with any material.
- They may have vivid dreams, which they describe in some detail.
- At school, such children are drawn to geography and maps and prefer to draw rather than write.

It is interesting that many dyslexics have very well developed spatial-visual skills, finding three-dimensional things much easier to 'read' or understand than two-dimensional ones and many move on to professions such as architecture.

Fostering a new Norman Foster

Encouraging this skill is mainly a question of recognising it and providing opportunities for the child to develop her ability. A few general points may be of help:

Children need the materials for drawing available to them. This includes a selection of differently coloured and textured paper or a large plain exercise book (which has the advantage of keeping the masterpieces in one place), wax block crayons that can be gripped using several fingers (also strengthening the child's whole-hand motor control before the fine motor skill of the fingers are engaged), thick wax crayons and later thick coloured pencils, a drawing board to protect tables and provide a firm surface to work on. Keep the drawings, dated, in a folder. In later years, the artist may be grateful. Reading children's drawings can also be a very revealing art.

Provide the children with modelling materials such as beeswax, modelling dough, even clay (as well as equipment such as plastic storage bins, hardboard or plywood boards, plastic aprons, a washable tablecloth, buckets, etc.).

When the children are old enough, say from 5 onwards, they can be shown how to work safely with craft knives, handsaws, wood glue, hammers and nails. Provide them with a good place to work in the garage or garden shed, with a work surface at a suitable height and lengths of light pine and thin plywood, and let them make things. They could fashion simple objects such as bird boxes as well as just be creative: they will make all kinds of imaginative boats, aeroplanes and the like. This is an activity that can benefit from having an adult working alongside on his or her own project. Paper and cardboard boxes can be used to make windmills, bridges, and houses although these usually have a shorter shelf-life.

Older children should have plenty of opportunity at school or at clubs to develop their drawing and modelling skills. Try to keep things concrete and three-dimensional before they get too engrossed in computer graphics. They need plenty of real experience of shape too. If you can, show them great works of art in galleries or in books in which the laws of perspective are apparent. You don't need to explain anything, admire it with them.

Take every opportunity to visit historical buildings such as old churches, castles, railway stations and airport terminals. Get them used to making sketches with a few notes. With architecture, it is important to experience what it *feels* like to be in such a building, to sense the quality of space, how the building relates to its surroundings, the quality of light and dark within the spaces. You don't have to be an expert. Just ask questions: *'What does it feel like when you look up at the tower inside the cathedral?' 'What does the front of that railway station say to us? Look how important I am or hurry up and catch your train?'* The good thing is that there are no right or wrong answers, just the chance for observation and discussion. It is surprising how much children read in architecture in their wonderful naivety, and you will soon discover who has visual-spatial intelligence.

Map-reading and drawing is a great way to nurture this ability, as is orienteering, which requires the ability to visualise space and how to move from A to B within it. From about the age of 11, children should be able to begin to read maps as long as they have had the symbols explained to them. Drawing their own maps of familiar (or even imaginary places) is also a stimulating and enjoyable activity.

Some children find it very helpful to make drawings or diagrams of things they have to learn, especially if it involves sequences that have to be remembered. This can be done in notebooks for later reference and is especially helpful if they have difficulty writing. Quick sketches of plants, landscapes, ships or science experiments can help a child who finds writing hard.

You can give your child picture 'dictations' to construct sketches from: *'I can see bright blue sky . . . a few wispy clouds . . . a horizon of mountains . . . in the foreground a single storey house painted red with a veranda . . . walking towards the road is a man with a Stetson hat and black boots . . .'* This drawing assumes the child is a reasonably good sketcher (not a brilliant artist but confident, which children with this intelligence often are). Also encourage children to draw cartoons that tell stories.

Bodily-kinaesthetic intelligence

A news clipping I recently used to light my wood-burning stove said *'Beckham as intelligent as Einstein'*. The article described how some researchers had measured bodily-kinaesthetic intelligence and reckoned the Manchester United footballer to be as intelligent in his field as the accomplished mathematician and musician Albert Einstein was in his. David Beckham's ability to make pinpoint passes at high speed, his general athleticism and tireless running are expressions of a great gift that is based on balance, body control, stamina and an ability to read the movement of others. This kind of intelligence enables an individual to co-ordinate her movements with a high degree of control and elegance, as well as economy of effort (which makes it look so graceful). It means having exceptionally good gross and motor control and hand–eye co-ordination. People with such ability make not only excellent sports people, but also dancers, craftsmen, surgeons, circus artists and gymnasts.

Identifying children with this intelligence

- They walk, run and jump in a well-co-ordinated and balanced way from the age of about 4 onwards (before that it is very difficult to tell).
- They can use their fingers in a skilful way quite early on to brush their teeth, hold and use scissors, tie knots and thread beads, etc.
- They prefer to move around when other children are sitting down, when listening to stories and even when eating for example.
- They like to handle things, open them, take them apart and explore them.
- They like to use tools early on, and they like working.
- Their balance is good, and they can climb stairs earlier than other children, stand on chairs, skip and run up steep slopes. This leads onto confidence in climbing, swinging, jumping and running. Later they may be attracted to daredevil activities and fair-ground rides.
- Their hand-writing is good, neat, keeps to the lines and is fluent.
- They like to practise skills in sport or their preferred movement.

Encouraging bodily-kinaesthetic intelligence

As in the other intelligences, we need to provide opportunity for meaningful and healthy activity that uses this ability, and avoid things that hinder it. In the film of the same name, would Billy Elliot have become a dancer if he had sat in front of the TV or computer for hours every day? Although in the movie, the boy's own will played a significant role, we as parents can assist by creating an environment in which regular movement (walking, swimming) is a part of life. The following suggestions follow a kind of progression from babyhood to adolescence.

- As I mentioned in Chapter 9, avoid using baby bouncers but let walking develop naturally. Once the child is walking, let her develop at her own pace with the opportunity to walk on uneven surfaces. Then let her walk, walk and walk.
- Children should have toys that stimulate their fine and gross motor skills.
- Encourage practical activities that involve hand–eye co-ordination (baking, sewing, gardening, painting and skipping)
- Do not enrol children for sport or dance training before they are physically able to take the stress and strain. If in doubt, ask a physiotherapist or someone trained in sports medicine.
- Play throwing and catching games with balls and beanbags to stimulate hand–eye co-ordination.
- Play lots of different sports to develop all-round skills before specialising in just one.
- Outward bound activities for adolescents are excellent, not only for character-building, but also to enable them to adjust to their new body shape. Climbing, mountaineering, canoeing, cycling and horse riding all help.

Having bodily-kinaesthetic intelligence as a one-sided ability is rarely enough to make a great or even a merely competent sportsperson. Other intelligences are needed, such as interpersonal skills, spatial-visual abilities and intrapersonal skills to know your own mind and cope with life's pressures. Apart from which, sport is a very short career.

Naturalist intelligence

What Professor Gardiner discovered as the basic intelligence that underlies an interest in and study of the natural world must in fact be one of the earliest human skills. Early humans must have evolved a highly developed ability to observe the world around them. In order to survive in hostile environments with powerful competitors such as cave bears, sabre-tooth tigers and lions, they had to be highly alert and observant. They needed to locate nutritious berries, nuts and ripe fruits, follow the tracks of others animals, understand the changing seasons and know what kinds of stone were useful for sharp tools. This Stone Age life skill has remained with us as the basis for science. Those who work as gardeners, farmers, fishermen, foresters, vets and meteorologists all depend on their naturalist intelligence, which enables them to understand the world of plant, animal and the natural environment.

Children with naturalist intelligence:

- show a lively interest in plants and animals
- like to play in the garden and go for walks in the park or woods
- like to collect shells, acorns, insects and flowers
- often know the names of many animals and plants
- enjoy being out in all weathers
- frequently like to draw plants and animals
- from about the age of 10 onwards takes a specific interest in keeping pets and can do so quite responsibly
- show an active interest in conservation.

It is to be hoped that all children will share this interest in the living world as a part of their lives whatever environment they live in.

> I believe that if children discover the butterflies and frogs, blackberries and birds nests, wasps and mice, in their backgarden, or local park, this will do more for their naturalist intelligence than any number of documentaries about the Grand Canyon or the last Siberian tigers.

Nature has become something we feel obliged to respect these days, and we equip ourselves expensively to survive it. But we must not think that learning about nature is only a matter of driving out to the nearest Forestry Commission car park and rambling for an hour or two, or canoeing down whitewater rapids. Nor is it about looking at diagrams of the food web in a GCSE course book.

Once most of mankind was relieved of the need to hunt, fish or farm, naturalist intelligence became increasingly applied to cataloguing nature, collecting and listing specimens. But today we have a new task – using our naturalist intelligence and intuition to support rather than conquer nature, and sustain our world. Too much intellect has left us with genetically engineered nature, rivers poisoned, global warming and a loss of biodiversity. What we need now are naturalists who love nature and can enhance sustainability, increase biodiversity and restore habitats, not as museum pieces but as economically viable landscapes in which nature and people can meaningfully co-exist.

Cultivating a real naturalist intuition starts with hands-on direct experience. A child who can regularly watch and refill a bird table will find those birds to be friends. The child will soon want to know, 'Where do they go?', 'Where do they sleep?' They will discover that the robin has a character different from that of starlings or noisy sparrows. All children benefit from the following practical activities, which provide an opportunity for them to establish a real relationship with nature:

- experiencing nature from an early age in the company of trusted adults, through being taken for walks in a backpack or off-road-style pushchair
- keeping nature tables with seasonal displays using twigs, grasses and flowers collected from the local hedgerows or garden. Better still, grow bulbs
- growing seeds and tending a few tubs even if you have no garden. Celebrate the emergence of the shoots and roots, learning to handle and distinguish between different plants and care for them
- learning about keeping a compost heap
- being encouraged to explore the locality at different seasons and in different weathers
- having the opportunity to experience animals as often as possible

in their natural surroundings – bird tables, nature reserves and
bird sanctuaries
- hearing nature stories involving animals and plants
- taking part in local nature conservancy tasks to maintain the
local environment.

Interpersonal intelligence

This means understanding other people and being able to get on
with them. You might think this is something that anyone can learn,
but life teaches us that unfortunately not everyone has as much of
it as they need. It is curious to consider this a form of intelligence,
but if you think about what getting on with others actually involves,
you can see it requires a wide range of abilities.

It means reading many very subtle signs and interpreting complex situations rapidly as people don't always say what they mean.
It means reading body language and other non-verbal signs, as well
as being able to observe other people's relationships with each other.
Furthermore, dealing with problems once they occur means planning actions and predicting their probable outcome. In many
complex social (or political or legal) situations, causes and effects
can be hidden, indirect, long term and disguised. It takes an astute
mind to act in a socially constructive way.

We sometimes call people who are socially gifted 'intuitive'. They
seem to know naturally how to behave, how to deal with people,
when and how to respond and above all how to make other people
feel relaxed. The main source of their ability, however, is the fact
that they can read situations quickly. This kind of intelligence is
especially important in, for example, police officers, emergency
service workers, counsellors, priests, teachers, journalists and man-
agers. Since the largest part of our economy today comprises the
service industries, most people in these will require a high level of
interpersonal skills as a basic qualification.

Children who are naturally gifted in these skills have the
following abilities:

- they are socially at ease, enjoying being with other people and
are not shy with strangers

- they play readily with other children
- when playing with others, they can be patient and wait their turn, and will help other children
- they like to arrange games and other events with other children
- they can show empathy with other children who are upset or who have hurt themselves
- when they are over the age of about 6, socially gifted children can explain other children's behaviour and know why things go wrong
- they will take the initiative in social situations.

How to help children to develop their interpersonal skills

All young children have natural interpersonal skills unless they have been forced or frightened into hiding their naturally social inclinations. Very young children open up towards other people and are instinctively very observant. If they grow up in an environment in which they observe people behaving with social skills, they will learn through assimilation, and as I pointed out earlier in the book, young children learn by example far more effectively than by merely being told. The follow suggestions should be seen as examples, but real life provides us with countless opportunities to show children how to develop their interpersonal skills taking their parents and teachers as role models.

Young children should be encouraged to listen when others are speaking. Learning respect towards others is important not only for its own sake but because real respect is based on an interest in the other person. Showing interest yourself in what others are doing or thinking is the best way to encourage children to take an interest.

Many social skills are based on creating a space for other people. That means learning how to welcome guests into your home, laying a place at the table and serving visitors first, making people feel at home and listening to them. Encourage children to invite their friends round and plan the events so that the occasion has a beginning, an end and a variety of activities. Playing host to visitors is very good practice. Making presents for others can also mean discussing what the other person might like, what their interests are and so on.

Encourage sharing not as something you *have* to do but as something that genuinely brings happiness.

Use thoughtful and considerate disciplinary methods at home, teach your children to get used to discussing things when they have calmed down and establish who has the final say – and stick to it (see Chapter 16).

As soon as the children begin to be able to determine their own limits (for example, when it is time to stop playing a certain game) and reflect on their behaviour, probably from 8 or 9 years old, take the opportunity to discuss with them how to make social situations better. Children's ability to do this will of course increase with age, but it is good to start in simple ways by factually discussing what worked socially and what didn't: how getting overexcited led to someone getting hurt, why someone was feeling left out, when people were getting too tired. With children from about 12 onwards, establishing forms of dialogue in which practically anything that crops up can be discussed is very important. This enables them to develop real negotiating and mediating skills.

The golden rules of interpersonal skills are (in that order):

- show an interest in those around you
- respect others
- respect yourself.

Intrapersonal intelligence

This is what used to be known as wisdom, and it is about knowing yourself. Self-knowledge is the most important kind of knowledge we can possess, not because we are the most important thing in the world but because, without self-knowledge, we can be a liability to the world. Knowing yourself is the precondition of being your own master.

This ability should not be confused with introspection. A person with insight into her own character will not dwell on it but will be able to act in an effective and responsible way in the world. Self-awareness is essential to self-development, both morally and otherwise.

If all the other aspects of development and all the various

intelligences are respected, intrapersonal intelligence will perhaps develop. It will help if you can cultivate the ability to reflect on your deeds and achievements, and make an honest assessment. This assumes self-honesty, courage and a certain amount of self-confidence.

Exercise 17

Of all the different kinds of intelligence described in this chapter, how would you rate yourself, your partner, your children and other people you know? Take the descriptions of how each mode of intelligence shows itself and assess how good each individual is in each area.

What would you do to foster each of these intelligences in your children?

16

Adolescence

*For the child, adolescence is a new territory, uncharted and unexplored.
Even parents often feel as if they are trying to navigate this unknown
territory without a map. Imagine how the adolescent feels!*
Betty Staley, *Between Form and Freedom*

The bad years

Imagine that you feel secure, happy and at ease with the familiar
world around you. You feel you have an unquestioned place in your
family and community. Time seems endless, free of pressure and
full of interesting possibilities. Of course life has its ups and downs,
but they soon pass. You barely feel the cold. You can play for hours
and never get tired. You can climb with the agility of a monkey. You
just are and do. This is what it feels like to be 11 years old.

Suddenly you wake up to realise that your surroundings seem
odd, both familiar and strange at the same time. It is as if the
quality of light had been changed to make everything look different.
You are no longer certain where you are or what you want to do, yet
you increasingly feel required to do *something*, go *somewhere*, meet
standards you don't quite understand. Life suddenly seems to be
full of unclear and complex rules you are expected to grasp and go
along with. There seems to be an urgency to get somewhere but no

obvious routes to follow. You get up (eventually) to find that your body is much heavier than you ever noticed. Your face seems bigger, fatter, thinner, your skin seems prickly, spotty, your hair greasy and the wrong colour. Your body no longer feels like yours, and everyone appears to be *looking at you and judging you*. This is what it can feel like once puberty starts.

The fall (for it is often experienced as such) from the grace of childhood into puberty can be like a bad trip. It is of course also a vital period of human development, the second most formative phase after early childhood. It is full of new potential, new challenges and discoveries. It is a great period of experimentation, of trying out who we are to become. It changes us forever. And it is fraught with risks.

The risks

The risks are well-known: drugs, depression, violence, crime, illnesses such as bulimia or anorexia, social and emotional alienation. In fact it is so risky that most societies try to prevent adolescents having access to things they might harm people with, things they are physically perfectly capable of doing. We try to stop them driving anything faster than a bicycle, using weapons, having sex or leaving home.

Most adults can neither remember nor imagine what it feels like to be in puberty. Our memories are clouded by a mixture of fear and nostalgia, with a strong topping of suggestion provided by stereotyped images from the media. Some adults literally fear teenagers, many feel nervous in their presence. It is not so much that they pose a physical danger to us but more that they are mysterious. They are no longer children – and therefore supposedly under adult authority – but they are not as predictable as adults.

They continuously surprise us, not least because they wear many disguises – challenging body decoration, clothing, hairstyles and posture. They may unnerve us at a much deeper psychological level because we don't know who they are and who they will become. Under their fragile exterior,

> they may even be our superiors. Youth is subversive of what
> *we are* because of what *it is*. It doesn't have to be
> revolutionary, it just has to be young.

Culturally, we are ambivalent too. We value youthful qualities but fear them when they are manifest in youth. We would prefer youthful vigour, beauty and energy – but combined with adult sensibilities. Many adults confronted with teenagers try to be liked and seek affirmation; others, perhaps recognising the futility of this aspiration, try to dominate. This tricky piece of folk psychology certainly complicates matters for the youngsters themselves.

Is puberty really that bad?

Back in the 1960s and 70s, professionals certainly used to think that it was. Puberty was dealt with as if it was some kind of pathology. The disharmony and disruption caused by wildly fluctuating hormone levels was seen as a kind of illness. But then many health professionals saw pregnancy and childbirth as being equally dangerous.

Teenagers were supposed to swing irrationally between extremes of aggression and depression, between arrogant self-confidence and crippling self-consciousness; between being totally inhibited and being rampant with sexual energy. But although puberty is a time of major change, it isn't quite that bad for most individuals. Most professionals do not now take such a dramatic view of things. Most adolescents do not go through extended trauma and emotional agony as a normal part of their development. In fact, most manage these undeniably significant changes with a balance of pragmatism and self-awareness. And they do readjust their attitudes and relationships as they make the transformation from childhood to adulthood.

The physiological changes, profound though they are, do not dictate to the psyche. Teenagers are not overwhelmed by physical processes because human beings are superbly adapted both biologically, to cope with inner change, and spiritually. It is their inner self-activity that gives them the energy and resources to grow through the changes, to undergo a true inner metamorphosis.

Initiation rites

We only need consider that, in most traditional and pre-industrial societies, the transition from childhood to adulthood appears to have occurred in a relatively short time without prolonged and major problems. It has often been said that this was because of the elaborate and sometimes painful initiation ceremonies that were performed, in effect terrifying the child into growing up. But the successful psychological effect of coming-of-age rituals to accept young people into the adult community undoubtedly arise from the *recognition* of maturity. In such societies, children received the education necessary to their practical and social needs (either formally in school or informally through simply taking part in life). After puberty and initiation individuals took a place in their society. They married and started a family as and when they were in a position to support one. The individual was treated first as an individual (mature or less mature) and then as an adult.

There is much that we can learn from these traditions without us necessarily trying to emulate them, most importantly that adolescents should be treated as individuals and as young adults. Modern European societies have extended the initiation rites in stages over many years with the modern equivalents of confirmation in the Christian faith, GCSEs and A levels, 18th and 21st birthdays and graduation. Teenagers retain their dependency for much longer and therefore often lose the experience of a single recognition and affirmation of their identity. The other extreme however, also occurs, namely that they are simply left to their own devices, either emotionally or materially, from about the age of 13. In either case there is no real recognition of the stages achieved.

The alternative to all this is a pseudo-recognition of growing up through the media in the created images of 'teenage-*ness*' in place of a recognition of real development. Many so-called teenage fads or fashions, youth cults and crazes are a picture of youth searching for identity. The media sometimes invents them, sometimes pick up on trends and broadcast them. This is of course a self-supporting system since crazes sell magazines, gear, clothes and music.

Spirituality

The search of young people (and they are getting younger still as social and cultural restraint weakens) for recognition and initiation is a powerful force. Drugs, music, dance and mass hysteria all play their role but are not causes of the search. They are simply the means to an end, the end being to get to another place, another inner space, with all the outer recognition and identification that goes with the search. And what is initiation? It is the ritual passage to another realm of consciousness and its celebration. Adolescence is a journey to another consciousness, to an inner place within oneself where one *is* oneself.

In the course of adolescence, the individual attains a new level of awareness and at the same time a new level of a personal accountability. When can an individual be held responsible for his or her actions? When can we expect the inner voice of conscience to say, '*Don't do that, it is wrong*'? When can an individual say, 'I want to do this or that and really mean *I* rather than simply acting out other people's expectations? At what point can individuals have the certainty that what they believe is what *they* believe?

The answers will be individual of course but they all have something to do with the age group we call adolescence. What we call the search for self goes back into childhood. At some stage between 12 and 16, the issue of the self – the '*Who am I*?' question – crystallises out. This often translates into a variety of questions: '*What do I want?*' '*What do I believe in?*', '*What ideals should I pursue?*' Such questions can find answers at all levels from the very mundane to the most sublime depending on cultural opportunity and individuality. But we can be sure that the question comes from the deepest core of the individual and is summoned forth by the higher self within the individual. And we would do well to respect the process. It is of a deeply spiritual nature and will infrequently manifest in a religious form, although it is more likely that a boy or girl will begin to look for ideals. But where will they find them?

The main problems for teenagers

The main problems that teenagers encounter and which may lead them to become antisocial, alienated, unhappy or even self-destructive are usually caused by the society around them rather than being internally determined by, for example, hormones. What causes adolescents problems are:

- adults who cannot cope with themselves and therefore cannot offer the support, understanding and recognition that young people need
- social and economic conditions that offer little hope for meaning-ful work, training or career prospects, leading many to lose hope and motivation
- schools that fail young people by offering them a diet of 'stones' instead of real nourishment, a string of half-baked ideas forming an exam syllabus. There is only so much motivation an adolescent can gain from the syllabus. There is only so much motivation an adolescent can gain from the mere need to get good marks in exams. There is little that inspires and little that really tackles the issues of the day. And overworked, underpaid and demoti-vated teachers are not in any position to radiate enthusiasm
- parents, educators and role models who lack spiritual or moral values, or who simply don't have real time and care for young people
- a mass media that offers a comfort blanket of banal entertain-ment, seductive but unattainable fantasies (become a millionaire, become a pop star), bizarre role models and commercial exploita-tion
- a thriving drug culture promoted by a well-organised criminal industry
- a prevailing social ethic of greed, short-termism and grab-what-you-can (a sort of Narcissus on ecstasy!)
- politicians who so obviously revert to self-interest at the first hint of a loss of tabloid support: little wonder that youth is so thoroughly alienated from politics.

None of this can be blamed on teenagers themselves, but *they* are the ones who suffer most from these adult-made problems. Why? Because they are looking to all these people and institutions for an ideal.

What most people don't realise is that adolescents are by nature highly idealistic and seek affirmation for their ideals. This may seem odd, especially if you have just been forced off the pavement by a loud group of threatening yobbos or your niece has just got pregnant at 14, but each joy-rider, each teenager drug-user, each girl having unprotected sex is an idealist. How can they be otherwise? And how can we grasp this?

Let us just for a moment go back to those traditional societies I mentioned above. Picture the following situation. The whole family are glowing with pride and admiration as the young couple take to the dance floor at the wedding. He is handsome, strong and skilful at his job. She is beautiful, graceful and accomplished in her roles too. They are happy, full of potential, dreaming of the future. And so they should be. They have reached by the age of 20 a certain culmination in their development. They are as healthy, strong, beautiful and fertile as they will ever be. They can really only get wiser. We can project this lovely image into a New Guinea hill tribe, a Sikh family in the Punjab, an orthodox Jewish family in Golders Green. In any of those cultures, these young people would be at their peak, fulfilling the expectations of their community and possessing a clear set of values. But we have to ask ourselves, what kind of values does our society offer youngsters? What kind of values do we offer our own children?

Even a generation ago, youngsters had a much clearer idea of the world into which they were growing up. Their parents had recognisable careers. The world of work was more visible and comprehensible; the steel works, shipyards and factories dominated the landscape both physically and economically. You might have rebelled against following your Dad down the pit, but at least you knew what the pit was. Now its hard for many youngsters to grasp what their parents actually do for a living: *'My Dad does something in an office'*, *'My Mum does something with computers'*. The *'something'* offers neither promise nor clarity.

In a post-industrial age, the image of progress is no longer the assembly line – raw materials in one end, products out the other.

We live in the age of virtual reality, globalisation and the Internet. Everything is instant and interlocked.

> In the past, you could say to your children, 'If you work hard and follow the right path, do this and then do that, you will achieve your goal.' But the dominant image for our times is 'It is all possible and happening now.'

This is of course a very confusing image and a hard one for adolescents to swallow, but they are far more able to swallow it than we are! It means we must shift our emphasis of advice and role-modelling. Working hard and taking things in stages is still important, but more important are the skills and qualities that belong to the individual, above all:

• being able to communicate your ideas
• understanding other people
• being flexible, creative and imaginative
• understanding the nature of development
• having a real sense of moral values and responsibility
• having courage to follow the truth.

These are the values parents, educators and society should be offering young people.

How long does adolescence last?

The period of puberty and adolescence used to be thought of as spanning the years from about 13 to 16, but nowadays it spans a much longer period, in fact from 10 to 20. There are obviously different phases within this decade, so I will briefly summarise the character of each stage.

Unlike the stages of early childhood, puberty and adolescence are very individual. Some children begin and finish early, some start late and mature late. Others seem able to condense the major physical and psychological changes into a relatively short number of years. There is no right or wrong path for the individual. The most noticeable trend, however, is towards an ever earlier onset of physical puberty and an ever longer period of psychological maturation. Therefore as a parent, do not be concerned when puberty starts. Your concern, especially if it becomes anxiety, will *not* help!

Pre-puberty, or the tweens

This phase is of great interest to commerce because this is the age at which brand-consciousness is at its most susceptible. This age group, especially girls, are precociously aware of appearance, fashion, musical taste, sexuality and identity. There is a vast literature of magazines aimed at this age range. It is worth collecting a few from the news-stand to get an impression of the mentality they aim at – being essentially gossipy, romantic, suggestively sexual, full of melodrama and portraying people at least 5 years older than the readership. This kind of literature has largely replaced horsey and 'Boys Own' type comics.

Pre-puberty ought really to be the heart of childhood, and I mean that not in any sentimental or nostalgic sense. In the couple of years leading up to puberty, between 10 and 12, children are at the most athletic, most physically graceful phase of their development before maturity itself. They are intelligent, astute, imaginative, lively and full of sparkle and energy. They are at the peak of their individual development. They have a keen interest in the world and are as yet not too burdened with self-consciousness.

> I personally find it sad that so many children are robbed of the heart of their childhood because they are seduced into this precocious pre-teenage thing.

On the other hand, it is worth remembering that they themselves will be mortified to recall what they were like at this age – skinny-hipped children in tube dresses and gory lipstick! To parents I can only say, don't get too upset about it as it will pass. Just try not to sell out to their demands and keep a healthy eye on common sense. They will be very grateful later. Above all, remember to picture what they are underneath it all.

Youngsters in pre-puberty and at the start of puberty have keenly alert intellects. Their cognitive development proceeds apace, but what they lack are experience, maturity and the ability to stand back and make sensible judgements. They are lacking in discrimination, taste and often social graces, so they are often convinced by what they hear from their friends or from the media. They don't always listen long enough to get the full facts, often jumping to conclusions, which can make them seem opinionated.

Well, they are opinionated! That these opinions will stand neither the test of time nor close scrutiny does not stop them being voiced with great conviction and passion. It is usually best not to meet this head on. Wait until the right moment before bringing the subject up again, and don't try to hold them to their previous opinions. That would be unfair as what they are in effect doing is trying out reality. Don't drive them into a corner by reminding them of their inconsistencies.

Girls, more frequently than boys, can use their intellect to manipulate others. They are capable of weaving complex webs of gossip, misinformation and downright lies to set up other people, which can have nasty results for all concerned, especially the perpetrator. The deviousness is a sign of identity insecurity. When they get caught, they are usually mortified and will go to great lengths of denial. It is no good punishing them as their behaviour is punishment enough. What they need is a combination of frank talking so that they can experience what effect this may have had on others and, strong affirmation: '*We like you anyway. You don't need to do this.*'

At this age, youngsters need to learn how to deal with information and make judgements; a good school will be meeting this need through its curriculum. New-found intellectual powers should be channelled into understanding the world rather than being driven inwards to introspection. The intellect needs to be schooled in such a way that their imagination can be engaged, otherwise they will soon lose interest or, more occasionally, become a victim of obsessive preoccupations, for example relentless beer mat collecting, computer software and travelling hundreds of miles to see the gates of their favourite pop star's mansion.

Puberty

Only 100 years ago the onset of physical puberty used to start in girls at the age of about 13 or 14. Now it is not unknown for girls to start their periods at 9 and 10, although 11 is now more typical, and in Europe the typical age is quoted as 12 years 13 months. It is a remarkable biological fact that a species can change something as fundamental in its lifeline as sexual maturity and has a profound significance for humanity as a whole.

Complex changes within the brain controlling the hormone balance within the body trigger the familiar symptoms of puberty. It is a massive physiological change. If it were not normal, we would call it a major illness, as many societies have done in the past. This hormonal instability goes on until the individual is about 20, but most of the changes occur in the first few years.

In boys (usually any time between the ages of 10 and 15), first the testicles grow in size. Somewhat later, pubic hair develops. Forty per cent of boys have a harmless phase of swollen breast glands. About a year after their testicles have started to grow, boys experience their first flow of semen, sometimes in their sleep but usually produced by masturbation. About 2 years after the appearance of pubic hair, they develop hair in the armpits, on the face and, in some boys, on the legs, lower arms and chest as well. By the age of 18–20, their body is fully developed.

Girls generally develop about 2 years ahead of boys. Their breasts begin to swell some time between their ninth and fourteenth years (such a wide range can cause concern, but 14 is not uncommon). At about the same time, the first delicate pubic hairs appear. Some 2 years after this, girls experience their first showing of menstrual blood. At first, there is no regularity to the rhythm, and the period is indeed often not accompanied by actual ovulation. The rhythm gradually establishes itself, and the breasts swell out to their full form. By the age of 16 or 17, most girls have reached full physical maturity.

Puberty is also accompanied by a significant growth of the whole body. Girls begin this around 11, boys by about 13. The growth comes literally in spurts and is by no means uniform throughout the body. This leads to all kinds of curious proportions until the adult shape is eventually reached. First the hands and feet grow, then the lower arms and legs, then the upper arms and thighs. In the girls the hips broaden. The breast or chest expands, along with the shoulders. Finally, the trunk catches up. This is why many teenagers appear to be, and often are, clumsy. Their stride has to take into account the fact that their feet are bigger. Try wearing shoes three or four times too big to climb the stairs and you will get some idea of what this means. Their arms are suddenly longer than they were. The body image in the teenager's movement perception is still the smaller one, but this no longer fits through narrow gaps and low doors. This takes some adjusting to.

From baggy to skin-tight

It is no wonder that youngsters at this age like to wear extremely baggy trousers and jumpers, covering up what is now a stranger's body. This goes with the generally slouching stature they adopt, as if dragging around an awkward ill-fitting body. And this is of course *exactly* what they are doing! The extra weight alone is a burden. It's like suddenly wearing clothes that are drenched in water. The normal development from baggy to well-fitting, even skin-tight, clothes is a clear indication that they no longer feel their body as awkward but quite the reverse; it has become their most expressive asset! Anyway, why shouldn't they show off their figures? They will never look so good again!

Other physical changes are even more of a burden. Acne and spots are the plague of teenage years. For something so common, it is remarkable that there is no real medical consensus on exactly what causes this problem, nor indeed is there any simple cure. It seems to be connected with hormonal and blood changes, as well as the maturing of the skin and hair follicles. Diet seems to be a factor too, but it is unfortunately also very individual. Some people can eat chips and peanuts until they burst but don't get spots. Others who follow a strict macrobiotic vegan diet (admittedly rare in the teenager) get plastered in the damn things!

During the early years of puberty and up to about the age of 15, youngsters tend to be self-conscious and apprehensive. This can manifest as shyness or provocative behaviour, but in both cases the need is for boundaries and affirmation.

The awakening intellect I described above now needs feeding with moral content and ideas. Teenagers are fascinated by the activity of thought itself and revel in grasping complex ideas as long as these can be presented in a lively way, since most teenagers have a short concentration span. They need to get to the point quickly, but once there they learn much faster than their teachers. The inexperienced teacher may miss this because their pupils' reactions won't reveal how much they are either interested or have understood. But nothing kills off a 15-year-old's interest faster than pedantic teaching or repetition.

Their intellect begins to acquire the character of cleverness. They can argue just for the sake of it and find logical inconsistencies in all your arguments. The positive (from their point of view) side of this is that they have a fine sense of hypocrisy, moral inconsistency and lies! Not only can they read an adult's intentions, but their innate sense of idealism is also offended.

A 15-year-old can feel as if she has been catapulted out of the world of childhood, this requiring the inner equivalent of relearning how to walk, talk and think. This explains occasional outbursts along the lines of *'Don't tell me how and what to think!'* They really want to learn things for themselves, and we should just give them the tools to do so.

Above all, adolescents of all ages will appreciate humour, as long as it is not ironic or demeaning. They appreciate best deprecating self-humour on the part of adults. Humour will loosen many a tight knot and deflate many an inflated balloon. It makes life's sometimes unbearable paradoxes and inconsistencies bearable. It breaks down barriers, and once these are down, one can offer much-needed and sought-for understanding, sympathy and advice.

Adolescence

This period, which I narrowly define as adolescence, really begins about the age of 16. A new seriousness can enter the young person's soul. For some, many boys, the age of 16 is the worst year of their life so far, the bottom of the hole – but it is also the turning point.

Youngsters have previously been satisfied with knowing *how things are*; now they want to know *how we know* and *how it came about*. Their critical faculties are fully awakened. They have never been more capable of making a cutting comment, yet never more prone to being hurt. Their inclination is to tear down what they see as the facades that hide the truth about life and expose the hidden inner side, yet they are more concerned than ever before to hide themselves. Whereas criticism, arguing and provocation were at the age of 15 a kind of intellectual sport, now they are for real.

I often think of youngsters at this age being the equivalent of medieval warriors on a quest. They may even adopt military-style clothing resembling armour – heavy boots, leather jackets, chains, thick belts, helmets and masks (either heavy black eye-liner or dark glasses). Beneath the martial exterior, there is, however, soft, delicate sensitivity. The armour is part display, part self-protection. It is no coincidence that the interest in fantasy literature, which adopts these heroic and brutally martial styles, begins at this age. There is a simmering, brooding quality of injustice, a lack of recognition, a winning back through unbearable suffering what rightly belongs to them. They can feel imprisoned or lost and yearn to break out. The wounds they bear are deep and slow to heal.

There is a heightened consciousness at this age, which may be hard to live with, and the temptations of losing it are great. The descent into drugs and mindless music is an escape from too much consciousness. But these warriors need the elevating quality of new ideals, a moral code and a spiritual direction or quest. '*Who am I?*' and '*How do I know?*' are the crucial questions at this age. But what answers do we give them? GCSE exams? I deeply hope that we, as parents and educators, can offer them some wider horizons.

As they emerge from this phase – as most of them do – they are more than ever before able to empathise with others, especially those less fortunate (i.e. who suffer more) than themselves. This is a great age to awaken social conscience through practical work, helping the elderly or the handicapped. The polarities of life are to be resolved by creative solutions that call for not only hard black and white logic, but also subtle judgements in which complex phenomena are weighed up. Environmental problems, the loss of biodiversity and the third world debt are the kind of issues 17-years-old can really get to grips with, issues that require subtle, complex creative solutions rather than simplistic slogans.

This is an age at which really deep meaningful relationships are formed. Young people ask themselves, '*Am I worthy of someone else's love?*', a question they also ask of the world at large. At this age, youngsters need the wise counsel of those who can answer this question, which may not be parents or teachers. Our role, however, is to recognise the need, even if we do not feel able to answer this question, which anyway leads an individual out into life, into the world.

What do teenagers need?

I conclude this chapter with a summary of teenagers' needs, which my colleague in California Betty Staley drew up. It consists, appropriately enough of opposites.

Physical activity and stillness

Growing into their new bodies, adolescents need physical activity to help the process, but this should avoid the risk of diving too deep. Too much physical strain leads to injury (a message difficult to get over to keen sportsmen who risk long-term damage by overdoing their training). The best activities are rhythmical and artistic with grace and control. Dance, eurythmy, gymnastics, t'ai chi and sports involving skill rather than muscle power are all helpful. The artistic element is particularly important, as of course is the social aspect of doing physical activities with other people. Being out in nature is also very important for teenagers, so outdoor activities such as hiking, canoeing and climbing are excellent. Not only is the fresh air and contact with nature important, but each of these activities has its own principles, logic and rules, many related to safety. Such principles are a kind of practical idealism. Many outdoor pursuits have a specifically environmental ethos too.

Meaningful activity and free time

This may seem very obvious, but young people are under increasing pressure to fill their entire lives with a timetable of activities. They also need a lot of sleep and pressure-free rest time. Meaningful activity implies mainly practical work such as gardening, forestry, crafts and artistic work in which natural intelligence is cultivated through the demands of the medium, be it wood, soil or textiles. Each handicraft has its own logic, its tools, its procedures, and each of these has evolved with an amazing degree of wisdom. In an age of electricity, it is so important to school the practical intelligence through manual skills, even if they are never literally needed. That is the point of culture. Culture is when we do things to create value even though it is not absolutely required by need.

Intensity and routine

New people, new experiences and new ideas are the stimulus for the developing young person. They yearn for excitement, novelty and adventure, and so they should! However, regularity and routine offer not only security, but also the chance to develop a sense of responsibility. Being part of the family meal-times, celebrating birthdays and festivals, doing homework, practising your musical instrument all have a calming, socialising effect. Teenagers obviously do not need mechanical boring routine, but they do need the support of familiarity and regularity in their lives.

The need to change the world and the need to be inward

Young people need to know that the world takes notice of them, that they can and do make a difference and that they contribute to changing the world – not necessarily all at once, now, but in the appropriate way. They need therefore to be involved at all the levels to which they can reasonably be expected to contribute. Family discussions, holiday plans, even parents' work plans are all topics they can share, even when the adults make the final decisions. The same goes for school. They need to know that they are stake-holders and that their views count. This goes too for wider community or environmental issues. After all, they have the energy and the brainpower to get things done. The other side of this is that they need to be able to reflect on their own and other's behaviour and circumstances. They need to be shown how to reflect on things, review how things went and be able to learn from past situations. Learning how to learn also means learning how to cope with conflict and the discrepancies between expectations and outcomes. This is not a solitary activity but needs to be undertaken with others in a constructive framework, either in the family, at school or in a youth club.

The need to belong and the need for separateness

Being part of a group is very important for teenagers, but they also need to know how to stand on their own feet. Some will need help to develop independence, to help them move out of the orbit of the group's influence. Others will need encouragement to get out of their isolation and join in with others. It is all about self-esteem. Parents and educators have to be very alert to the needs of youngsters in this respect as it is obviously a very touchy subject.

The need to need and the need to be needed

Closely related to the last point, this refers to the need of the adolescent to find companionship that goes beyond what a group can offer. It is one to one and more intimate. It is about recognising when a teenager needs help (and how to offer it – not by saying, *'What a mess, let me do it for you'*). It is also about knowing when to let them get on with it on their own. Teenagers are not always good at indicating when they need help. They may just be sullen and uncommunicative or put on a display of bravado, but they are really a bundle of nerves before a performance, an exam or even a visit to the doctors. It is better to ask if they are all right. If this is done without any hint of nagging or being overprotective, they are more likely to respond. As in all dealings with teenagers, it is better to come straight out and ask, and then leave the door open for them to come back and say, *'Well, actually Mum, I am a bit worried.'*

Letting teenagers know that *they* are needed is also very important. In earlier times, adolescents were given many responsibilities:

looking after children, shopping, working on the farm and generally helping out. Many modern families have got out of this habit, but it is very helpful to adolescents to be given tasks (not just paid jobs like baby-sitting or cleaning the car). First, they can show how competent they are (and they usually are surprisingly good at child-minding and helping out at parties for younger children), and it also makes them feel grown up and accepted. It keeps them in touch with home life too, helping them learn to appreciate just how much Mum and sometimes Dad actually do for the family. Helping outside the home, in the wider community, is also a very valuable experience for all concerned.

The need for fact and the need for imagination

The awakening intellect of the adolescent needs feeding with objective information, and their developing powers of thinking need to be challenged. They also, however, need their imagination to be stimulated. They need to be able to engage in fantasy, imagining how the world could be and being able to give artistic expression to that. There is a whole world of literature to expand their minds, not least the myths and legends that earlier cultures used as ways of discussing their deepest concerns. Mythology is practical psychology packaged in an exciting and involving format. The great legends and teaching stories of earlier cultures such as the Native Americans, the Celts and the Vikings are full of issues such as parentage, loyalty to friends and family, the challenge and temptations of evil, the quest for truth, love and loss, the search for individuality, justice and revenge, forgiveness and sacrifice – all the issues that concern adolescents.

Dialogue

Betty Staley sums this up beautifully:

> *the needs expressed in adolescence become the needs of the adult. In the dialogue between the world and the adolescent's own soul, the youngster experiences the dilemma of human life. Maturity, or integration, has to do with the reconciling of opposites or allowing of polarities to meet in the middle, where a third possibility may arise.*

Healthy development lies in the balancing of opposites: 'Thus our lives become quests and the visions of our adolescent *strivings provide light on our journey for all our years to come.*'

Exercise 18

Reflect back on your own puberty and adolescence. As we did earlier with childhood memories, try to focus on a few situations, reconstruct them and answer the following questions:

- What did you think about the people around you (parents, teachers, brothers and sisters, friends), and how did you feel towards them?
- What did you think of yourself?
- Where were your dreams, wishes and plans at that age?

If you can, choose several different ages and reconstruct each one separately. Then compare your notes and try to describe how you changed.

Exercise 19

Use your diary to record events involving your children, issues that arise, problems that occur. It is even helpful to note unusual occurrences good and bad. Note your own observations and reflections. This journal will be of great help for your parenting skills and will provide invaluable data for doctors, teachers and other professionals who may get involved in your child's life at that point.

References

The references below give full details of the publications cited in the text.

Arnold JC, *Endangered: Your Child in a Hostile World* (Plough Publishing, 2000).

Baldwin Dancy R, *Special Delivery: The Complete Guide to Informed Birth* (Celestial Arts, 1986).

Baldwin Dancy R, *You Are Your Child's Frist Teacher: What Parents Can Do with and for their Children from Birth to Age Six* (Celestial Arts, 1989).

Biddulph S, *Raising Boys* (Thorsons, 1977).

Bryson B, *Mother Tongue* (Penguin, 1990).

Buzzell K, *The Children of Cyclops: The Influence of Television Viewing on the Developing Human Brain* (AWSNA Publications, 1998).

Carey D and Large J, *Families, Festivals and Food* (Hawthorn Press, 1982).

Colum P, *The King of Ireland's Son* (Floris, 1999).

Cordes C and Miller E (eds), *Fools Gold: A Critical Look at Computers in Childhood* (Alliance for Childhood, 2000).

Cromer RF, *Language and Thought in Normal and Handicapped Children* (Blackwell, 1990).

Dahl R, *Charlie and the Chocolate Factory* (Puffin Books, 1964).

Druitt A, Fynes-Clinton C and Rowling M, *All Year Round* (Hawthorn Press, 1998).

Engel S, *The Stories Children Tell: Making Sense of the Narratives of Childhood* (WH Freeman & Co., 1995).

Flanagan G, *Beginning Life* (Dorling Kindersley, 1989).

Gibran K, *The Prophet* (Heinemann, 1979).

Glöckler M and Goebel W, *A Guide to Child Health* (Floris Books, 1990).

Heaney S, *Beowulf* (Faber and Faber, 1999).

Heckmann H, *Nøkken: A Garden for Children* (AWSNA, 2000).

Johnson S, *Strangers in our Homes: TV and our Children's Minds* (a pamphlet published by Kimberton Waldorf School, 1999).

Kitzinger S, *The Experience of Childbirth* (Penguin, 1987).

Kitzinger S, *Freedom and Choice in Childbirth* (Penguin, 1987).

Kitzinger S and Nilsson L, *Being Born* (Dorling Kindersley, 1986).

Lutzke P, *The Sense of Word* (*Der Sprachsinn*), (Verlag Freies Geistesleben, 1996).

Pierce JC, *Evolution's End: Claiming the Potential of our Intelligence* (Harper, 1992).

Pinker S, *The Language Instinct* (Penguin, 1994).

Pinker S, *Words and Rules* (Penguin, 1999).

Rawson M and Rose M, *Ready to Learn: From Birth to School Readiness* (Hawthorn Press, 2002).

Sanders B, *A is for Ox: The Collapse of Literacy and the Rise of Violence in an Electronic Age* (Vintage Books, 1994).

Schacter DL, *The Seven Sins of Memory: How the Mind Forgets and Remembers* (Houghton Mifflin, 2001).

Staley B, *Between Form and Freedom: A Practical Guide to the Teenage Years* (Hawthorn Press, 1988).

Sutcliff R, *Dragon Slayer* (Puffin, 1978).

Sutcliff R, *The High Deeds of Finn MacCool* (Puffin, 1982).

Sutcliff R, *Outcast* (Puffin, 1984).

Sutcliff R, *The Sword and the Circle* (Knight Books, 1983).

Sutcliff R, *Tristan and Iseult* (Puffin, 1981).

Thomson J B (ed.), *Natural Childhood: A Practical Guide to the First Seven Years* (Gaia, 1994).

Tilley S-J and Welby S, *The Dough Craft Sourcebook* (Chancellor Press, 1995).

Wilkomirski B, *Fragments* (Picador, 1995).
Wills C, *Children of Prometheus: The Accelerating Pace of Human Evolution* (Penguin, 1998).

GEO Magazine: Childhood and Youth (*Kindheit und Jugend*) Special Edition, 1995.

Further reading

The literature on childhood and parenting is vast and the books listed below are simply those I know, use and think are valuable. Most contain their own bibliographies, leading to several more paths to follow. When doing this, bear in mind your own children (or those you know) and look for information that helps you to make up your mind.

Baldwin Dancy R, *You Are Your Child's First Teacher: What Parents Can Do with and for their Children from Birth to Age Six* (Celestial Arts, 1989).

Bartz R, *Festivals with Children* (Floris Books, 2001).

Berger T and Berger P, *The Christmas Craft Book* (Floris Books, 1990).

Berger T and Berger P, *The Easter Craft Book* (Floris Books, 1993).

Biddulph S, *The Secret of Happy Children* (Thorsons, 1998).

Brooking-Payne K, *Games Children Play* (Hawthorn Press, 1996).

Brown EE, *Tassajara Bread Book* (Shambhala Publications, 1993).

Bruce T, *Time to Play* (Hodder & Stoughton, 1992).

Carey D and Large J, *Families, Festivals and Food* (Hawthorn Press, 1982).

Caroll L and Tober J, *The Indigo Children: the New Kids Have Arrived* (Hay House, 1999)

Clouder C and Rawson M, *Waldorf Education* (Floris Books, 1998).

Cooper S, Fynes-Clinton C and Rowling M, *The Children's Year: Crafts and Clothes for Children and Parents to Make* (Hawthorn Press, 1986).

Cornell JB, *Sharing Nature with Children* (Exley Publications, 1998).

Druitt A, Fynes-Clinton C and Rowling M, *Birthday Book* (Hawthorn Press, 2002).

Engel S, *The Stories Children Tell: Making Sense of the Narratives of Childhood* (WH Freeman & Co., 1995).

Evans R, *Helping Children to Overcome Fear* (Hawthorn Press, 2000).

Fenner P and Rivers K, *Waldorf Education: A Family Guide* (Michaelmas Press, 1992).

Fitzjohn S, Weston M and Large J, *Festivals Together: A Guide to Multicultural Celebration* (Hawthorn Press, 1993).

Friends of the Earth for Real Food, campaign and action packs, (Freephone 0808 800 1111).

The Complete Grimm's Fairy Tales (Routledge and Kegan Paul, 1975).

Haller I, *How Children Play* (Floris Books, 1991).

Hauschka R, *Nutrition* (Rudolf Steiner Press, 1989).

Healey JM, *Endangered Minds: Why Children Don't Think – and What We Can Do About It* (Simon & Schuster, 1996).

Healy JM, *Failure to Connect: How Computers Affect our Children's Minds – for Better or Worse* (Simon & Schuster, 1999).

Hix M and Godson S, *Eat Up: Food for Children of All Ages* (Fourth Estate, 2000).

Jacobs J, *Celtic Fairy Tales* (Senate Editions, 1994).

Jaffke F, *Advent for Children* (Floris Books, 2000).

Jaffke F, *Toy Making with Children* (Floris Books, 1988).

Jaffke F, *Work and Play in Early Childhood* (Floris Books, 2000).

Jenkinson S, *The Genius of Play* (Hawthorn Press, 2001).

Johnson CM, *Discovering Nature with Young People* (Greenwood Press, 1998).

König K, *Brothers and Sisters: the Order of Birth in the Family* (Floris Books, 2000).

Large M, *Who's Bringing Them Up?* (Hawthorn Press, 1990).

Lievegoed BCJ, *Phases of Childhood* (Floris Books, 1997).

Lines K, *The Faber Storybook* (Faber & Faber, 1961).

Mander J, *Four Arguments for the Elimination of Television* (William Morrow, 1979).

Mellon N, *Storytelling with Children* (Hawthorn Press, 2000).

Nye R, *Classic Folk Tales from Around the World* (Random House, 1996).

Patterson B and Bradley P, *Beyond the Rainbow Bridge: Nurturing our Children from Birth to Seven* (Michaelmas Press, 2000).

Petrash C, *Earthwise: Environmental Crafts and Activities with Young Children* (Floris Books, 2000).

Postman N, *Amusing Ourselves to Death* (Penguin Viking, 1985).

Postman N, *The Disappearance of Childhood* (Delacorte, 1982).

Purvis L and Selleck D, *Tuning into Children – Understanding a Child's Development from Birth to Five Years* (BBC Education, 1999).

Rawson M and Rose M, *Ready to Learn: From Birth to School Readiness* (Hawthorn Press, 2002).

Rawson M and Richter T, *The Educational Task and Content of the Steiner Waldorf Curriculum* (SWSF Publications, 2000).

Salter J, *The Incarnating Child* (Hawthorn Press, 1987).

Sanders B, *A is for Ox: The Collapse of Literacy and the Rise of Violence in an Electronic Age* (Vintage Books, 1994).

Schacter DL, *The Seven Sins of Memory: How the Mind Forgets and Remembers* (Houghton Mifflin, 2001).

Shah I, *World Tales* (Allen Lane, 1979).

Sherwood C, *Naming: Choosing a Meaningful Name* (Hawthorn Press, 1999).

Staley B, *Between Form and Freedom: A Practical Guide to the Teenage Years* (Hawthorn Press, 1988).

Starting Point series: Spring, Summer, Autumn, Winter (Frankland Watts, 1991).

Stern DN, *Diary of a Baby – What your Child Sees, Feels and Experiences* (HarperCollins, 1990).

Strauss M, *Understanding Children's Drawings* (Rudolf Steiner Press, 1978).

Thomas A and Thomas P, *The Children's Party Book* (Floris Books, 1998).

van Leeuwen M, *The Nature Corner* (Floris Books, 1999).

Waldorf, Waldorf, Waldorf: An Illustrated companion to the Exhibition Celebrating 75 Years of Waldorf Education at UNESCO in Geneva.

Wills C, *Children of Prometheus: The Accelerating Pace of Human Evolution* (Penguin, 1998).

Winn M, *Unplugging the Plug-in Drug* (Penguin Viking, 1985).

Magazines
Natural Parent: Your Guide to Holistic Family Living
Available from: Mothers Know Best Ltd., Tower House, Sovereign Park, Market Harborough, Leicestershire LE16 9EF, UK; E-mail: wddty@zoo.co.uk

Renewal: A Journal for Waldorf Education
Available from: AWSNA, 3911 Bannister Road, Fair Oaks, CA 95628, USA.

Steiner Education
Available from: The Sprig, Ashdown Road, Forest Row, East Sussex, RH18 5BN, UK; Telephone: 01342 822115

Useful addresses

Steiner Waldorf education

Steiner Waldorf Schools Fellowship
Kidbrooke
Forest Row
East Sussex RH18 5HG

Tel: 01342 822115
E-mail: mail@waldorf.compulink.co.uk
Website: www.Steinerwaldorf.org.uk

Association of Waldorf Schools of North America (AWSNA)
3911 Bannister Road
Fair Oaks
CA 95628

Tel: (916) 961-0927
E-mail: awsna@awsna.org

Association of Rudolf Steiner Schools in Australia
213 Wonga Road
Warranwood
Victoria 3134

Tel: (03) 9876-2633

Federation of Rudolf Steiner Schools in New Zealand
PO Box 888
Hastings
Hawke's Bay 4201

Tel: (06) 878-7363
E-mail: mailto:waldorf@voyager.co.nz

Federation of Waldorf Schools in Southern Africa
Centre for Creative Education
McGregor House
4 Victoria Road
Plumstead 7800
Cape Town

Tel: (021) 797-6802
E-mail: mailto:fedwald@mweb.co.za

Other organisations

Alliance for Childhood
Website: www.allianceforchildhood.net

This is an international forum for partnerships of individuals or organisations who work together out of a respect for childhood in a worldwide effort to improve children's lives. It is committed to fighting poverty and neglect, to promoting better health, to protecting children from commercial pressures, to countering children's dependence on electronic media, to improving childcare facilities, to promoting a play-based early years curriculum and to strengthening family life. The Alliance has centres in Australia, Belgium, Brazil, Germany, Sweden, Switzerland, Thailand, the UK and USA.

Childline
Freepost 1111
London N1 0BR
UK

Tel: 0800 1111

Childline is the free, national helpline for children and young people in danger and distress. It provides a confidential phone counselling service for any child with any problem 24 hours a day, every day.

Let the Children Play
Hillview, Portway Hill
Lamyatt, Shepton Mallet
Somerset BA4 6NU
UK

Website: letthechildrenplay.org.uk

An organisation of parents campaigning for play-based education for young children.

National Childbirth Trust
Alexandra House
Oldham Terrace
London W3 6NH
UK

Tel: 020 8992 8637

Information and support for expectant and pre-school parents.

Parent Network
Room 2 Winchester House
Kennington Park
11 Cranmer Road
London SW9 6EJ
UK

Tel: 020 7735 1214

This is a support organisation that was established as a registered charity for parents. It offers training for parents, grandparents and carers from all backgrounds and ethnic groups. The Network offers excellent accredited courses.

Parentline Plus
520 Highgate Studios
53–79 Highgate Road
London NW5 1TL
UK

Tel: 0808 800 2222
Website: www.parentlineplus.org.uk

Offers support, advice and information to anyone parenting a child.

Sport England
16 Upper Woburn Place
London WC1H 0QP
UK

Tel: 020 7273 1500

Sport England (previously known as the English Sports Council) is responsible for developing and maintaining the infrastructure of sport in England. Its aims are: more people involved in sport; more places to play sport; more medals through higher standards of performance in sport.

Index